Building Powerful Numeracy for Middle and High School Students

Building Powerful Numeracy for Middle and High School Students

Pamela Weber Harris

HEINEMANN
Portsmouth, NH

Heinemann

361 Hanover Street

Portsmouth, NH 03801–3912

www.heinemann.com

Offices and agents throughout the world

Library of Congress Cataloging-in-Publication Data

Harris, Pamela Weber.

    Building powerful numeracy for middle and high school students / Pamela Weber Harris.

        p. cm.

    Includes bibliographical references.

    ISBN-13: 978-0-325-02662-6

    ISBN-10: 0-325-02662-9

  1. Numeracy—Study and teaching (Middle school). 2. Numeracy—Study and teaching (Secondary).   I. Title.

    QA135.6.H38 2011

    510.71'2—dc23   2011022811

Editor: Katherine Bryant

Production editor: Sonja S. Chapman

Cover design: Matthew Simmons

Interior design: Catherine Arakelian

Compositor: Eric Rosenbloom, Kirby Mountain Composition

Manufacturing: Steve Bernier

Printed in the United States of America on acid-free paper

17 PAH 7

dedication

To my four children,

Abby, Craig, Matthew, and Cameron,

who have taught me so much.

You are my best guinea pigs!

contents

Acknowledgments ix
Foreword by David C. Webb x
Introduction xii

Chapter 1   **Numeracy** 1
             Kim or Dana 2
             Understanding Numeracy 2
             The Importance of Representation 5
             Problem Strings 6

Chapter 2   **Addition and Subtraction: Models and Strategies** 11
             Addition: A "Digit Approach" 12
             The Open Number Line 13
             Addition Strategies 13
             Subtraction: A "Digit Approach" 15
             Subtraction Strategies 16
             Implications for Higher Mathematics 19

Chapter 3   **Addition** 29
             Give and Take 30
             Doubles 35
             Comparing Strategies 37
             Clarifying Understanding 37

Chapter 4   **Subtraction** 41
             Difference Versus Removal 41
             Constant Difference 45
             Comparing Strategies 49
             Clarifying Understanding 50

Chapter 5   **Multiplication and Division: Models and Strategies** 52
             Multiplication: A "Digit Approach" 52
             The Ratio Table and the Array 54
             Multiplication Strategies 56
             Division: A "Digit Approach" 62
             Division Strategies 63
             Implications for Higher Mathematics 66

Chapter 6   **Multiplication** 73
             Using Proportional Reasoning 73
             Doubling and Halving 76
             Chunking: The Distributive Property 79
             Over and Under 81

5 Is Half of 10 84
Comparing Strategies 84
Clarifying Understanding 89

Chapter 7 **Division** 89
Quotative and Partitive Division 89
Connecting Multiplication and Division 90
Partial Quotients 94
Over and Under 97
5 Is Half of 10 Strings 98
Constant Ratio Strategy 99
Comparing Strategies 102
Clarifying Understanding 102

Chapter 8 **Decimals, Fractions, and Percents: Models and Strategies** 105
Decimals 105
Rational Numbers 106
Equivalent Fractions: The Double Number Line Model 109
Fraction Addition and Subtraction 111
Fraction Multiplication 112
Fraction Division 114
Percents 115
Using Fractions and Decimals in Whole Number Operations 120
Implications for Higher Mathematics 121

Chapter 9 **Decimals and Fractions: Addition and Subtraction** 125
Decimal Addition 125
Decimal Subtraction 127
Comparing Strategies: Decimals 128
Fraction Addition and Subtraction 129
Comparing Strategies: Fractions 142
Clarifying Understanding 142

Chapter 10 **Decimals and Fractions: Multiplication and Division** 145
Decimal Multiplication 145
Decimal Division 149
Comparing Strategies: Decimals 155
Fraction Multiplication 156
Fraction Division 160
Comparing Strategies: Fractions 165
Clarifying Understanding 166
Conclusion: Bringing It All Together 168

References 170

acknowledgments

A huge thank-you to:

The good Lord, by whose grace all of this was possible.

My son, Matthew, who did most of the illustrations for me.

My family, for all of their love and support.

Amy Arick, Abby Sanchez, and Rick Sanchez, who allowed me access to their expertise and their experiences in their classrooms.

The six elementary teachers—Candice Underwood, Dana Fincher, Kim Montague, Mary Ramirez, Shannon Waits, and Stephanie Lugo—who jumped off a cliff with me fifteen years ago to try something new because you had my kids.

The Hays Consolidated Independent School District, which allowed me the privilege of working with its teachers and students for many wonderful years.

The Hays CISD math leaders, who tirelessly worked with me to improve instruction for the whole district, benefitting my kids.

Texas Region 14, especially Kathy Hale, for believing in me, helping me, and letting me develop my numeracy right along with you.

T³ (Teachers Teaching with Technology), who gave me my start at professional development and writing curriculum.

The Texas Statewide Systemic Initiative, the Dana Center, Texas State University, and Dr. Paul Kennedy, who gave me my start in the great state of Texas.

The teachers, the best in their field, who have presented with me: Andi Bosar, Dana Fincher, Lisa Deland, Monica Hettenhausen, Debbie Keitz, Mary Ramirez, Melisa Williams, and especially Sarah Hempel, Kim Montague, and Ann Roman.

Susan May for checking my calculus.

Garland Linkenhoger, who taught kindergarten in the morning and calculus across the street in the afternoon, for cleaning up my mathematical language.

Michelle Mueller, for all the support and the last minute detail help.

My wonderful editor, Katherine Bryant, and everyone at Heinemann.

foreword

Our educational institutions often separate mathematics education into two camps, primary and secondary. From established teacher licensure programs to the organization of schools, resources, materials, and methods often are used within two related but distinct domains that rarely intersect except for the students who matriculate from one to the other. In spite of this disconnect, we expect coherence to exist in curriculum, standards, and sequences of instructional activities. What Pam Harris has offered in this book is a compelling approach for achieving greater coherence in the development of secondary students' numeracy and computational fluency.

The number strand is usually an afterthought in secondary mathematics classrooms. With algebra and geometry as the prevailing priorities, why should we investigate number strings and pairs of numbers on a number line? In addition to the related algebraic extensions that are articulated in many of these chapters, number strings are designed to help learners generalize and make connections among the set of tasks. Numeracy becomes a context for further investigation of patterns and generalization. In fact, the way in which Harris organizes familiar tasks reminds us that relational thinking can be promoted in ways that are accessible to all students.

Numeracy also involves understanding the structure of number and relationships between numbers. Harris discusses how models and tools such as the empty number line, area model, and fraction bar, can be used with students to visually convey constant differences between number pairs, the distributive property, and division of fractions as well as other concepts. While these visual models will be familiar to elementary teachers, their role may be less evident to secondary mathematics teachers—and this may be the great contribution of this book. At best, secondary mathematics classrooms include students with a wide range of experience and expertise with numeracy. To support their students' learning, secondary teachers need to understand the potential prior knowledge of their students and how to use tasks, strategies, and models (students may or may not be familiar with) in productive ways. The collection of vignettes included by Harris serves as a reminder of how student numeracy is supported through student communication, both to articulate their solution strategies and listen to the strategies of others.

As the Common Core Standards for School Mathematics usher in a renewed national focus on school mathematics, it is important for teachers to recognize that students need to have opportunities to make sense of mathematics. Pam Harris provides an abundance of such opportunities in the chapters that follow that will undoubtedly improve student numeracy, confidence with computation, and motivation to investigate other mathemati-

cal patterns. As Deborah Ball and Hyman Bass described ways to make school mathe -
matics more reasonable,[1] Pam Harris is a reasonable voice to consider in the national
debate about algorithms and invented strategies.

—**David C. Webb**
University of Colorado at Boulder
Executive Director, Freudenthal Institute USA

---

[1]Ball, D. L., and Bass, H. 2003. Making mathematics reasonable in school. In G. Martin
(Ed.), *A research companion to the Principles and Standards for School Mathematics*
(pp. 1–39). Reston, VA: National Council of Teachers of Mathematics.

introduction

I can remember trying to reteach basic facts in general math. It was almost like putting a coin into a soda machine and having the machine reject it; the coin just falls through. Teaching computation over and over again is much the same; students just pass through, and none of the ideas stick.

GAIL BURRILL, NCTM PRESIDENT'S MESSAGE, 1997

Carl Sandburg once said, "Arithmetic is where numbers fly like pigeons in and out of your head. . . . It is numbers you squeeze from your head to your hand to your pencil to your paper till you get the answer." We can chuckle at Sandburg's insight and humor, and as math teachers we can all certainly agree that this is not how we want our students to feel. Instead, we want them to develop flexibility with numbers, to look to the numbers first before they calculate, and to choose an elegant, efficient strategy given those numbers. We want them to have a deep understanding of place value and properties of operations, and a repertoire of strategies for computation based on these understandings. This repertoire should include the standard algorithms with an understanding of the place value and properties involved, while at the same time recognizing that, depending on the numbers, they are often not the most beneficial strategies to use.

Before handheld calculators, emphasis was placed on paper-and-pencil arithmetic, but in today's world mental arithmetic strategies and the ability to judge the reasonableness of an answer have risen in importance. When the numbers are messy and the calculations are too difficult and cumbersome to do mentally, we usually reach for the calculator, not pencil and paper. Using algorithms, the same series of steps with all problems, is antithetical to calculating with number sense. Calculating with number sense means that one should look at the numbers first and then decide on a strategy that is fitting—and efficient.

As secondary teachers, we are often frustrated by the lack of number sense in our students. Students seem to either reach for a calculator or just shrug and say, "I don't know" when asked simple arithmetic questions. They seem ill-prepared to learn higher math because they have not memorized basic facts. Many students make careless errors with nonsensical results, yet do not recognize how far off their answers are. We are in the age of *algebra for all*, yet we have students who were obviously never in the *arithmetic for all* movement.

Recently, pockets of elementary students have begun to experience reform mathematics efforts. These students may use strategies you do not recognize. The Common Core State Standards (CCSS) consistently call for students to use "strategies and algorithms" and be able to "understand and explain why the procedures work." (Common Core State Standards Initiative 2011) As more states implement the CCSS, more students will arrive with alternative strategies. How do we support, not supplant, such learning?

This book is written for secondary mathematics teachers who wish students came to them with more arithmetic skills and more confidence in learning higher math. We want to encourage students to look not only at the operation in a problem but also at the numbers in the problem before they decide on a strategy. We also want them to have multiple strategies on hand to be able to check their solutions and have more confidence in their answers. We want students to have models in their heads with which to think about numbers and their relationships.

Since students don't always come to us that way, how can we help them? Solid research at the elementary level is showing us how to help all students be mathematically proficient by redefining what it means to compute with number sense, but since the literature is aimed at elementary teachers, it is largely unknown to secondary teachers. This book is an attempt to bridge that gap, to bring these insights to the secondary world.

For the last ten years, I have worked with this research and the resulting reform math materials with elementary teachers and students. As a graphing calculator expert, frequent secondary workshop presenter, and secondary curriculum writer and developer, I purposefully scrutinized it all, saw what worked and what didn't work, always with an eye to success in higher math. I was and continue to be amazed at the power we can harness in our secondary students by teaching ourselves and our students real numeracy.

The linchpin of this book is that when we help students construct numerical relationships, they begin to believe that mathematics is understandable, that it is not all about memorizing abstract, counterintuitive rules, but instead an arena in which they can reason and use their intuitive sense. We can develop their numeracy and use this understanding to build higher math. Chapter 1 provides a brief set of lessons learned from elementary reform. The rest of the chapters will focus on the main strategies, big ideas, and models for each operation; how those strategies, ideas, and models relate to higher mathematics; and how to help students construct these critical numerical relationships.

CHAPTER 1 *one* 1 ⊛.

Numeracy

Anytime I am given a calculation problem (add, subtract, multiply, divide, percents, fractions . . . anything!), it's like I can see all these different ways to solve it running through my head like a ticker. Then I'm standing there trying to pick the quickest or most efficient way.

TEACHER AT NUMERACY WORKSHOP

Kim or Dana

Kim and Dana are two elementary teachers who have classrooms next door to each other. When I first began working with them, they told me very different stories about their math experience. Blushing, Kim told me that she did a lot of math in her head, but she assured me quickly that she knew and taught her students "the right way." Kim also stated, a bit shamefacedly, that, while she had gotten fine grades in math, her brother was really the mathy one. She could follow what her teachers wanted her to do, but she preferred to think about it her way. When Kim calculated, she played with the numbers until she found a strategy that made the problem as easy as she could.

Dana, on the other hand, followed what she called "all the rules." She made excellent grades in math, too, but by meticulously repeating exactly the steps that she was taught. Dana believed that mental math meant performing the algorithms in your head, and she claimed with conviction that people who were good at mental math were those who could "hold all of those numbers and the little slashes in their heads while they went through all of the right steps." She readily admitted that she wasn't good at (her version of) mental math, but that it didn't matter because she could always find a pencil if need be.

Do you see yourself in either of these reactions? Imagine that you are out at a rather nice restaurant for lunch with 11 friends. The check comes and the 12 of you decide to split the bill evenly. The bill is $249. You do a quick mental estimate of a 15% tip, add it on, and round up to $300. Now, how would you do the division to find out how much you each owe? Do you perform the standard long division algorithm on paper or in your head, as Dana would do, starting with "12 goes into 30"? Or do you play with the numbers, as Kim would do, perhaps seeing it immediately as equivalent to 100 divided by 4? When you were in school and the teacher said, "Show me your work," did you carefully mimic the teacher's procedures? Or were you more likely to play with the numbers?

I was a Dana, through and through. I made the grades and set the curves, but I had very little conceptual understanding of number. If I was in the grocery store and didn't have a pencil or calculator or couldn't hold all of those numbers in my head as I tried to figure the price per ounce, then I had a strategy. My strategy was simply to buy the bigger box. Surely the bigger box had to be the better buy, right? I, like Dana, thought that people good at mental math could do long division in their heads. I simply had no concept that there was a whole realm of numerical relationships that I could play with, manipulate, and use to my advantage to solve problems.

If you are more like Kim, this book offers you a structure and framework to guide students who are more like Dana and to help students who are like yourself to expand their natural tendencies. If you are like Dana, you can sympathize with your students who may think, as you once did, that mental math means doing algorithms in their heads and help these students develop the numerical power that will allow them to move away from these "imaginary" algorithms, while helping the Kims in your class build their numerical power. Helping students learn to choose appropriate strategies and models, and developing their understanding of why the procedures work, will build your students' numeracy.

Understanding Numeracy

All humans are born with the perceptual intuitive ability to compare amounts and to even see small amounts like two or three as subunits, or groups, without needing to count them (Dehaene 1999). As children learn to count, they construct the idea that the counting numbers grow by 1 (though this linear relationship usually breaks down for them as the numbers grow larger). Unfortunately, children's early intuitive number sense was not discovered until recently, and so rather than building upon it, well-meaning teachers have often worked against it by emphasizing procedures and sacrificing the development of number relations. As a result, many learners (like Dana) abandoned their intuitive math sense in order to adopt the procedures being emphasized. They lose sight of how the numbers are related to each other.

Researchers now believe that people with good number sense (like Kim) have capitalized on their own natural innate math sense despite the emphasis placed on procedures in most schools (Stein 2008). Over the last several years, pockets of elementary students have begun to experience mathematics based more on numeracy and less on algorithms. You may have some of these students, but others may still come to you without this strong foundation.

Numeracy, at its heart, is using mathematical relationships to reason with numbers and numerical concepts. The diagram in Figure 1.1 shows the components of numeracy.

FIGURE 1.1

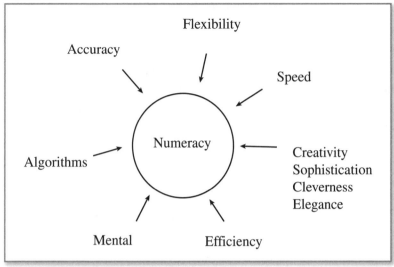

Flexibility

We want students who will look at the numbers in a problem and consider more than one way to solve the problem. This flexibility allows students to have more confidence in their solution because they see relationships in the numbers more clearly.

Efficiency

Give students experience with different strategies and problem types so that they will know which kinds of problems lend themselves to which strategies. We want students to consider the numbers in a problem, not just the operation, before they decide on an efficient strategy to solve it.

Accuracy

Getting the right answer has traditionally been the focus of math instruction. While accuracy is important, it is not the only part of numeracy that matters. As students begin exploring which strategies work nicely for certain numbers with an eye for clever, efficient, or even elegant strategies, they will actually get more answers correct because the emphasis is on relationships.

Creativity, Sophistication, Cleverness, and Elegance

"Mathematics is a highly creative activity. Mathematicians solve problems but they also pose problems. They inquire. They explore relations, investigate interesting patterns, and craft proofs. They present their ideas to the mathematics community and those ideas hold up only when the logic of the argument is accepted" (Fosnot et al. 2008; www.contextsforlearning.com/seriesOverview.asp). When mathematicians write proofs, they seek to make their work clean, concise, and understandable. The process is much less about brute force and much more about creativity and elegance. When students compute, they can seek clever and sophisticated strategies based on the relationships they are learning. They can play with the numbers, bringing their creativity to bear.

Algorithms

The common arithmetic algorithms have a place in numeracy. We can study why they work, how place value is used to create such compact processes that work for all such problems. Indeed, that each algorithm works for the entire class of problems is a wonderful historic feat. The invention of these algorithms allowed even those not trained in the use of the abacus to compute. We should study why these processes work. However, how often should we actually use them? In today's world, we have other, even quicker and far more accurate methods of computing (such as calculators and spreadsheets) when we are faced with dealing with many large numbers. If the algorithms are students' only computation strategy, the algorithms' *digit approach* may inadvertently affect students' progress in higher math. It is possible for students to be successful with the addition and subtraction algorithms using counting strategies instead of additive strategies and with the multiplication and division algorithms using additive instead of multiplicative reasoning. If students have not developed additive and multiplicative reasoning, it will be very difficult for them to reason proportionally and algebraically as they will need to in secondary mathematics.

In a study of forty-four mathematicians' computation strategies, Ann Dowker (1992) found that "mathematicians tended to use strategies involving the understanding of arithmetical properties and relationships rather than strategies involving the use of school-taught techniques" (52). To these mathematicians, solving these problems "seemed to involve an enjoyment of thinking about and playing with numbers, rather than rote memorization" (52). For all the mathematicians and all the problems, they only used an algorithm 4% of the time. "Most mathematicians used a wide variety of strategy types during the task and, if retested, often used different strategy types for the same problem on the two occasions" (53).

Speed

We, as secondary math teachers, were generally very good at the algorithms. We practiced them and have used them successfully for a long time, so naturally, they will be faster for us initially. But with a little practice, more often than not, a more transparent strategy is at least as fast as the algorithm. The sophisticated strategies in this book combine both speed and greater understanding of the mathematics involved.

Mental

Doing mental arithmetic does not mean doing it all in your head. Instead, it implies that you are using your head to reason. Many who employ the strategies suggested in this book use paper and pencil to keep track of their mental steps. This is different from writing down numbers and performing a predetermined set of steps that have been memorized without understanding.

The Importance of Representation

How do we build numeracy? One key lesson from elementary reform efforts is the importance of representation. The representation of student strategies on models such as the open number line, the open array, and the ratio table promotes discussion on relationships rather than on procedures. For example, consider the subtraction problem 36 − 19. Before you read on, find an answer. What strategy did you use?

Several strategies for solving this problem can be shown on an open number line. Perhaps you subtracted an "easy" number first: 36 − 16 − 3 = 17; or 36 − 10 − 9 = 17. This strategy can be modeled on an open number line as shown in Figure 1.2. You could oversubtract and adjust: 36 − 20 + 1 = 17. On an open number line this would be modeled as in Figure 1.3.

FIGURE 1.2

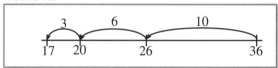

FIGURE 1.3

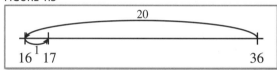

Many people would rather add up than remove. They know that 36 − 19 can be thought of as "19 plus something is 36." So 19 + 1 = 20, then 20 + 16 = 36. This can also be modeled on the number line as in Figure 1.4.

FIGURE 1.4

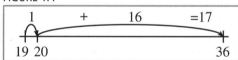

Some people would rather keep the difference constant but make the problem easier, turning 36 − 19 into 37 − 20. This can be modeled on the number line as shown in Figure 1.5.

FIGURE 1.5

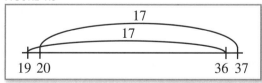

When you model student strategies, it is a model *of thinking*. As students *see their thinking*, they can begin to use the model as tool to solve problems, a tool *for thinking*.

(Gravemeijer 1999). Students begin to operate using the model. Then students continue to develop more sophisticated strategies using the model as a tool, as we'll explore with two additional examples.

For multiplication, arrays are useful models. For example, consider 5 × 13. One strategy for solving this problem is to start with a 10 × 13 array. For many people, finding 10 × 13 is easy: 130. If you cut that array in half, you can see that 5 × 13 is half of 10 × 13, or 65. The array in Figure 1.6 models this strategy.

FIGURE 1.6

A ratio table is a useful tool for division. For example, remember how you and 11 friends split a $300 tab? Consider the ratio of $300/12 people. This can be simplified to $100/4 people and $25/person. Note that with the ratio table (see Figure 1.7), we could also answer a proportion question such as, "If a meal costs $300 for 12 people, how much would it cost for 15 people?"

FIGURE 1.7

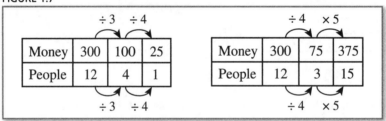

Using a number line, array, and ratio table requires an understanding of number relations, getting right to the heart of numeracy.

Problem Strings

In my experience, many well-meaning teachers ask students to show their work. But they do not really mean, "Show *your* work." They actually mean, "Show *my* work. Mimic *me*. Show all of *my* steps in solving that problem." These teachers may have found success in school mathematics by carefully memorizing and painstakingly imitating the rules and procedures they were taught. Like me, they had been successful with just such learning.

But is the best way to *do* a problem necessarily the best way to *learn about* solving those kinds of problems, to learn about the concepts involved? What does it mean for us to skip over the *understanding* part to the *doing* part? What do we lose or gain in the process? Superimposing a rule, even a "good" rule, can force learners to abandon the meaning they were starting to construct. Thus we end up with some students who can solve textbook problems very nicely, but not problem solvers who can adapt their understanding to new contexts and situations. We also end up with other students who believe they can't solve problems because for them, the memorized rules never worked.

By allowing students to solve problems in their own way and then modeling, comparing, and discussing different strategies with the rest of the class, we honor the students' thinking and nudge students toward more efficient and sophisticated thinking. One way of achieving this result is through problem strings.

A *problem string* is a purposefully designed sequence of related problems that helps students mentally construct numerical relationships and nudges them toward a major, efficient strategy for computation. This method of teaching was introduced by Cathy Fosnot and her colleagues (2008) in the Young Mathematicians at Work series. "Our goal in designing these strings was to encourage children to look to the numbers first before they decided on a strategy and to develop a sense of landmark numbers and a toolbox of strategies in order to calculate efficiently and elegantly—like mathematicians who employ a deep understanding of number and operation." Fosnot and her colleagues have written at length on strings for elementary and middle school students in Young Mathematicians at Work and the Contexts for Learning series. As I have used their materials extensively with students and teachers for the past several years, I have adapted some of their strings and added many of my own.

In general, the following approach works well for introducing problem strings. Depending on how easy the first few problems are for your students, give more or less wait time.

- ▶ The first problem is often an easy one, the foundation to build on. Write it on the board and ask students for the answer and how they solved the problem. Write the answer and model the strategy.

- ▶ Write the next problem and give appropriate think time. Encourage students who succeed with one strategy quickly to try to find a more efficient or sophisticated strategy to solve the same problem. Note that it is always important for students to find the answer themselves first, before other students begin explaining their strategies. Each student must have a sense of the relationships between the numbers in the problem before seeing other strategies. Also note that we want students to show their strategies so we can understand their thinking.

- ▶ Walk around and find a student who has used the goal strategy and one or two students who used different strategies.

- ▶ Ask the one or two other students to explain as you model their strategies on the board. Then ask the student who used the target strategy to explain as you model the strategy. For each strategy, ask students how many of them used that strategy.

- ▶ Continue the same approach with the other problems in the string.

- ▶ As you reach the end of the string, you may want to ask for fewer strategies to be shared and instead focus on the target strategy, depending on the length of the string and, more importantly, where students are in their understanding. If this is their first time with the strategy, then you might take longer and elicit more strategies. If students have worked with this strategy before, you might spend less time on extraneous strategies and focus on what makes a strategy suitable for a given problem.

- ▶ We want to encourage students to be guided by the numbers in the problem to find efficient and even clever or elegant solution strategies. The goal is for students to make connections between the numbers in the problem and different strategies; if you just start telling students which strategies go with which kinds of problems, it will become just another bunch of tricks to memorize. We want students to construct the relationships and be able to use them fluently, not memorize them. Our goal is to learn as much mathematics as we can, with as little memorization as possible.

► The last problem is usually a bit different than the other problems, using bigger or less friendly numbers, where the connection to the target strategy might not be as obvious. By this point, some students will see the connections and use the target strategy. Do not fret about the other students. With more time and experience, they will continue building their numerical power. The goal is not simply to have students discover the strategy, but for them to construct numerical relationships and to begin to use those relationships to solve problems.

Figure 1.8 shows an example of a string designed to teach a particular addition strategy, that of going slightly over and adjusting to find the correct sum. The following steps show how you might use this string in class.

FIGURE 1.8

An Example: Addition Over Strategy
57 + 10
57 + 9
57 + 19
57 + 49
46 + 39
46 + 99
215 + 495

1. Write *57 + 10*, pause briefly, ask students for the answer, and write *= 67*. This problem is easy, but to set up the pattern for the rest of the string, model the problem on an open number line, as shown in Figure 1.9.

FIGURE 1.9

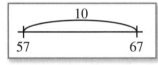

2. Write *57 + 9* on the board, and ask students for the answer. Ask if anyone used the previous problem to help. Again, this is easy, but draw the model (Figure 1.10) and then write the answer, *= 66*.

FIGURE 1.10

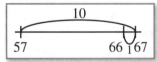

3. Give students the next problem, 57 + 19. Circulate and find someone who used the "over" strategy and someone who used another strategy, such as splitting the numbers into place-value chunks. Encourage students to show their thinking.

4. Bring the group back together for discussion. Ask the student who used the splitting strategy to describe what he or she did, write the answer, and model the strategy. Then do the same for the student who used the target "over" strategy. See Figure 1.11 for the models.

FIGURE 1.11

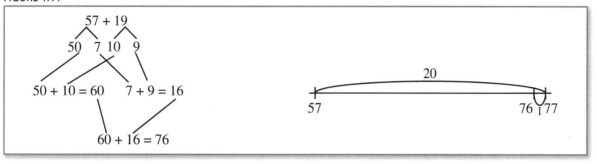

5. Repeat with the next problem, 57 + 49. As before, find a student who used the target strategy and one who used a different strategy. Model both strategies (as in Figure 1.12) as students discuss them.

FIGURE 1.12

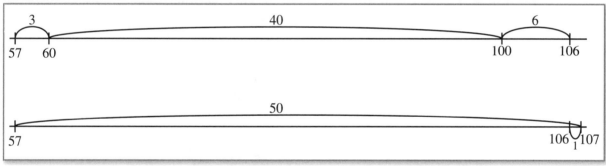

6. Continue with the next two problems, focusing on the over strategy. Model students' work as in Figure 1.13.

FIGURE 1.13

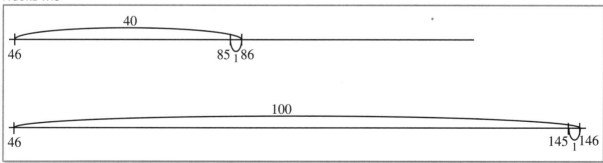

7. Encourage students to discuss what they have been doing. Have them turn and talk to a partner about the strategy they've seen. Then bring students back together and discuss as a group.

8. After students have discussed the strategy, give them the final, more challenging problem, 215 + 495. When you've given them time to think, have them discuss the strategy as you model it (Figure 1.14). Then ask students what they might call this strategy, developing language they can use in later discussions.

FIGURE 1.14

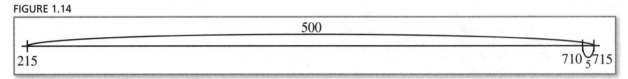

This string encourages using the relationships of the numbers to find sums. Note that while the teacher mostly modeled the target over strategy, students were asked to solve the problems in ways that made sense to them. The discussion promotes numeracy as students see strategies modeled, compared, and discussed. The teacher supports the students' understanding by generalizing why the over strategy works well for the numbers in these particular problems.

If some students have not tried your target strategy by the end of a string, encourage them to do so, but don't force anyone. They may not be ready now, but they may be the next time around. Problem strings for a particular strategy are meant to be done more than once, and each time students will bring to the strings more and more numerical power. As Fosnot and Uittenbogaard (2007, 10) caution, "The intent is not to get all learners to use the same strategy at the end of the string. That would simply be discovery learning. The strings are crafted to support development of computational fluency, to encourage students to look at the numbers and to use a variety of strategies helpful for working with those numbers." Note that the problems and problem strings are not intended to be used all at once, handed out as worksheets, or used as independent work for students.

In the chapters that follow, you will find examples of problem strings for different operations useful to secondary students, as well as some guidelines for creating your own problem strings.

By using models and problem strings in a systematic way, with an eye toward the major, efficient strategies, we can help secondary students construct mental numerical relationships. For those students who come to us with some elementary work in numeracy, we can build on their current understanding and support their continued development, while at the same time helping those who lack that understanding gain the foundation they need. When we give secondary students this numerical power, we also help them engage in learning higher mathematics with more confidence and more success.

CHAPTER 2

Addition and Subtraction: Models and Strategies

I was more like Dana. I did what I was told. I loved math, but I didn't understand it. Now I do!

Numeracy Workshop Participant

I was a Dana and now I will be a Kim. I will be playing with numbers with my students instead of just memorizing and following the rules.

Numeracy Workshop Participant

I was definitely a Kim. I have always been able to see numbers in my head and pull them apart. It has made me successful in math and I've always loved it. However, being a Kim has made it very difficult for me to teach math. It's easy for me to know what to do but difficult to explain it. This workshop has helped me be able to explain what I've been doing in my head and gives me ideas to be able to show this method to my students to help them be more successful.

Numeracy Workshop Participant

This chapter discusses the ramifications of secondary students' numeracy, or lack thereof, with addition and subtraction. We'll describe some of the more transparent, sophisticated strategies that can improve students' numeracy and fluency with these operations. Then we'll examine how building numeracy can improve students' understanding of higher mathematics.

Addition: A "Digit Approach"

Many secondary students come to us with a "digit approach" to whole number operations. For example, they might look at 6,994 + 219 as a series of digit calculations. They first add 4 and 9, write down a *3* and carry a 1, then 9 and 1 and 1 is 11, write down *1* and carry a 1, and so on. Notice how these steps refer to digits.

We want students to look at a number like 6,994 and see it simultaneously in many ways. One of these is that 6,994 is a big number close to 7,000. We would also like students to have the correct sense of place value so that $6,994 = 6(1,000) + 9(100) + 9(10) + 4(1)$ or $6,994 = 6 \cdot 10^3 + 9 \cdot 10^2 + 9 \cdot 10^1 + 4 \cdot 10^0$. These are the concepts used in the traditional American addition algorithm. However, I submit that it is never helpful (nor mathematically correct) for students to "see" the 6,994 as 6, 9, 9, 4. In reality, however, that is how many students come to us.

Consider how this plays into misconceptions in symbolic representations. As students look at an expression such as $3x$ or $5xy^2$, what are they thinking? Do they bring their digit approach with them? Does $3x$ mean 3, *x*? Does it mean 3 and *x*? If I am adding $3x$ and $5xy^2$, can I line them up and do what I have been taught that addition means? (See Figure 2.1.) We clearly *tell* students that $x + x + x = 3 \cdot x = 3x$, but if students come from a digit approach, this will be a leap of faith, a thing to memorize.

FIGURE 2.1

$$
\begin{array}{r}
3x \\
+ 5xy^2 \\
\hline
8x^2y^2
\end{array}
$$

What if, instead of a digit approach, students thought of 6,994 + 219 as "a number close to 7,000 and about 200?" This is far more than just an estimating or rounding strategy. It is about keeping a sense of the magnitude (size) of each addend throughout the process. So, 6,994 + 219 can be thought of as "I only need 6 more to make 6,994 into 7,000. Then the problem becomes 7,000 and 213, which I know is 7,213."

Place-Value Splitting

An important thing we have learned, and research has shown (Fosnot and Dolk 2001, 101), is that given the opportunity, students will indeed invent their own strategies, learning many great and important things in the process. Frequently, these invented strategies will be place-value splitting strategies. For example, consider the sum 47 + 29. As shown in Figure 2.2, students group like numbers together, 40 + 20 and 7 + 9, and then add those parts together. Because students are thinking of 40 and 20, they are considering the *magnitudes* in the problems, not just the digits, which helps them make a decent estimate.

FIGURE 2.2

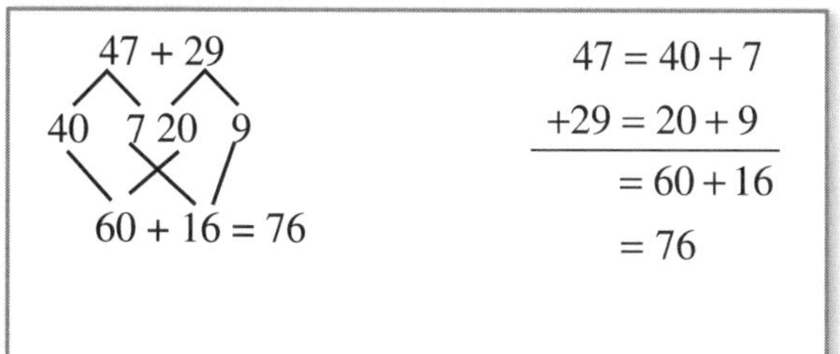

$$47 + 29$$

$$40 \quad 7 \quad 20 \quad 9$$

$$60 + 16 = 76$$

$$47 = 40 + 7$$
$$+29 = 20 + 9$$
$$= 60 + 16$$
$$= 76$$

Place-Value Splitting Strategy

Place-value splitting is a fine strategy for young students because it shows some understanding of place value and it can lead to insight into the addition algorithm. Students can often do this mentally with success. But place-value splitting is relatively inefficient when compared to other addition strategies, and it doesn't lead to the more sophisticated subtraction strategies. So we need to nudge students onward and upward. They need experience keeping one addend whole, an important element of the more sophisticated addition and subtraction strategies.

The Open Number Line

While a closed number line has numbers and tick marks already provided, an open number line is a more flexible tool, allowing students to use the numbers that are useful to solve problems. As the teacher models students' thinking on an open number line, students can see the numerical relationships in a visual, spatial sense. Students can then begin to use the open number line as tool with which to compute.

Precisely because number line representations require learners to operate (for example, to ask themselves what the landing point would be when a jump of 10 is taken), the focus is immediately on number relations. A strong sense of number relations correlates positively with accuracy of magnitude comparison (Siegler and Laski 2007) and overall math achievement test scores (Booth and Siegler 2006; Siegler and Booth 2004).

Addition Strategies

Keeping One Addend Whole: Friendly Numbers and Give and Take

When young students start keeping one addend whole, they often start by "adding a friendly number." Frequently, this means adding 10 first, since many students find adding 10 to be easy to do mentally. Teachers can encourage students to use larger friendly numbers to reduce the number of jumps, as shown in Figure 2.3.

FIGURE 2.3

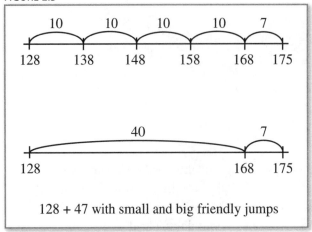

128 + 47 with small and big friendly jumps

While this strategy is useful, it can get cumbersome as the numbers become greater. An alternative strategy encourages students to *get to a friendly number*. Instead of adding a friendly number, students add on just enough to *get to* a friendly number and then deal with the rest in manageable chunks. For example, for the problem 289 + 24, consider the first approach in Figure 2.4.

FIGURE 2.4

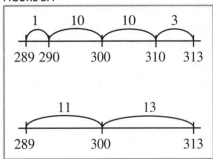

The first number line represents a student using the number line as a tool to find 289 + 24 by adding in small and easy-to-handle chunks: start at 289, then add 1 to get to the friendly number 290. Now add 10 to get to the friendly number of 300. Now, how much is left to add? We've added 11, so that means we need to add 13 more. So, add 10 to 300 to get 310, and then 3 more to get 313.

While adding all of these small chunks is manageable now, it will be more difficult as the numbers get bigger. After adding each chunk, the student needs to consider how much more to add. This becomes unwieldy and tedious. We want students to add fewer, larger chunks. Therefore, we can nudge students toward adding larger chunks by juxtaposing the two strategies, lining up the numbers so students can see the smaller jumps encompassed by the larger jumps and begin to look to add larger numbers, which leads them to begin to give and take simultaneously: Add 11 to 289 to get to 300. That means you have 13 left to add, which gives the total 313. Giving and taking the larger chunks (adding 11 to the 289 and taking 11 from the 24) begins to happen less step-by-step and more in chorus: "I need 11 and I'll get it from the 24. That leaves 300 + 13." Instead of proceeding to add bit by bit as with get to a friendly number, the process is more fluid in give and take.

This give and take can happen with much larger numbers. Try this one: 3,965 + 2,347. Grab 35 from 2,347 and give it to 3,965. You now have 4,000 + 2,312, which is easier to solve mentally. You'll find many examples in Chapter 3 of how to help build mental numerical relationships so that your students can use give and take fluently.

As you reflect on these addition strategies, note that they are all about chunks of numbers and jumps on a number line, the bigger the better. Keeping track of chunks of numbers like this requires students to unitize, to consider more than one number as one chunk. What was many is now many and one at the same time. "Unitizing is a shift in perspective" (Liu, Dolk, and Fosnot 2007, 6). When students count by ones to add, they are using counting strategies. If they are using counting strategies, they have not made the shift to additive reasoning. When students split up numbers by place value, maintaining magnitude, and bring the chunks back together, they are reasoning additively, as they are when they give and take strategically to make the problem easier. Making this shift is vital for subtraction and imperative to developing multiplicative reasoning. If you find that your students are counting by ones to add, use the strings and activities in Chapter 3 to help them construct additive reasoning.

Subtraction: A "Digit Approach"

Students frequently come to us with a "digit approach" to subtraction, as they do for addition. For example, an item on the fifth-grade high-stakes Texas test read, "Alaska, the largest state in the United States, has an area of 656,424 square miles. Rhode Island, the smallest state, has an area of 1,545 square miles. What is the difference between the areas of these two states?" (Texas Education Agency 2003). How would you solve this problem? Traditionally, this is a subtraction problem, involving regrouping (borrowing) as shown in Figure 2.5. Before reading on, actually compute the answer and take note of how many steps it takes.

FIGURE 2.5

$$
\begin{array}{r}
\overset{5\ \ 13\ 11\ 14}{65\cancel{6},\cancel{4}\cancel{2}\cancel{4}} \\
-\ 1,545 \\
\hline
654,879
\end{array}
$$

Notice that when using the common subtraction algorithm as shown, this subtraction problem turns into a digit-oriented problem, where students focus on the correct steps in the correct order and not the magnitudes involved in the problems. They focus on "taking 1 from the 2 to make the 4 into 14" instead of dealing with 24.

This digit approach can have the same impact on polynomial subtraction as it does on addition: for $4x^2 - 3x$, do I line them up and take away? However, for subtraction there is an additional consequence of this narrow understanding. With the algorithm, students perform several *removal* (take away) steps, as in $14 - 5$, $11 - 4$, $13 - 5$, and $5 - 1$. Even though the original problem was about the *difference* between the two numbers, the procedure requires *taking away*.

Subtraction Strategies

Two Meanings for Subtraction

For greater understanding in higher math, it is important for students to understand two meanings of subtraction: taking away (removal) and finding the difference (distance) between two numbers. In other words, 63 − 27 can be thought of in two ways. One is removing 27 from 63. The other is finding the difference between 27 and 63. Figure 2.6 shows these two interpretations.

FIGURE 2.6

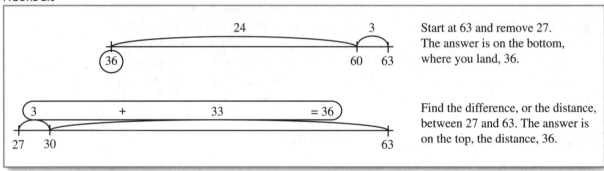

Start at 63 and remove 27. The answer is on the bottom, where you land, 36.

Find the difference, or the distance, between 27 and 63. The answer is on the top, the distance, 36.

The common subtraction algorithm uses the removal meaning of subtraction because each digit is subtracted from another digit (or two-digit number if you borrowed). Because of this, most of our students come to us with primarily a removal meaning for subtraction.

Adding On Versus Removing

It's halftime at the basketball game and the score is 38 to 43. How many points do you need to catch up? Many people would find the difference between 38 and 43 by adding up from 38 to 43 as shown in the first number line in Figure 2.7. But what if the score at halftime were 51 to 3? Most people would just take away or remove 3 from 51. When the numbers are far apart relative to each other, like the football scores 3 and 51, simply removing the smaller number can be easy. When the numbers are relatively close together, like the basketball scores 38 and 43, finding the difference between these close-together numbers can be easy.

FIGURE 2.7

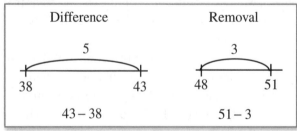

Many people would rather add up to find the difference between two numbers to solve "subtraction" problems.

Of course, I am not suggesting that the "removal" meaning of a subtraction problem should be abolished. Sometimes, it is an accurate and useful interpretation. Rather, the goal is that students have facility with interpreting subtraction both as removal and as finding the difference, as appropriate. These students better understand the relationship between addition and subtraction, and they are better prepared for concepts such as absolute value and subtraction of polynomials. Finding the difference between numbers being represented by subtraction has huge implications for learning in higher mathematics, which is the focus of the latter part of this chapter.

As you work with students to develop both meanings of subtraction, you may find that, as in addition, students can get bogged down when subtracting too many small chunks. You can, again, encourage them to subtract bigger chunks, as for 762 − 45 in Figure 2.8.

FIGURE 2.8

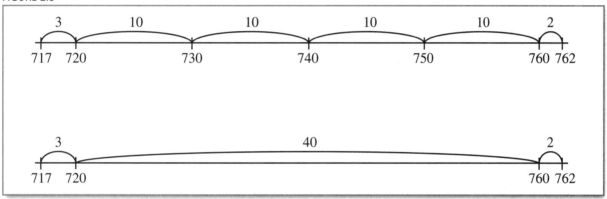

The "Constant Difference" Strategy

One powerful subtraction strategy based on finding the difference is the constant difference strategy. Figure 2.9 shows a series of subtraction problems. What do you notice about them?

FIGURE 2.9

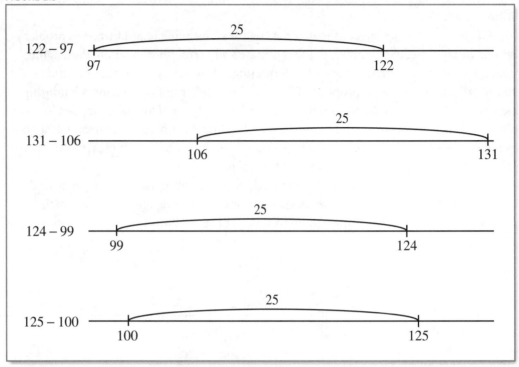

The distance between the numbers is the same in each problem, therefore making equivalent expressions: $122 - 97 = 131 - 106 = 124 - 99 = 125 - 100$. Of the four subtraction problems, which would you rather solve? The constant difference strategy, fully explored in Chapter 4, allows you to shift the problem up or down the number line to create a problem that is easier to solve.

At a training for fifth-grade teachers, several teachers raised the concern that it was fine for younger students to play around with subtraction on a number line, but that the problems their students faced required the most efficient method, the common algorithm. They even had an example ready for me—the high-stakes test question earlier in the chapter: "Alaska, the largest state in the United States, has an area of 656,424 square miles. Rhode Island, the smallest state, has an area of 1,545 square miles. What is the difference between the areas of these two states?"

They said that their students were taking too long to subtract off 1,545 and getting lost in all of the pieces. As they removed to get to friendly numbers, keeping track of how much was left to remove was arduous and tedious. They would start at 656,424 and remove 24 to get to 656,400. Now they would reason that they still had $1,545 - 24 = 1,521$ to remove. So they would remove 400 to get to 656,000 and still have $1,521 - 400 = 1,121$ to go. And so on. Now, each of these pieces was not difficult, and the students were keeping a sense of magnitude with transparent steps, but I agreed that there were more steps than I wished.

However, what about the constant difference strategy? Before you read on, try to shift the distance between 1,545 and 656,424 to a friendly place, where the problem becomes easier.

Note that 1,545 is 455 from 2,000 and therefore adding 455 to both the subtrahend and the minuend can turn the problem into $656,879 - 2,000$ (see Figure 2.10). Notice that the addition of 455 to 656,424 requires no regrouping. Also notice that the resulting subtraction again needs no regrouping. Contrast these three steps with the algorithm; its regroupings requiring more than ten steps.

FIGURE 2.10

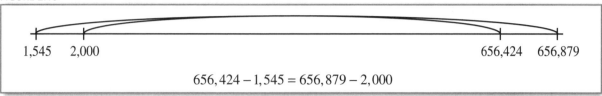

$$656,424 - 1,545 = 656,879 - 2,000$$

To me, this problem exemplifies the numerical power to be had by all and allows the problem to be solved quickly as well. But if all we wanted were fast solutions, we could reach for a calculator. What we really want is for students to have numerical power and learn higher math better. The application of these ideas to higher math in the next sections makes it all worth it.

Implications for Higher Mathematics

If students understood both the removal and difference meanings for subtraction, how might that affect their understanding of higher math? Let's consider a powerful example. Recall the formula for the slope of a line: slope $= \frac{y_2 - y_1}{x_2 - x_1}$. Do the subtractions have to do with removal, or with finding the distance between coordinates? See Figure 2.11 to see clearly that this formula has everything to do with the distance definition of subtraction. Rate of change is a major concept that flows through much of secondary mathematics. Wouldn't it be nice if students realized that what they are finding is the ratio of distances? How might that impact their concept of rate of change?

This is just one example of how helping students become more numerate increases their success in higher mathematics. The rest of this chapter will illustrate how several concepts, processes, and formulas can be built from or made clearer by a facility with numeracy. As you read, notice how many topics and formulas in higher math are based on the idea that subtraction is conceptualized as both removal and difference.

FIGURE 2.11

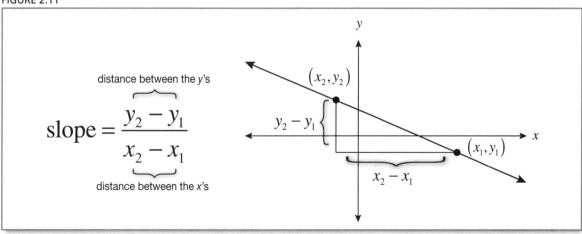

Decimal Subtraction

If students have constructed numerical relationships where both removal and difference can be represented by subtraction, consider how they may approach problems like 20.02 − 0.93. A student skilled in regrouping may use a removal strategy, by regrouping at least three times. If a student has constructed the big idea of *subtraction as difference* and the strategy of *constant differences* to subtract, the student could use the number line in Figure 2.12 to reason that 20.02 − 0.93 = 20.09 − 1.00 = 19.09.

FIGURE 2.12

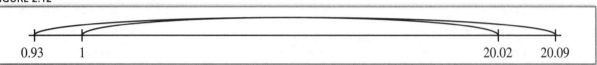

Similarly, 37.042 − 28.899 = 38.143 − 30.000 = 8.143 because, as one ninth-grade student said, "I can add to both numbers until I get a nice number to subtract. Why? Because the distance between them stays the same." Because students are dealing with the magnitudes involved, their answers have a much better chance of being reasonable. Their work becomes an extension of their work with the same strategies using whole numbers, as we'll look at more closely in Chapter 9.

Integer Addition and Subtraction

When students are comfortable using an open number line as a model to solve problems, they can set up integer addition problems and know what to do to find the answer, without memorizing tons of rules. A student reaching into rote memory might think, "Let's see, I'm adding and the numbers have different signs so I subtract the two numbers and take the sign of the larger." In contrast, a student who uses open number lines to model the problem can *see* what to do. Once students have an understanding of negative and positive integers, they naturally add on an open number line without much instruction. For example, Figure 2.13 shows how −14 + 27 can be solved as *starting on −14 and adding* 27. Similarly, −57 + −29 can be solved by *starting with −57 and adding a debt of* 29. Note that we are not using the procedure commonly called *walking the number line*, a system of having students start on the first number and then turn in a certain direction according to the operation and then walk a certain direction according to the sign of the number. If students have facility with adding and subtracting whole numbers on an open number line, none of that extra memorizing is necessary.

FIGURE 2.13

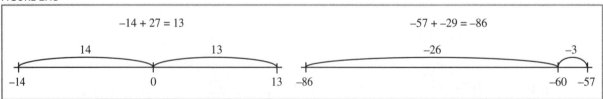

And what about integer subtraction? Even with the best models, integer subtraction is more difficult than addition. There are many fine models that can aid in understanding integer subtraction, such as two-color counters, debt, elevation, and thermometers. While I don't advocate the open number line as the only model to use for integer addition and subtraction, I do suggest that students with numeracy can readily use their constructed understanding of whole number operations and the open number line to their advantage. If students are well versed in the idea that subtraction can be thought of as the *distance* or *difference* between two numbers, then they can look at $-2 - (-5)$ as the difference between -2 and -5 (see Figure 2.14). How far apart are -5 and -2? We can use an open number line to see that the difference between -5 and -2 is 3. And it is true that $-2 - (-5) = 3$.

FIGURE 2.14

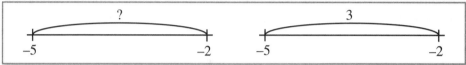

Does that always work? Can we just find the distance between any two integers when asked to subtract? Not quite; we have to consider direction. If the problem involves subtracting a lesser number from a greater number, the answer can be found simply by finding the difference between them. If the problem involves subtracting a greater number from a lesser number, then the answer will be negative.

We can also use the constant difference strategy to make equivalent, easier problems. For example, for $-5 - (-17)$, use give and give to shift the distance between -5 and -17 up by 17 so that you have $-5 - (-17) = (-5 + 17) - (-17 + 17) = 12 - 0 = 12$. Similarly, for $3 - 42$, use take and take to shift the distance down 3 between 3 and 42 so that you have $3 - 42 = 0 - 39 = -39$, as shown in Figure 2.15.

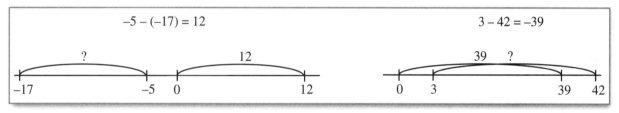

Working with integer subtraction includes juxtaposing the strategies of subtraction as difference and adding the opposite. When you put the two strategies side by side and students see that they produce the same result, students can then use the strategy that makes the most sense depending on the situation. So, with the problem $2 - 5$, you can look at the difference between 2 and 5 and, considering direction, you get -3 (see the first number line in Figure 2.16). However, many students conceptualize the same $2 - 5$ with money and debt. "I have \$2. I spend \$5, so now I am in debt \$3." This meaning can be represented by the second number line in Figure 2.16, which uses the removal meaning of subtraction: start at 2 and add negative 5 (remove 5). Students need to wrestle with the connection between this and the difference strategy so that they have both strategies in their repertoire.

FIGURE 2.16

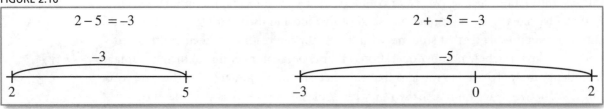

This understanding actually leads very nicely into vectors, commonly studied in physics, precalculus, and beyond. Two vectors are equal when they have the same magnitude (length) and direction. A negative vector (shown in Figure 2.17) is a vector that has the same magnitude, but the opposite direction. Thus, the opposite direction has the opposite sign, which is supported by students' experience subtracting on a number line.

FIGURE 2.17

This also applies to a concept in integral calculus as shown in Figure 2.18. When the curve is above the x-axis, the area is the same as the definite integral, Area $= \int_a^b f(x)\,dx$. When the curve is below the x-axis (where the y-values are negative), the definite integral is negative and the area is given by Area $= -\int_a^b f(x)\,dx$. Note again the relationship between opposite direction and opposite sign, a relationship that students will grasp more easily if they are familiar with subtracting on the number line.

FIGURE 2.18

When the function is **above** the x-axis, the area is the **same** as the definite integral.

$$\text{Area} = \int_a^b f(x)\,dx$$

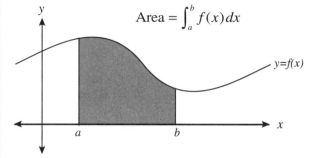

When the function is **below** the x-axis, the definite integral is negative, so the area is the **opposite** of the definite integral.

$$\text{Area} = -\int_a^b f(x)\,dx$$

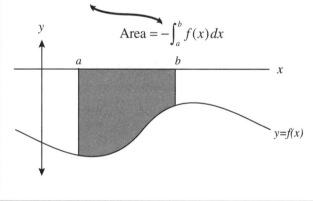

The Distance Formula

When students move from one-dimensional number lines to the two-dimensional coordinate plane, they bring with them all of the understanding and sense of space that they have constructed from one-dimensional lines. They also bring any misconceptions or incomplete understanding.

Consider, for example, the formula to find the distance between two points. Many students and teachers approach the distance formula in a strictly procedural way—subtract the x's and square, subtract the y's and square, add, take the square root. How can improved numeracy aid in finding the distance between two points? First, consider building from the Pythagorean theorem to the distance formula. The distance formula becomes far less about subtracting x's and y's and far more about finding the lengths of the sides of a triangle. For this operation to have meaning, students need to understand that subtraction can be used to find the distance between two points, as shown in Figure 2.19. This idea will play out later in the arc length formula in calculus.

FIGURE 2.19

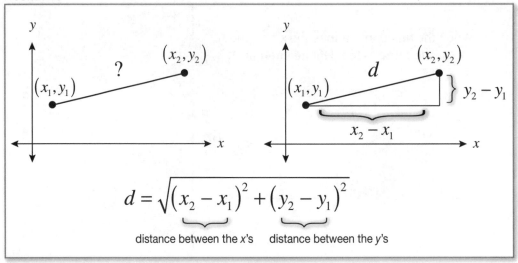

$$d = \sqrt{\left(x_2 - x_1\right)^2 + \left(y_2 - y_1\right)^2}$$

distance between the *x*'s   distance between the *y*'s

Differential Calculus: Rate of Change

In calculus, differentiation involves finding the slope of the tangent line to a curve—thus finding instantaneous rates of change for any curve and at any point. This major concept in calculus draws on the same slope formula students learn in algebra 1, but now it is complicated by the idea of a limit, as shown in Figure 2.20.

Students in calculus will have a much easier time understanding the slope of a tangent line if they are not stuck with "take away" as their only way of thinking of $f(x + h) - f(x)$. A more helpful interpretation here is that students are finding the difference between the two *y*-values: $f(x + h)$ and $f(x)$. Thus, the fairly complicated formula can be more transparent, a "grown-up" version of the earlier slope formula. With that understanding, students can concentrate on new ideas (what does it mean to find the limit?) because they understand the basic underlying concept.

FIGURE 2.20

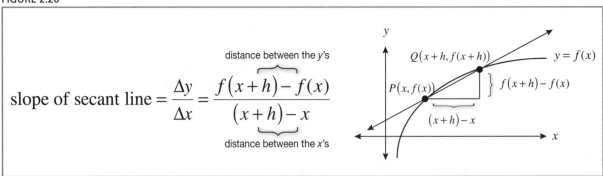

$$\text{slope of secant line} = \frac{\Delta y}{\Delta x} = \frac{f\left(x + h\right) - f\left(x\right)}{\left(x + h\right) - x}$$

Integral Calculus: Area Under a Curve and Volume of a Solid

At its core, integration is a systematic way of finding sums of very narrow partitions. We can use integration to find the area under a curve. We will discuss this topic more in

Chapter 5 when we discuss multiplication, but the understanding of subtraction as difference is key as well.

To find the area under a curve, you use calculus to add up all of the areas of the infinitely skinny rectangles that make up the curve. To do this, we need the height of the rectangles, which is the distance from the x-axis to the function, which is the function value, $f(x)$. However, when finding the area between two curves (see the lower diagrams in Figure 2.21), the height of the rectangles is now the difference between the function values and hence the formula is $\int_a^b f(x) = g(x)dx$. Does the subtraction mean to remove $g(x)$ from $f(x)$? No, it means to find the distance between the y-values of each function.

FIGURE 2.21

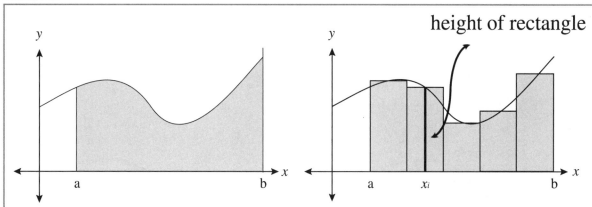

Height of the rectangle is the function value, $y = f(x_i)$

Area under the curve $= \int_a^b f(x)\,dx$

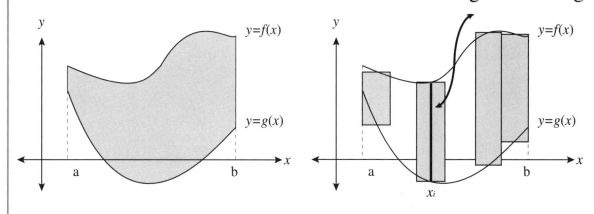

Height of the rectangle is the difference of the functions, $f(x_i) - g(x_i)$

Area between curves $= \int_a^b f(x) - g(x)\,dx$

Finding Volume

Another topic in integral calculus is rotating the area under a curve to find the volume of the region created. One method is shown in Figure 2.22. In order to find the volume of the "wavy cylinder-like solid," you find the volume of the disk shown and then use calculus to add up the volumes of all of the disks. The area of the base of each disk, a circle, is found by πr^2, but how to find the radius? Note that in the solid on the left, the function is rotating about the x-axis, so the radius is the distance from the x-axis to the function, which is the function value, $f(x)$. However, in the figure on the right, the solid has been shifted up, where the function is rotating about the line $y = c$, and therefore the radius is the *distance* from the function, $f(x)$, to the axis of revolution $y = c$. So, again, the formula can be more transparent when students can recognize $f(x) - c$ as the distance from the function value to the line $y = c$.

FIGURE 2.22

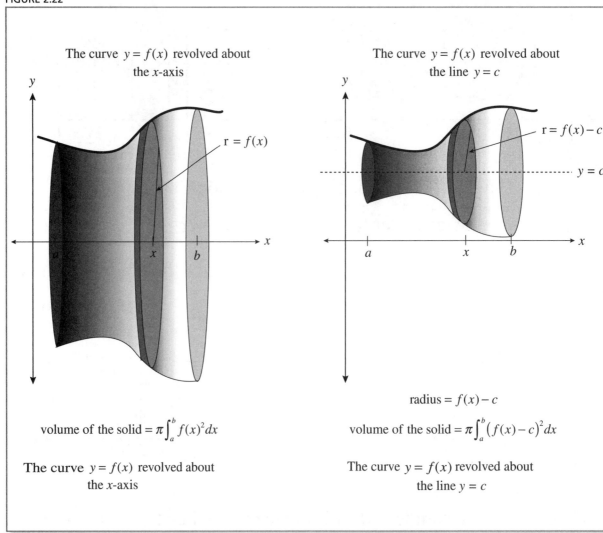

The curve $y = f(x)$ revolved about the x-axis

$r = f(x)$

volume of the solid $= \pi \int_a^b f(x)^2 dx$

The curve $y = f(x)$ revolved about the x-axis

The curve $y = f(x)$ revolved about the line $y = c$

$r = f(x) - c$

$y = c$

radius $= f(x) - c$

volume of the solid $= \pi \int_a^b (f(x) - c)^2 dx$

The curve $y = f(x)$ revolved about the line $y = c$

Similarly, there is another method to find the volume of solids created by rotating curves about axes of revolution, this time finding the volume of shells (like hollowed-out cylinders) and using calculus to add up the volumes of the infinite number of shells (as shown in Figure 2.23). In this example, the height of each shell is simply the function value, $f(x)$. So to find the volume of the solid, you use calculus to add up all of the shells' volumes where each shell's volume is: Volume $= 2\pi x f(x)\Delta x$, where x is the radius of each shell.

FIGURE 2.23

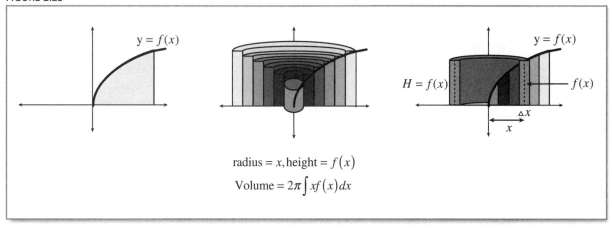

$$\text{radius} = x, \text{height} = f(x)$$
$$\text{Volume} = 2\pi \int xf(x)dx$$

But what if the rotating shape is the area between two curves, $f(x)$ and $g(x)$? (See Figure 2.24.) Then the height of the shells can be found by subtracting the function values, $f(x) - g(x)$.

FIGURE 2.24

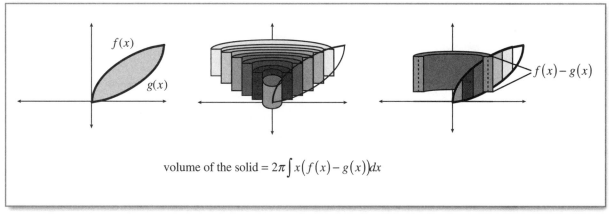

$$\text{volume of the solid} = 2\pi \int x\big(f(x) - g(x)\big)dx$$

Delta-Epsilon Definition of a Limit

Last, consider the ominous delta-epsilon definition of a limit, as shown in Figure 2.25.

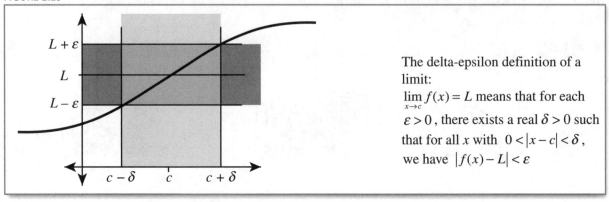

The delta-epsilon definition of a limit:
$\lim\limits_{x \to c} f(x) = L$ means that for each $\varepsilon > 0$, there exists a real $\delta > 0$ such that for all x with $0 < |x - c| < \delta$, we have $|f(x) - L| < \varepsilon$

This formal definition involves several big ideas, but let's limit (pun intended) the conversation here to the subtractions: $0 < |x - c| < \delta$ and $|f(x) - L| < \varepsilon$. Both of these sentences express the relationships of intervals around c and L involving the distances represented by the variables δ and ε. If a student is left with only a sense of removal, this notation to represent intervals will be very difficult if not impossible to understand.

The previous examples demonstrate the increased depth of understanding that students can gain when they approach secondary mathematics with a strong numeracy background. The next two chapters will show you how to develop this background in addition and subtraction with your students.

Addition

Addition and subtraction are not problems that I need to answer, they are numbers with relationships I need to discover, and there is logic and structure to those relationships.

NUMERACY WORKSHOP PARTICIPANT

One of my favorite questions to ask when I walk into a classroom is, "What is 99 plus anything?" Within a minute, I have students hooked on wanting to know more about numeracy. First, though, most students just stare. "Seriously," I say, "What is 99 plus any two-digit number?" Pause. "Ok, pick one—pick an ugly two-digit number," I continue, calling to one of the students looking at me. "47, 29, 74," are some of the ugly two-digit numbers they offer. "So, what is 99 and 47?" Pause. And then I say slowly, "99 and 47 is 100 and . . ." When several students call out 46 and eyes light up, I've almost got them. "So, what's 99 and 29? 99 and 29 is 100 and . . . ?" Pause. "Turn to the person next to you and explain what you just did." Then I ask for someone to explain to the class how you can figure 99 plus anything. After someone explains that "99 plus anything is just 100 plus 1 less than the thing," I ask them to consider 999 plus anything. And I sit back and smile.

As I listen to the sometimes tentative, sometimes excited discussion of this transparent, understandable, and useful strategy, I am struck by the students' reactions. Many students are intrigued at the idea that they can compute those sums so quickly. Some are considering such an idea for the first time. Others had long ago constructed this strategy, but have rarely heard anything like it in a math class. At this point, many students are hearing it only as a trick and, if they are seeing math as billions of tricks to memorize, they will probably not be interested in one more trick. But with this hook, I find that a critical mass of students will allow me some latitude and they will engage in work on numeracy.

Give and Take

The discussion in an algebra 1 class might continue like this as the teacher, Abby, asks students to solve problems in ways that are transparent. She begins by asking students to consider the 99 and 999 plus anything idea. "Why does that work? Here is a model of what I heard you say as I walked around." She draws models on the board (see Figure 3.1).

FIGURE 3.1

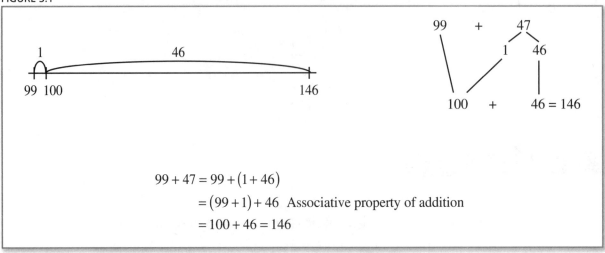

$$99 + 47 = 99 + (1 + 46)$$
$$= (99 + 1) + 46 \quad \text{Associative property of addition}$$
$$= 100 + 46 = 146$$

She continues by connecting this experience to notation students may be more familiar with. "I'll write this another way, with a different model, using numbers and properties of our real number system" (see the bottom part of Figure 3.1).

After pausing for a bit to give students time to think, Abby continues, "The associative property of addition was helpful, wasn't it? We can use this associative property to make many addition problems into easier problems. If someone just walked in the room right now, how would you explain how the associative property helps make addition problems easier?" She pauses and then asks students to discuss with their partners.

After some partner time, she asks, "How can you use the associative property of addition to help you with a problem like 1,997 + 2,989?"

Jonas says, "You can give 3 to make the problem 2,000 plus 2,986 and that's 4,986."

Richard adds, "Or you can take 11 from the 1,997 and make the problem 3,000 + 1,986."

Abby records their strategies (Figure 3.2) and uses the students' language. "So you were giving to one number what you are taking from the other? Could you use this give and take strategy for 7.98 + 2.19?" She then gives students time to work on this problem. As they work, she circulates and observes their strategies. Not all students are using the give and take strategy. Some are using the traditional American addition algorithm. Some students try a mental strategy and then use the algorithm to check their work. Abby expects this and encourages students to use a method that makes sense to them. At the same time, she purposefully chooses problems and numbers that will lend themselves to the give and take strategy. As she circulates, she highlights the target strategy by calling on two students to write their strategies on the board (see Figure 3.2).

FIGURE 3.2

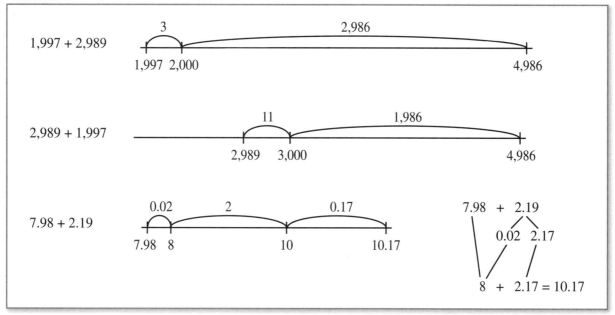

After a brief discussion, she gives students a fraction problem, $5\frac{3}{4} + \frac{1}{2}$, and asks, "What might be a friendly number for this problem?"

In this discussion, the teacher used the string of problems in Figure 3.3. This string was purposefully constructed to bring out certain ideas: addition can be transparent; keeping one number whole; friendly numbers; the associative property of addition; the idea of give and take; and the idea that there is more than one way to add. In fact, there are many ways to add that are quicker and easier than the way many students are used to.

FIGURE 3.3

$$99 + 47$$
$$99 + 29$$
$$1{,}997 + 2{,}989$$
$$7.98 + 2.19$$
$$5\tfrac{3}{4} + \tfrac{1}{2}$$

Notice that the teacher modeled students' strategies and brought in the appropriate mathematical reasons for steps. Students' own strategies were honored as they were asked to solve the problems in ways that make sense to them. Students were encouraged to make sense out of the target strategies. Problem strings are a powerful way to help students construct numerical relationships and apply those in efficient and even elegant ways.

Figure 3.4 lists problem strings that use the associative and distributive properties to develop the give and take strategy. Notice that strings for sixth graders have more examples. As you work with students with more experience, the numbers get bigger and smaller, there are fewer examples in each number system, and you also vary the order of the addends sooner.

Early Middle School	Late Middle School (Algebra 1)	Algebra 2/Precalculus
$48 + 26$	$58 + 36$	$67 + 28$
$139 + 52$	$4,996 + 528$	$5,989 + 2,222$
$2,997 + 317$	$2.7 + 5.9$	$1.06 + 7.98$
$1.9 + 4.8$	$0.15 + 7.99$	$3.099 + 0.023$
$7.99 + 0.15$	$5\frac{3}{4} + \frac{1}{2}$	$19\frac{5}{6} + \frac{5}{12}$
$2.33 + 4.98$	$99\frac{2}{3} + \frac{4}{9}$	$32\frac{8}{9} + 3\frac{1}{3}$
$2\frac{3}{4} + \frac{1}{2}$	$9\frac{4}{5} + 2\frac{3}{10}$	$\frac{5\pi}{4}, \frac{7\pi}{3}$

To write a give and take string for your class, you might first consider your current topic and how give and take or any of the accompanying concepts (friendly numbers, associative and commutative properties, etc.) might relate to that topic. So, let's say you are working with triangle and trapezoid midsegments in a geometry class. Since the length of the midsegment of a trapezoid is the average of the bases, students will most likely need to add the two bases when averaging. To write a string that will support their fluency in this addition, you might start with a problem like 38 + 24, for which students' strategies will likely vary. Plan to model a couple of these different strategies. If students don't suggest it, model the strategy of giving 2 to 38 to make the problem 40 + 22 as well.

You can write the next problem with bigger numbers, such as 497 + 214. Notice that if you give 3 to 497, you still have 211—a slightly more difficult number to add than a multiple of 10. If your students need more support, you could use a problem such as 497 + 213, which could lead to using 500 + 210.

Since addition is commutative, take and give works too, so for the next problem, you can switch the order of the addends, such as 4,632 + 4,997. Notice that at the same time, the numbers got bigger and the subtraction got harder. With this problem, when students give 3 to get 5,000, they'll have to take 3 from 4,632, which takes a little more work.

The string so far includes 38 + 24, 497 + 214, and 4,632 + 4,997. Next, you could change to decimals or fractions as in the strings in Figure 3.4, or instead you could make the give and take amount less obvious, such as in 176 + 446. The use of 176 takes advantage of students' experience with quarters, because it's so close to 175. The 24 necessary to make 176 into 200 subtracts easily from 446, to make 176 + 446 = 200 + 422. Another problem that takes advantage of quarters could be something like 774 + 239 = 800 + 213. An even more obscure reach could be 445 + 7,265 = 500 + 7,210; this is a nice problem to use near the end of the string, because it could also be solved by taking from the first addend instead of the second, as in 445 + 7,265 = 410 + 7,300. A nice conversation will arise when you juxtapose the two strategies and ask, "Which is easier for you—giving 55 to 445 to get 500 or giving 35 to 7,265 to get 7,300?" This will continue to encourage students to look to the numbers first before deciding what to do. You could end the string by encouraging students to consider using some of these strategies and ideas as they approach the midsegments topic in the rest of the lesson.

If your students are not ready for this more sophisticated addition strategy of give and take, you may first want to use the strings in Figure 3.5 to guide them to add friendly numbers, which can be considered a precursor strategy. These problem strings are intended to help students develop the strategy of keeping one addend whole and adding a friendly number. The first two strings encourage students to add multiples of 10 and then adjust at the end. The third string encourages students to add a friendly number that is just too much and then adjust back.

FIGURE 3.5

Add Friendly Numbers		
27 + 10	356 + 100	19 + 10
27 + 40	356 + 120	19 + 9
27 + 45	356 + 125	29 + 9
59 + 10	678 + 200	29 + 19
59 + 30	678 + 210	47 + 19
59 + 33	678 + 217	33 + 18
38 + 27	529 + 372	145 + 99

With the first two strings, you can model smaller and greater jumps to encourage students to work toward bigger chunks (see Chapter 2).

Some students will quickly grasp the idea of keeping one addend whole; others are still constructing place value and will want to split both addends into place-value parts. You will want to model those splitting strategies for a while but move quickly to nudge students toward keeping one addend whole. Throughout, encourage discussions of:

▶ What does it mean to split a number into its place-value parts?

▶ What makes a number "friendly" for a particular problem?

▶ How would I get to that friendly number?

▶ How much do I have left (still to add)?

▶ Which strategy seemed more efficient for this problem? Why?

▶ Which strategies seemed transparent?

An Algebra 1 String: Generalizing with Variables

After discussing the give and take strategy using the algebra 1 string shown in Figure 3.4, how could you help students generalize what they have learned and apply it to variables? Let's go back to the classroom.

After recording students' strategies and discussing them, Abby ends the string by asking, "So, why is it that you can take from one number and give it to the other and still get an equivalent sum? Why does this give and take strategy work? Discuss that with your partner."

After some partner discussion, she brings the class together. Knowing that she wants to move the group to abstraction, she asks students to discuss the strategy in general. "So, if you are adding two numbers, say a and b, then . . . ?"

Matt: "You add something to a and subtract it from b."

Abby writes this on the board as $a + b = (a + c) + (b - c)$. (See Figure 3.6.) "Where did c come from?"

Craig: "Well, c is part of b."

FIGURE 3.6

$$9\frac{4}{5} + 2\frac{3}{10} = \left(9\frac{4}{5} + \frac{1}{5}\right) + \left(2\frac{3}{10} - \frac{2}{10}\right) = 10 + 2\frac{1}{10} = 12\frac{1}{10}$$

$$9.8 + 2.3 = (9.8 + 0.2) + (2.3 - 0.2) = 10 + 2.1 = 12.1$$

$a + b$ If we partition b, $b = c + d$

$$a + b = (a + c) + (b - c) = (a + c) + d$$

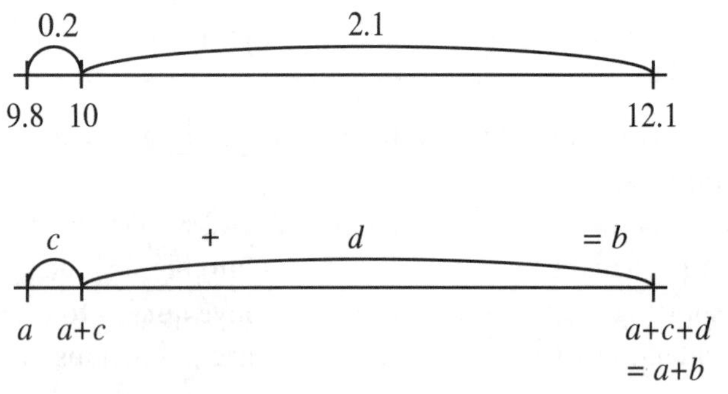

"So, if we partition or split up b, then we have c and what's left. Let's call that d." She records this as $b = c + d$. "What did you do once you gave something to a and took it from b?" Students realize that they are adding the friendly number, $a + c$, to what's left over, d.

Notice that the teacher is modeling these students' general discussion of a numerical strategy using variables and equations. Students see how variables represent the numbers they were just working with. These students are learning to connect their understanding of numerical relationships to symbolic representations.

A Precalculus String

The friendly number concept developed in the previous give and take strings can also apply to trigonometry. Let's say that you are planning a give and take string in precalculus during a trigonometry unit. How could you connect that to your students' current learning? What is a natural outcome upon which you could capitalize?

Because you know that students need strong facility with special angles and reference angles, one route is to ask students to consider how the idea of friendly numbers plays out in trigonometry. If you're going to focus on these friendly angles at the end of the string, it is important that, during the discussions throughout the string, you ask students to describe the friendly numbers they used in the string and what made them friendly in the particular problems. In a string like that in Figure 3.4, students will likely mention concepts such as multiples of ten, tenths, and one (for fractions).

At the end of the string, you could ask students to consider radian measure and friendly numbers. Based on the unit circle (see Figure 3.7), what are some friendly numbers you can think of? Following are some students' ideas.

FIGURE 3.7

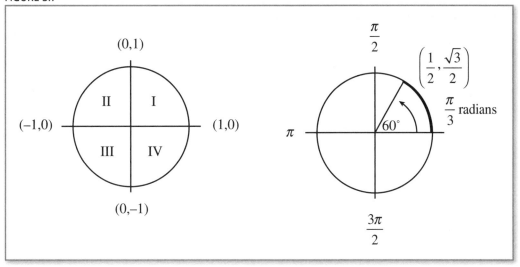

▶ "To find $^{5\pi}/_4$ radians on the unit circle, I compare it to π. It's more than 1 π and less than $^{3\pi}/_2$ so I know it's in the third quadrant. So I guess my friendly numbers were π and $^{3\pi}/_2$."

▶ "It's sorta like where the axes are: 0, $^{\pi}/_2$, π, $^{3\pi}/_2$, and 2π. They are friendly because you know where they are and you can use them to compare other angles to."

▶ "If you are finding the sine of $^{5\pi}/_3$, it's in the fourth quadrant, well, you know it's negative, but you also have to know what's the sine of $^{\pi}/_3$. That's $^{\sqrt{3}}/_2$ so sin $^{5\pi}/_3$ = $-^{\sqrt{3}}/_2$."

▶ "When we had to use the identities to find stuff like sin ($^{7\pi}/_{12}$), we had to break the numbers up into friendly numbers. We had to know that $^{7\pi}/_{12} = ^{\pi}/_3 + ^{\pi}/_4$."

These students are using examples of friendly numbers and generalizing in the world of radian measure on a unit circle. They are relating and connecting ideas and processes.

Doubles

Another important addition strategy is using doubles. When I began researching elementary math, I ran across suggestions that students should learn their doubles. I mentioned this in passing to a group of participants in an algebra 2 workshop, and one participant enthusiastically agreed. She was so enthusiastic that I asked her to explain. "Well, doubles are everywhere and so handy," she replied, "You really should know your thirty-fives, forty-fives, fifteens." I was surprised by her choices, "Thirty-fives?" "Well, yes, you know 3.5, 35, 350, 0.35—once you know that double 35 is 70, then you know all of the rest, like double 3.5 is 7, double 350 is 700." Well, she was right—doubles are very handy in many situations. Given a problem like 3.49 + 3.52, you can build off of 3.50 + 3.50 = 7.00 and then give and take a little for 3.49 + 3.52 = 3.50 + 3.51 = 7.00 + 0.01 = 7.01.

The strings in Figure 3.8 can help your students construct some doubles relationships. Let's see how this string could work in a classroom.

FIGURE 3.8

Middle School	High School
$75 + 75$	$15 + 15$
$749 + 752$	$1.52 + 1.49$
$7.44 + 7.58$	$\frac{3}{2} + \frac{3}{2}$
$0.76 + 0.71$	$45 + 45$
$\frac{3}{4} + \frac{3}{4}$	$4.45 + 4.54$
	$4{,}511 + 4{,}499$
	$0.43 + 0.46$

After quickly agreeing with students that 75 + 75 is 150 and 750 + 750 is 1,500, the teacher asks students to find 749 + 752. Several students line up these numbers and regroup. Some students add 51 to 749 to get 800 and then add the remaining 701. Claire explains her strategy, "Since 750 and 750 is 1,500, I gave 1 to the 749 and then you have 750 + 751 so it's 1,501." She used doubles and compensation as shown in Figure 3.9.

After students work on the next problem, 7.44 + 7.58, the teacher asks if anyone had approached it in a way similar to Claire's doubles strategy. Several hands go up. Noah explains, "I used the double of 7.5. That's 15, and I realized that you are 0.02 over, so that's 15.02."

To tease out more of the place-value connections, the teacher asks the group to write down all of the doubles used so far: 75 + 75 = 150, 750 + 750 = 1,500, and 7.5 + 7.5 = 15. The teacher then asks students to consider 0.76 + 0.71 and what double they might use. After a minute, Brandon explains, "I know 75 cents and 75 cents is $1.50. So, it's really like you've got 75 cents and 72 cents, so 3 cents less is $1.47."

Finally, to connect fractions and decimals, the teacher gives the students the last problem of ¾ + ¾. "Do any of the problems that we've just done influence your thinking about this fraction problem?" Students offer the following explanations as the teacher models them on the board.

"Three-quarters of a dollar and three quarters of a dollar is one and a half dollars, so 1.5."

"Three-quarters is like 75; it's just point 75. Double 75 is 150 so double point 75 is 1.5."

"I thought of it like fractions. Three-quarters is seventy-five–hundredths, $\frac{3}{4} = \frac{75}{100}$. So double seventy-five–hundredths is one hundred fifty–hundredths, $\frac{150}{100} = 1.50$."

FIGURE 3.9

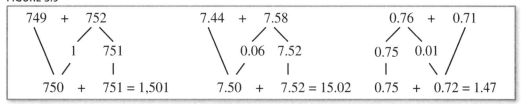

These students are thinking flexibly among representations of rational numbers and using place value to evaluate related problems.

The doubles strategy is also useful with angle measures such as 30°, 45°, 60°, 90°, 180°, and 360°. For example, students can relate the sum of the measures of the angles of a triangle to the sum of the measures of a quadrilateral. By cutting or partitioning the quadrilateral into two triangles, they see that the sum of the measures of the angles of the quadrilateral is just twice the sum of the measures of the angles of the triangles. Since the sum of the measures of the angles in each triangle is 180°, they can then double 180° to get 360°. This generalizes to all polygons and can be used to help students generalize to the formula for the sum of the measure of the interior angles of any polygon.

Comparing Strategies

A key lesson to take away from this chapter is that students need to have a repertoire of strategies. Understanding numerical relationships gives students the freedom to choose a strategy, rather than being stuck with only one way. Consider the following students and their responses to these three addition problems: 35.72 + 34.98; 2,378 + 6,743; 2.0613 + 7.9254.

For 35.72 + 34.98, Claire explained, "I gave 2¢ to 34.98 to get 35 and that leaves the 35.72 at 35.7. I know double 35 is 70. So, the answer is 70.7."

For 2,378 + 6,743, Raul also used a give and take strategy. "I thought about giving 22 to 2,378 for 2,400, but I didn't like that. So, instead I got 6,743 to 7,000 by adding 257. So that leaves 2,121 + 7,000 = 9,121."

For 2.0613 + 7.9254, Illiana shrugged. "I just added. When I looked at both numbers, I realized I could just line them up and add, without having to carry. So, it's 9.9867."

Each student chose a strategy that made sense for the problem. Having worked through well-chosen problem strings, the students were able to evaluate the numbers in the problems and choose an effective strategy.

Clarifying Understanding

But do they get it? Students who have come to you from a "math is memorization" world may try to memorize these powerful addition strategies rather than understand them. "Give and take—got it. Can we move on now?" It takes effort and engagement to construct the mental numeric relationships that make the strategies accessible, so that students become more naturally inclined to use strategies that make sense to them. Consider the following activities to help see the extent to which your students understand and use the numerical relationships involved in addition, rather than just memorizing.

As Close as It Gets

Look at the problems in Figure 3.10. Instead of asking students to *solve* these problems, ask them to choose the *closest* answer from among those given. Then discuss the problems, one at a time, as a class. Model these relationships as they come up. The power in these exercises comes as students discuss how they see the relationships. Students who come to you with a rule-based, digit-oriented approach are freed up to reason about the quantities because they do not have to compute an exact answer. In a sense, when you trust them with such large and small numbers, they become empowered to think about the quantities involved instead of reverting to a memorized rule. These are not the typical rounding or estimation problems, though they might appear to be. Since students must choose among given answers, they cannot just round. They must reason.

FIGURE 3.10

As Close as It Gets		
$409 + 1.19$	$13.2 + 1,989$	$\dfrac{1}{42} + \dfrac{12}{13}$
a) 400 b) 410	a) 14 b) 1,900	a) 0 b) 0.5
c) 419 d) 500	c) 2,000 d) 2,100	c) 0.75 d) 1

When students look at a problem like $409 + 1.19$, they might think of 409 and about 1, which is about 410. If they round, they might mistakenly choose 400. If they are lining up the numbers incorrectly (a common error), they might choose 419 or 500. For the next problem, $13.2 + 1,989$, students may reason, "You are adding about 13 to about 2,000, which is about 2,000." The last problem threatens to send most students into memorized rules, but in this context allows students to just consider the quantities involved and reason. A student might say that adding $\frac{1}{42}$ to $\frac{12}{13}$ is like adding practically 0 to practically 1, which gets you about 1.

Relational Thinking

Another teacher-led activity can help with reasonableness, sense making, and avoiding reactionary memorization. This activity, relational thinking, can help repair some misconceptions while encouraging algebraic reasoning. Carpenter, Franke, and Levi, in *Thinking Mathematically: Integrating Arithmetic & Algebra in Elementary School* (2003), discuss research about students' reasoning about the relational symbol of equality, the equal sign (=). They suggest that many students (and teachers) see it less as a relational symbol of equality and more as a "do it" symbol. For example, "$2 + 3 =$" might be thought of as "do $2 + 3$." So these students would look at a sentence like $16 + 7 = \underline{\hspace{1cm}} + 3$ and incorrectly fill in the blank with "23." They "do" $16 + 7$ and find 23, but this results in the obviously incorrect $16 + 7 = 23 + 3$. Instead, to reason about filling in that blank, students could use a give and take strategy. If you take 4 from 7 to get 3, you can then give it to the 16 to get 20. So the correct equation, expressing the relationship of equality, is $16 + 7 = 20 + 3$.

The misunderstanding of the relational symbol "=" is found sometimes as secondary students record their equation solving. For example, we might see the equation $3x - 5 = x$ solved as sort of a run-on sentence, where the first step, subtract x from both sides to get an equivalent statement of $2x - 5 = 0$, is written incorrectly as $3x - 5 = x = 2x - 5 = 0$. The student could then continue to record incorrectly the rest of the steps as $3x - 5 = x = 2x - 5 = 0 = 2x = 5 = \frac{5}{2}$. This shows the equal sign as more of a connector than a relational symbol expressing equality. The student writes an equal sign to connect to the next step. Students could more correctly use a "therefore it follows" symbol like $3x - 5 = x \Rightarrow 2x - 5 = 0 \Rightarrow 2x = 5 \Rightarrow x = \frac{5}{2}$. Or they could simply start over each time so that each sentence expresses equality.

$3x - 5 = x$

$2x - 5 = 0$

$2x = 5$

$x = \frac{5}{2}$

The relational thinking activity asks students to give and take mentally and to shift quantities around to keep the equality of the sentence true. Notice that the first sentences in Figure 3.11 have blanks to fill in. Students are instructed *not* to compute the sum on the left, but instead to compensate in order to fill in the blank, requiring them to reason relationally. The next type of question is a true-or-false question. For example, "Is it true that $19.8 + 2.03 = 20 + 0.03$? Why or why not?" This activity not only helps students to give and take, but also helps to build the correct meaning of the relational symbol of equality. As the Common Core State Standards state, "One hallmark of mathematical understanding is the ability to justify, in a way appropriate to the student's mathematical maturity, why a particular mathematical statement is true." (Common Core State Standards Initiative 2011).

FIGURE 3.11

Relational Thinking
Fill in the blank:
$36 + 97 = \underline{\hspace{1cm}} + 100$
$3{,}554 + 2{,}849 = 3{,}403 + \underline{\hspace{1cm}}$
True or false? Why?
$19.8 + 2.03 = 20 + 0.03$

A Last Word About Addition

On the first day of a K–2 training session, I was leading teachers in a whole number addition string. Near the end of the string, I put up "$215 + 495$." A woman excitedly gasped, "Oh!" I turned to see what was up. She was pointing to the board with a look of wonder.

"I can do that! It's just 500 plus 210 and that's easy—710!" I smiled, "Great!" "No, you don't understand," she exclaimed. "I could never do stuff like that. I memorized and worked hard, but I could never do math. But I can!" This is a college graduate. How many of our secondary students would love to have that moment too? The approach in this chapter can help you get them there.

four **4** ▥ ....

Subtraction

Math makes sense when you trust students enough to let them play with numbers long enough to understand relationships.

NUMERACY WORKSHOP PARTICIPANT

As shown in Chapter 2, having a strong understanding that subtraction can mean finding the difference between numbers has huge implications for learning in higher mathematics. This chapter contains examples of how to use problem strings to help students construct subtraction strategies in secondary classrooms.

Difference Versus Removal

Let's join Amy in her middle school class in the middle of a difference versus removal string. She wants her students to experience problems that are easier to solve with one or the other strategy. As she juxtaposes those problems, she'll engender some healthy disequilibrium. As students discuss their strategies, they'll be practicing addition (when they find the difference) and subtraction (when they remove) and also building relationships in whole numbers, integers, and fractions. Amy starts by posing the basketball score (38 to 43) and football score (3 to 51) scenarios from Chapter 2.

"Who can summarize the football and basketball halftime scores question?" asks Amy.

Denae volunteers, "You add up when it's a close game."

"And you subtract when it's a blowout," adds Christian.

"With that in mind, what is $811 - 22$?" continues Amy with the next problem.

Most students remove 11 from 811 and then 11 more to land on 789. Amy models this on an open number line (see Figure 4.1). Knowing that her students need to solidify these ideas, she asks, "Would you also please find the difference between the two numbers?"

Even though it is very efficient to just remove 22 from 811, Amy wants students to compare for themselves, to feel the relationships, not just memorize them.

Some students are not sure where to start. "Who can give a helpful hint to those who are unclear here?"

"Finding the difference is like finding the distance between the two numbers, like we did in the football game," suggests Suzanne.

After students work, Amy models finding the difference between 22 and 811, and she writes this next to the removal strategy, as in Figure 4.1. "Look at both of these strategies for 811 − 22. Talk with your partner about where on the number line the answer is when you found the difference between 811 and 22 and where the answer is when you removed 22 from 811. Why are the answers where they are?"

FIGURE 4.1

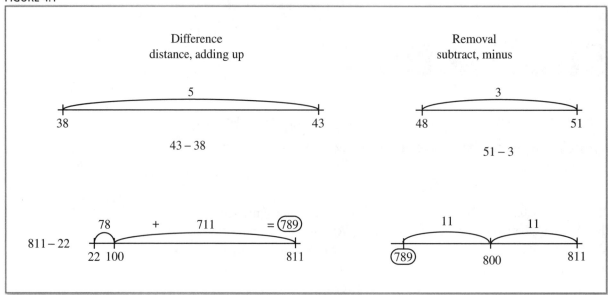

After a few minutes of partner discussion, Amy asks Suzanne to circle the answer in each strategy. Connecting to previous work, Amy asks, "Where are the answers in our addition strategies on a number line?"

Gabe answers, "The answers were where we landed. We started on one number and took jumps on the number line to add the other number. We landed on the answer."

Mariah adds, "Yes, and that is like the minus strategy. You start on one number and then subtract off the other number, so you land on the answer."

"Good descriptions. And what about finding the difference? Where is that answer?" asks Amy.

John David replies, "When you find the difference, it's like finding the distance between the numbers, so the answer has to be on top because that tells you how far apart the numbers are."

At the end of the string, Amy puts up one more problem, −5 − (−8) and asks, "Can you find the distance, the difference, between these numbers?"

After students work for a bit, Amy asks Edwin to explain. He says, "I put both numbers on the number line. Then it was easy—they are just 3 apart. So the answer is 3." (See Figure 4.2.)

FIGURE 4.2

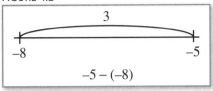

Amy then asks the students to find $-3 - 5$.

Tim responds, "Well, I am still looking at the difference between -3 and 5, which is 8, but this time the answer is -8 because you went the other way."

Amy asks him to clarify. "What do you mean, 'went the other way'?"

Tim answers, "You are subtracting a big number from a small number, so it has to be negative."

Amy pushes for more, knowing that not all of the students are clear yet, "Why does it have to be negative? Turn to your partner and discuss please." After some discussion, Amy brings the group back and asks Shelby and Mason to report.

Mason says, "If you subtract like normal, a big number subtract a small number, then you just get the difference. But if you go the other way, then it has to be negative."

Shelby adds, "Yes, because a small amount of money minus a large amount puts you in the hole."

Amy knows that they have a lot more work to do with integer operations, but this will be a nice piece of their work. These students are able to apply the finding the difference strategy to integers. They are using a model and strategy that is good for more than just whole numbers and decimals; it carries through to integers and can be used to build even more mathematics.

Figure 4.3 shows some possible problem strings for building this important understanding in different contexts.

FIGURE 4.3

Difference Versus Removal		
Middle School	**Algebra 1**	**Precalculus**
$51 - 3$	$52 - 47$	$32 - 5$
$42 - 38$	$61 - 4$	$53 - 48$
$9.2 - 0.5$	$811 - 22$	$2{,}001 - 1{,}989$
$7.1 - 6.7$	$253 - 238$	$7{,}122 - 133$
$21\frac{5}{9} - 20\frac{7}{9}$	$19.28 - 1.39$	$\frac{3\pi}{2} - \frac{\pi}{4}$
$3\frac{1}{5} - 2\frac{4}{5}$	$5.44 - 4.99$	$\pi - \frac{5\pi}{6}$
	$6\frac{1}{5} - \frac{3}{10}$	
	$8\frac{1}{3} - 7\frac{5}{6}$	
	$\text{slope} = \dfrac{y_2 - y_1}{x_2 - x_1}$	

Algebra 1

Let's look at the end of a difference versus removal string in an algebra 1 class. Abby, the teacher, continues with the problem $6\frac{1}{5} - \frac{3}{10}$. Because $\frac{3}{10}$ is relatively small compared to $6\frac{1}{5}$, many students choose to remove, starting with the $6\frac{1}{5}$ and removing $\frac{1}{5}$ to land on 6, and, since $\frac{1}{5} = \frac{2}{10}$, removing one more tenth, $\frac{1}{10}$, to land on $5\frac{9}{10}$. Abby models this (see Figure 4.4). She then asks, "Now, how about $8\frac{1}{3} - 7\frac{5}{6}$?"

As students work, Abby looks for students who use a difference strategy and models that strategy as shown in Figure 4.4. Since the $7\frac{5}{6}$ and the $8\frac{1}{3}$ are relatively close to each other, it is easy to find that relatively short distance between them. Notice that students do not have to change each mixed number to an improper fraction, find a common denominator, and then subtract. Instead, they can use the fractions' relative positions on the number line to operate, either by removing when the distance is large or finding the distance when the distance is small.

FIGURE 4.4

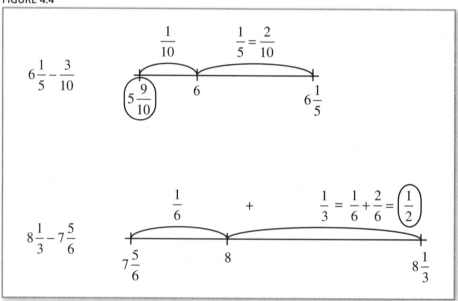

Abby ends the string by writing the formula for the slope of a line, $m = \frac{y_2 - y_1}{x_2 - x_1}$, and asking, "Tell me about the two subtraction signs in this formula. Do they mean 'remove' and 'take away'? Or do they mean 'find the distance between coordinates'?"

With the understanding that subtraction can denote finding the distance between two numbers, these students can better understand this fundamental formula in algebra. For them, the formula can be less procedural and more conceptual. This will probably help students remember the formula and apply it to find the slope between two points, but it also has implications for the very understanding of slope itself: that slope could be the ratio of distance traveled to the elapsed time, or the ratio of two differences between start and end values. They will be better able to grasp that rate of change is the ratio of changes or differences.

Precalculus

Let's examine how the problem string from Figure 4.3 can help in a precalculus class working on radian measure. At the end of the string, the teacher, Rick, gives the students the following two subtraction problems and asks which problem might be easier to solve by removal and which by finding the difference: $\frac{3\pi}{2} - \frac{\pi}{4}$ and $\pi - \frac{5\pi}{6}$.

As students work, Rick circulates and hears a conversation between two students. He asks them to share with the class, and he models their discussion (see Figure 4.5).

Brittney begins, "We were saying that it's like the number line has been wrapped around the circle. We are doing the same things around the unit circle that we did on the number line."

"Yeah, for the first problem ($\frac{3\pi}{2} - \frac{\pi}{4}$), since $\frac{\pi}{4}$ is little, you just start on $\frac{3\pi}{2}$ and then remove $\frac{\pi}{4}$ and you land on the answer, $\frac{5\pi}{4}$," explains her partner, Marcus.

Brittney finished, "But for the second problem ($\pi - \frac{5\pi}{6}$), they were close together, so we found the difference. Put both $\frac{5\pi}{6}$ and π on the unit circle and you can see that they are just $\frac{\pi}{6}$ apart."

Notice how students are able to operate on the unit circle and use it as a model to think with and solve problems.

FIGURE 4.5

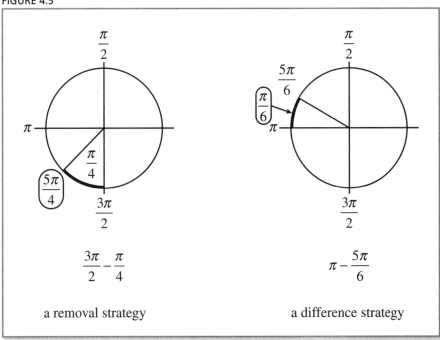

a removal strategy   a difference strategy

Constant Difference

Once students construct both notions of subtraction and can find the difference between two numbers, then we can really empower them with the constant difference strategy for subtraction. Let's look at a sample middle school string in Figure 4.6.

FIGURE 4.6

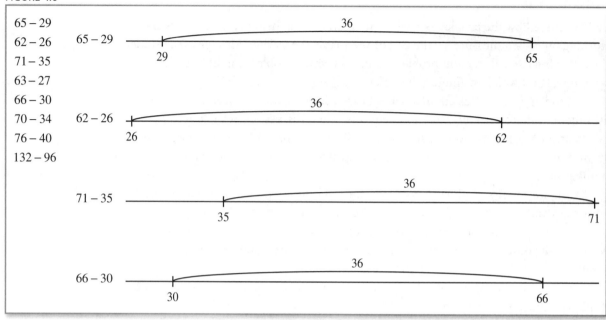

65 − 29
62 − 26
71 − 35
63 − 27
66 − 30
70 − 34
76 − 40
132 − 96

The string begins with a problem that uses "middling numbers"—numbers that do not immediately lend themselves to either finding the difference or removal, such as 65 − 29. Some students will most likely use each strategy. The teacher models both strategies on the board and then presents a new problem: 62 − 26. Students work on this problem, again with each student using her preferred strategy, and the teacher models both strategies. The next three problems are 71 − 35, 63 − 27, and 66 − 30. For these problems, the teacher models only the difference strategy.

Throughout the string, students begin noticing that all of the problems have the same answer, 36. One student exclaims, "The numbers are all 36 apart, just at different places. The 36 is shifting." The teacher has intentionally tried to engender intrigue and puzzlement. She wants the students to wonder why this is happening and to seek to figure that out. At this point in the string, the teacher asks students to discuss this with a partner, "Why is this happening? Why might I want to shift the distance around?" During the following class discussion, students commented:

"All of these are 36. You're just moving it around on the number line."

"The numbers are all 36 apart, just at different places. The 36 is shifting."

"Of all those problems, I'd rather do the last one."

"Yeah, since this works, if we get a hard problem, we can just move the distance somewhere nicer."

"For that first problem, 65 −29, instead of borrowing or making lots of jumps, I could just shift both numbers up one to 66 − 30 and then it's easy."

These students are reasoning about a sophisticated subtraction strategy, the constant difference strategy, using the number line to justify their thinking. They have a model with which to think and reason. They are constructing numerical relationships as their teacher leads them through purposefully constructed strings of problems. They haven't fully vetted the constant difference strategy, though. Students are now intrigued that they can shift the difference to make an equivalent problem, but many are not sure where to shift. Should they make the minuend or the subtrahend a nice number? The teacher could offer two problems, such as $70 - 34$ and $76 - 40$, to help students differentiate between the two. Which do you find easier?

For most students, the last problem is much easier to solve. Through the discussion, the teacher guides students to realize that they can shift a problem on the number line, keeping the difference constant, to friendly numbers that make the problem easier.

In an algebra class, after doing constant difference strings with much shifting up and down the number line, the students are ready to connect their numerical understanding to algebra. The teacher starts the students with $a - b$ and asks them to work with a partner to show what is happening using variables. Students first recognize that when they shift the distance along the number line, they are adding the same amount to both numbers. The teacher records their results: $a - b = (a + c) - (b + c)$. Students agree that this matches their description, and they begin to realize that the right side of the equation can be simplified to match the left side. This equivalence can be shown as follows: $a - b = (a + c) - (b + c) = a + c - b - c = a - b$. Students also note that subtracting a constant amount works, which the teacher records similarly: $a - b = (a - c) - (b - c) = a - c - b + c = a - b$.

Students may refer to these strategies as "give and give" or "take and take," by analogy with the give and take strategy for addition discussed in Chapter 3. The key understanding students construct from this discussion is that as long as the distance stays the same, you can shift the problem up or down the number line to wherever the problem is easier.

These students are using variables to represent a sophisticated subtraction strategy, the constant difference strategy. They are generalizing a connection between a geometric representation of shifting a distance up and down the number line and an algebraic representation using variables to demonstrate the relationships. They are also ready to apply this strategy to much harder subtraction problems.

Writing a Constant Difference String

So, say you are in the midst of teaching domain and range, or perhaps solving inequalities in an algebra class. These topics all deal with ranges of numbers on a number line; for domain, range, and single-variable inequalities, it's a number line, while with two-variable inequalities, it's the coordinate axes. Some of the big ideas undergirding these topics, like the continuity of the number system, the continuity of measurement (distance), and the density of the number line, are all supported by the use of the open number line in general and constant difference strings specifically.

To support this understanding of ranges of numbers, you could do some constant difference strings with your students, where they will deal with the distance between endpoints on a number line.

As you saw in Figure 4.6, one type of string that helps students build the constant difference strategy consists of several subtraction problems that have the same difference. As students solve these problems using any strategy, they begin to notice that the answers are all the same. Modeling the difference strategy for each problem allows students to see the common distance being shifted up and down.

So, to write such a string, you could begin with a final, easy problem in mind, such as $59 - 30 = 29$. Notice that 29 and 30 are roughly half of 59. Using these middling numbers means that the problems we create will not be obviously removal or difference problems. So, what are some other problems that have a difference of 29 but where the answer is not as obvious? You could shift that distance between 30 and 59 up by 9 to get $68 - 39$. If students use the algorithm, they'll have to regroup to solve this problem. (Notice that if we shifted it up 10, 11, or 12, we would have $69 - 40$, $70 - 41$, or $71 - 42$—much too easy to start with.) Now you could choose the next problem to be shifted down a bit, such as $63 - 34$ (which still requires regrouping). Next, you could shift up, perhaps to $70 - 41$. You will want to model these on a number line to make sure that it gives you the "look" you want; all of the differences should be the same and distributed seemingly randomly but not too closely around the first problem.

The next two problems, shifting down and up, could be $61 - 32$ and $66 - 37$. You may want to hold one problem (such as $67 - 38$) in reserve, in case the class is working hard but not seeing the differences shifting. If things are going well, you could skip to $59 - 30$. If students are comfortable shifting the difference, you may ask them to come up with a problem that would be made extremely easy by shifting the difference. Then, of course, you'll want to have them discuss *why* that problem is easier than the rest. If students are not yet ready, giving them a problem like $59 - 30$ may prompt the beginning of such a discussion.

If you are working with integer operations, you could similarly write a string beginning with the idea that $0 - 20 = -20$. Now shift that around and your string could become: $-7 - 13$, $-11 - 9$, $-4 - 16$, and $0 - 20$, with the last two problems having different answers, $-6 - 19$ and $-12 - 15$. Students focused on the number line, watching the 20 shift around, now have to decide where to shift these new problems. If students had been catching on to the common answer for the first set of problems, they may stop working and just guess, "I bet the next one's negative 20!" So, giving the last two problems gives everyone a chance to try the constant difference strategy independently. Figure 4.7 summarizes these two strings.

FIGURE 4.7

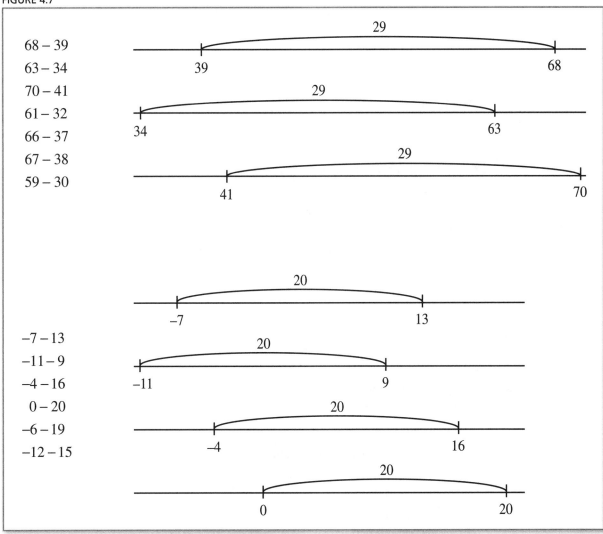

Comparing Strategies

As with addition, students need a repertoire of subtraction strategies and the ability to consider the numbers before they operate, in order to choose the most efficient strategy.

Consider these three problems. Before reading on, think about which strategy you would use to solve each one.

    a. $5{,}367 - 5{,}298$

    b. $52{,}632 - 1{,}521$

    c. $100{,}021 - 132$

For $5{,}367 - 5{,}298$, Caleb used a constant difference strategy. He explained, "It was easy to add 2 to both numbers and make the problem $5{,}367 - 5{,}298 = 5{,}369 - 5{,}300 = 69$."

For $52{,}632 - 1{,}521$, Micheala explained, "I simply subtracted—I didn't have to do anything else. I just lined them up and got 51,111." It is noteworthy that she subtracted left to right, big to small, keeping a sense of magnitude.

For 100,021 − 132, Mike explained, "I subtracted 21 to land on 100,000. Then I subtracted the remaining 111 to get 99,889. But you could also add 68 to both numbers and the problem becomes 100,089 − 200."

Try the following problems. What strategies work best for you?

a. 9.012 − 3.989

b. 7.462 − 5.351

c. 60.12 − 0.23

Clarifying Understanding

Students who have long been in the atmosphere of "math is memorizing" will still be at risk for trying to revert to memorizing strategies. Can we give and take or give and give or take and take? Which strategy works when? Try some of the activities that follow to help students realize that they can just think about the numbers and feel the relationships, instead of memorizing.

As Close as It Gets

As with the addition strategies in Chapter 3, the "As Close as It Gets" exercises in Figure 4.8 can help keep students aware of the magnitudes involved in the problems and make sure they are reasoning about the quantities instead of mimicking a set procedure. Remember, the power is in the discussion of students' reasoning as they identify which choice is closest to the correct answer.

FIGURE 4.8

As Close as It Gets		
$14,009 - 9.19$	$1,002 - 899$	$5\frac{1}{9} - 1\frac{12}{13}$
a) 14,000 b) 5,000	a) 3 b) 100	a) 5 b) 6
c) 13,000 d) 4,000	c) 200 d) 300	c) 4 d) 3

Relational Thinking

Now that students have explored several addition and subtraction strategies, they may be tempted to misapply the "rules" from one situation to another. Remember that our goal is for students to construct numerical relationships so that the strategies arise from those relationships. Otherwise, students could be left with memorized rules and confusion: Can you give and take with addition, subtraction, or both? Some relational thinking activities, such as those in Figure 4.9, can help your students clarify their understanding, help you see how well your students understand the numerical relationships, and help you identify any places where they may still be struggling or trying to mis-apply memorized rules.

For example, with the problem "Does 6.2 − 3.8 = 6 − 4?" you could ask students to model each side of the equation on an open number line as in Figure 4.9. When they *see* that giving and taking with subtraction results in the distance between the numbers changing (shrinking, in this case), they will better understand that they cannot give and take if they want the distance to remain constant. Similarly, if you model both sides of the statement $500 - 312 = 512 - 300$ on the open number line, you can easily see that the distance increases and the statement is false.

FIGURE 4.9

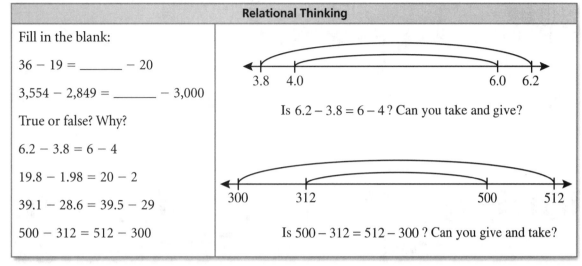

Relational Thinking	
Fill in the blank: $36 - 19 = \underline{\hspace{1cm}} - 20$ $3{,}554 - 2{,}849 = \underline{\hspace{1cm}} - 3{,}000$ True or false? Why? $6.2 - 3.8 = 6 - 4$ $19.8 - 1.98 = 20 - 2$ $39.1 - 28.6 = 39.5 - 29$ $500 - 312 = 512 - 300$	Is $6.2 - 3.8 = 6 - 4$? Can you take and give? Is $500 - 312 = 512 - 300$? Can you give and take?

A Last Word About Subtraction

Consider a class of subtraction problems that many people find very difficult with the standard algorithm, those where the minuend is mostly zeros (for example, $2{,}000 - 549$). Can you see now that you could shift by 451 to get the equivalent $2{,}451 - 1{,}000$? Or what about something like $50{,}010 - 39{,}999$? Shifting by just one creates the simple problem $50{,}011 - 40{,}000$. Because the minuend contains mostly zeros, adding anything to it as you shift up the number line is always relatively easy. Using strings like those in this chapter will help your students become fluent in using this powerful constant difference strategy.

CHAPTER 5

Multiplication and Division: Models and Strategies

I feel very empowered and excited to share these strategies and activities with students—and anyone else that will listen to me!

NUMERACY WORKSHOP PARTICIPANT

This chapter sets the stage for whole number multiplication and division, discussing the ramifications of the current elementary approaches and proposing the models and strategies that secondary teachers can employ with their students. In Chapters 6 and 7, you'll find examples of how to help students construct these numerical relationships and strategies with problem strings and other activities.

Multiplication: A "Digit Approach"

As with the addition and subtraction algorithms, the digit approach is implicit in the common algorithm for multiplication. In a problem like 49 · 35, students start by multiplying 5 × 9 to get 45, write down the *5*, and put the *4* above the 49, as shown in Figure 5.1. They then find 5 × 4 (20), add the 4 to get 24, and write that down, and so forth. Each of these steps focuses on a one-digit-times-one-digit problem, ignoring the magnitudes (i.e., that 5 × 40 is 200, hence the 245). The next steps in the algorithm can further confuse the issue as students are instructed to write a *0* on the next line as a "placeholder." Many students have no idea (and do not care) why they put that 0 there. Then the algorithm proceeds with more digit-by-digit problems, ending with an addition problem that again uses the digit approach. Focusing on the individual digit problems and the mysteriously appearing zeros, students end up with little sense of magnitudes for large multiplications.

FIGURE 5.1

```
   4                2̶
  49               49
 × 35             × 35
 ────            ────
 245              245
                 1470
```

Because students can successfully use counting or additive reasoning throughout these digit manipulations, they may not be using multiplicative reasoning. As we saw in the addition and subtraction algorithms, students who use a digit approach may be stuck using counting strategies or, at best, additive strategies. If they use counting strategies, it will be very difficult for them to multiply. If they use additive reasoning (such as skip-counting), they will be able to find answers to multiplication problems, but only with much effort and without thinking multiplicatively.

What does it mean to think multiplicatively? Students have to keep track of the number of groups and the number represented by each group simultaneously, in a process called *unitizing*.

Unitizing requires that children use number to count not only objects but also groups—and to count them both simultaneously. The whole is thus seen as a group of a number of objects. The parts together become the new whole, and the parts (the objects in the group) and the whole (the group) can be considered simultaneously. . . . For learners, unitizing is a shift in perspective. . . . It is a huge shift in thinking for children, and in fact, was a huge shift in mathematics that took centuries to develop. (Fosnot and Dolk 2001, 11)

If students have not made this shift, they may find the answer to a multiplication question by labor-intensive repeated addition or skip-counting, but they are not thinking multiplicatively. And if they cannot reason multiplicatively, they will not reason proportionally, which is the underpinning of rational number work (as we'll discuss in Chapter 8) because "proportional-reasoning tasks involve comparing quantities by using multiplication and division" (Miller and Fey 2000, 310).

Therefore, we must help students gain a deeper understanding of both multiplication and division. This chapter will discuss the models and strategies that we can use as secondary teachers to help students make this shift to multiplicative and proportional thinking.

Single-Digit Multiplication Facts

Seven times eight, like the garden gate, is made of sticks, rhymes with fifty-six.

A similar poem, along with many others, hung on the wall of my son's third-grade classroom. His well-meaning teacher did not "do math" personally, but planned to help her students be more successful than she was. She was determined to find ways to help her students memorize those beastly facts, and the poems were one of those ways. Her understanding of multiplication facts was that they should be memorized, each and every one. She did not realize that students could reason using relationships to figure out single-digit facts.

Consider the following approaches to finding 7×8.

▶ "Well, I know that 10 sevens is 70, but I only need 8 sevens, so 70 − 14 is 56."

▶ "7 × 7 is 49, but I need 8 sevens, so 49 + 7 is 56."

▶ "I know 4 × 7 is 28, so double that to get 8 × 7 is 56."

The students in the three examples have a good sense of the magnitudes involved in the problem. They have a mental picture of number relationships and can manipulate those relationships to solve the problem. Of course, we want the facts to be automatic for our students. By emphasizing reasoning and sense making, we can help students have the facts at their fingertips and also have models with which to reason about higher mathematics. We can help students build mental pictures of multiplicative relationships by using ratio tables and array models.

The Ratio Table and the Array

For multiplication and division, the ratio table and the open array are key physical representations to aid in understanding relationships. Using these representations, we can model how to chunk numbers in multiplicative situations, and students can then use these models to think as they compute.

Ratio Tables

The ratio table is an example of the familiar paired number table. A ratio table is a special paired number table in which the ratios of $\frac{y}{x}$ in each pair are equivalent and therefore the ordered pairs represent a proportional relation, $\frac{y}{x} = k \Rightarrow y = kx$. Because all of the ratios $\frac{y}{x}$ are equivalent, they are related multiplicatively, $\frac{y}{x} = \frac{ay}{ax}$ (see Figure 5.2).

FIGURE 5.2

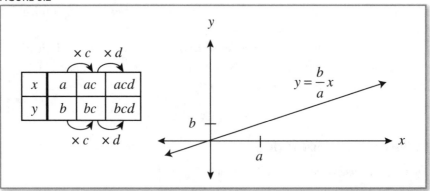

The three strategies for finding 7×8 that were shown previously can be modeled with ratio tables as in Figure 5.3, in which each ratio is equivalent to the others in the table.

FIGURE 5.3

1	10	2	8
7	70	14	56

1	7	8
7	49	56

1	4	8
7	28	56

The website for Catherine Twomey Fosnot and colleagues' Contexts for Learning curriculum states, "In the Netherlands, the ratio table is the prevalent model for multiplication and division (rather than the array, which is more typical of US materials). Thus proportional reasoning is emphasized at the start, as soon as multiplicative thinking is being developed" (2008; www.contextsforlearning.com/faqs.asp). Thus we can use the ratio table to build multiplicative and proportional reasoning at the same time. This proportional reasoning is key to several concepts in higher math: finding common denominators for fraction operations, representing more complicated proportional situations where the ratio is not a unit ratio, and solving proportions. It also helps students understand concepts such as slope, rate of change, and rational functions. (See Chapters 8–10 for more on these concepts.)

The Array Model and the Area Model

The rectangular array model is useful in developing many multiplicative and geometric concepts. It can be used as a tool with which to compute multiplication and division problems. Some real-world examples of arrays are boxes of fruit arranged in rows, columns, and layers; rows of desks neatly lined up in a classroom; and a rectangular football field where the area can be measured in square yards, square feet, and so on.

An example of the array model is the area model, a continuous rectangle of adjacent rows and columns of square units. The open arrays shown in Figure 5.4 for the three students' strategies for finding 7×8 are examples of area models. The problem 7×8 can be read as 7 by 8, a rectangular array that is 7 units long by 8 units wide. Thus by finding 7×8, we are finding the area of a 7×8 rectangle. Look at the diagrams in Figure 5.4 and match them with the verbal strategies from page 54. Do you recognize the relationships?

FIGURE 5.4

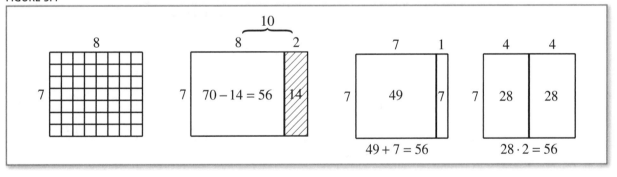

That you can take the number of columns and multiply by the number of rows to get the number of square units is more than just a procedure. Because area and perimeter problems are often so easy to solve when presented formulaically, students and teachers miss rich opportunities to build multiplication concepts such as the associative property, the commutative property, and the distributive property, and at the same time support the development of spatial sense and geometric reasoning. What happens to the area if you cut one dimension in half? What happens if you chunk the area into manageable pieces? Which pieces are the most advantageous for solving problems? The array model helps students explore these questions and more.

Multiplication Strategies

The Importance of "Times 10"

The effect of multiplying by 10 is one of the remarkable aspects of our base ten number system. We know that 9×10 is 90, 9×100 is 900, and $9 \times 1,000$ is 9,000. Now, for students, the idea that 9 tens (9×10) is 90 isn't too bad. But what about 10 nines (10×9)? If students can use only additive reasoning, they will start adding nines: 9, 18, 27. . . . If they use the commutative property, the problem becomes much simpler. But it's one thing to just tell students that $10 \times 9 = 9 \times 10$, and it's quite another thing for students to *own* the relationship. Using the array model can help because, while the orientations are different, the area of a 9-by-10 rectangle is equivalent to the area of a 10-by-9 rectangle. Therefore the products are equivalent.

A related notion can be shown in the following series of connections. 7×30 can be understood as repeating 3 groups of 7×10, and then to doubling 7×10 and adding one more group, and finally looking at 7×30 as $10 \times (7 \times 3)$. This can be expressed as: $7 \times 30 = 7 \times 10 + 7 \times 10 + 7 \times 10 = 2(7 \times 10) + 7 \times 10 = (7 \times 3) \times 10$. In other words, students can reason that 7×30 can be thought of as ten 7-by-3 rectangles as shown in Figure 5.5.

FIGURE 5.5

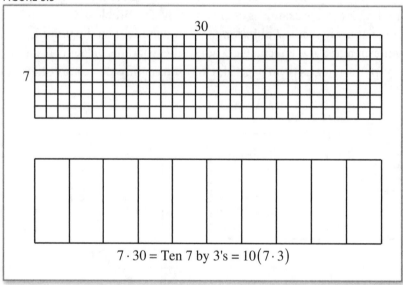

$7 \cdot 30 = $ Ten 7 by 3's $= 10(7 \cdot 3)$

Extending this pattern gives the relationships $23 \times 40 = (23 \times 4) \times 10$ and $60 \times 92 = 10(6 \times 92)$. These are all, of course, demonstrations of the associative property, $a \cdot (b \cdot c) = (a \cdot b) \cdot c$. Students can construct these relationships as they work with array models.

5 Is Half of 10

At one point, I checked in with my oldest son, then in fifth grade. "Do you know the multiplication facts? Like, do you know your fives?"

He briefly paused and then shook his head no. "Not really." He did not seem bothered by this.

You might imagine that I was more than a bit bothered. "What do you mean?"

"Well, Mom, I don't really have to know the fives, because I know the tens," he answered.

"Give me an example," I asked, trying to figure out what he meant.

He sighed. "Well, 5 × 9. I know 10 × 9 is 90, and 5 is half of 10, so 5 × 9 is 45."

Does that always work? "Give me another example."

He sighed again, "Um, OK, 23. 23 × 10 is 230. Half of 230 is 115."

Figure 5.6 shows how this might be modeled by an array and ratio table. Notice that his strategy is helpful for far more than just the single-digit multiplication facts for 5. It is useful for 5 times anything! In fact, this strategy can be stretched to find 50, 500, and even 0.5 times anything.

FIGURE 5.6

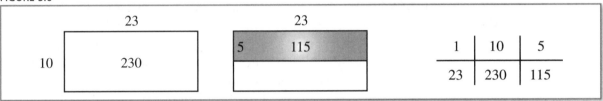

Which student would you rather have—a student with the "fives facts" rotely memorized, or a student who knows and can work with the fact that 5 is half of 10? I would argue that my son did know his fives because he could figure them so quickly, for single-digit and much bigger numbers.

Associative and Commutative Properties: Doubling and Halving

Consider a 16 × 12 rectangle. What happens if you double one dimension and halve the other? In other words, what happens to the area if you cut the array in half and rearrange the pieces as shown in Figure 5.7?

FIGURE 5.7

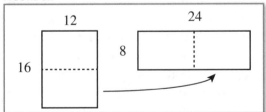

The area, of course, remains the same, demonstrating spatially that $16 \cdot 12 = 8 \cdot 24$. Keep doubling one dimension and halving the other, and you get equivalent problems: $16 \cdot 12 = 8 \cdot 24 = 4 \cdot 48 = 2 \cdot 96$. Geometrically, we are watching the area remain constant as we rearrange pieces of an array. Algebraically, we are seeing the associative property of multiplication, the multiplicative inverse, and the multiplicative identity at work: $a \cdot b = a(1)b = a(2 \cdot \frac{1}{2})b = (a \cdot 2)(\frac{1}{2} \cdot b) = 2a \cdot \frac{1}{2}b$.

In general, because $c \cdot \frac{1}{c} = 1$, you can not only double and halve, but also triple and divide by 3, quadruple and divide by 4, and so on. In our original 16×12 rectangle, quadrupling and dividing by 4 yields $64 \cdot 3$ or $4 \cdot 48$. Try this on a problem like $25 \cdot 26$, $125 \cdot 12$, or even $3\frac{1}{2} \cdot 21$. This strategy builds useful geometric concepts of area, specifically chunking area into manageable pieces, which comes into play in many places in higher math.

Another way to look at the doubling/halving in Figure 5.7 is by factoring and reassociating: $16 \cdot 12 = (8 \cdot 2) \cdot 12 = 8 (2 \cdot 12) = 8 \cdot 24$. With this in mind, we could factor and associate in many different ways, one other being $16 \cdot 12 = 16 \cdot (3 \cdot 4) = (16 \cdot 3) \cdot 4 = 48 \cdot 4$. Each of these expressions gives the dimensions of a rectangle that has an area of 192 square units. In fact, we could rearrange all of the factors of both 16 and 12 for many different equivalent problems, representing many different rectangles with the same area. As students investigate these equivalent problems, they gain spatial experience in the ideas of prime and composite numbers, prime factorization, and uniqueness found in the Fundamental Theorem of Arithmetic, which, in informal terms, states that every positive integer (except the number 1) can be expressed as a unique product of primes. Working with both algebraic and geometric representations serves to strengthen students' multiplicative thinking and builds toward such concepts as exponentiation (repeated multiplication), greatest common factors, and least common multiples.

As students work with these models and strategies to find multiples of numbers, they construct mental numerical relationships and have most of the facts at their fingertips. For those few facts that they don't have memorized by this point, they can reason so quickly to find them that often you can't tell the difference.

The Distributive Property of Multiplication over Addition

In many cases, we can find answers to multiplication and division problems by "chunking": separating problems into more manageable problems. This chunking is frequently referred to as *using partial products*. This approach takes advantage of the distributive property of multiplication over addition, which is the underpinning of the multiplication algorithm.

First, let's look at how using a proportional situation modeled in a ratio table can support this development of chunking of multiplication. (The ratio tables in this book are all shown as horizontal tables so that more will fit on the page. In classrooms, ratio tables should be shown both horizontally and vertically.) For example, consider packs of chewing gum that contain 16 sticks each. This is a proportional situation because of the constant ratio of 1 pack to 16 sticks. Because the ratio is constant, students are clear that when you double the number of packs, you also double the number of sticks, so 2 packs: 32 sticks and 4 packs: 64 sticks. They are also clear that if you add a pack, you also add 16 sticks, so in 5 packs you have $64 + 16 = 80$ sticks. You can show this in a ratio table as in Figure 5.8.

FIGURE 5.8

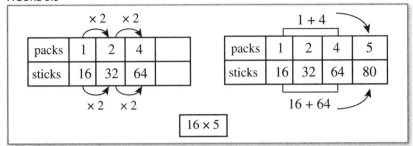

When the teacher records this thinking in a ratio table, that table can start to become a tool with which to operate. For example, to find 7 × 16, you could use a table to record this thinking: 1 pack has 16 sticks, so 2 packs have 32 sticks. Add 1 more pack to get 3 packs with 48 sticks. Double the 2 packs to get 4 packs with 64. Now add the 3 and the 4 packs to get 7 packs with 48 + 64 = 112 sticks. This reasoning is straightforward and shown in the first ratio table in Figure 5.9. It could be written 7 · 16 = (3 + 4) · 16.

FIGURE 5.9

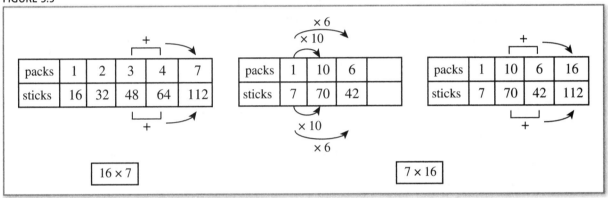

However, if I were given the naked expression 7 · 16, I might change the representation to be 16 packs with 1 pack holding 7 sticks. Then you could find 10 packs of 7 sticks to have 70 sticks and 6 more packs to have 42 sticks, so 16 packs would have 70 + 42 = 112 sticks. This strategy could be written 7 · 16 = 7(10 + 6).

Similarly, if asked to find 12 · 16, you could reason that for packs that hold 16 sticks, you need to find the number of sticks for 12 packs. So 10 packs is 160 sticks, 2 more packs is 32 sticks, so 12 packs hold 160 + 32 = 192 sticks. This strategy could be written 12 · 16 = (10 + 2) · 16 and is shown in Figure 5.10. Or, for 17 · 16, you could reason that for packs that hold 17 sticks, you need to find the number of sticks for 16 packs. So 10 packs is 170 sticks. Half of that gives you 5 packs, for 85 sticks. Add those to get 15 packs, for 170 + 85 = 255 sticks. Now you just need 1 more pack for 255 + 17 = 272 sticks. This strategy could be written 17 · 16 = 17(10 + 5 + 1).

FIGURE 5.10

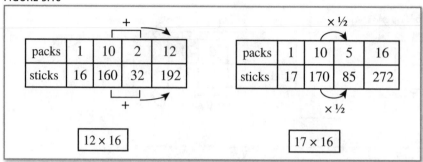

Note that the strategies discussed here are not prescribed moves; they are based on the numbers and their relationships. For a different problem, different steps might be appropriate. Susan Lamon, in her *Teaching Fractions and Ratios for Understanding*, notes that in a ratio table, "strategy cannot be taught directly; ratio tables are individual constructions that record personal thought processes" (Lamon 2005, 107). When you model students' thinking in a ratio table and they realize how their thinking is represented in such tables, students are then better able to understand other strategies modeled in ratio tables. They then begin to use the ratio table as a tool to apply those strategies. Often a student will start with the information given and a goal at the "end" of a ratio table, and then they will work up to that goal. They think, "What can I do to reach that goal?" See Figure 5.11 for an example.

FIGURE 5.11

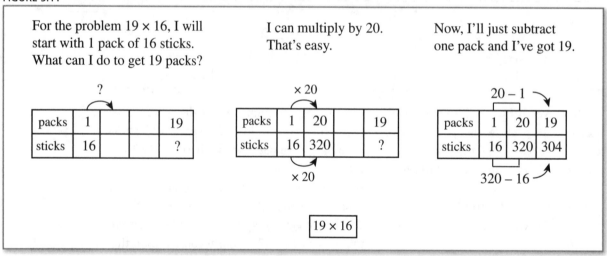

Partial Products and Place Value

The strategies discussed earlier involve chunking numbers and can be called *partial product strategies*. Using partial products, however, usually refers to using place-value chunks. For 17 · 16, for example, this would mean breaking both the 17 and the 16 so that 17 · 16 = (10 + 7)(10 + 6). All of these pieces are manageable, and because they maintain their magnitude, students already have a decent estimate of the product. They don't have to ask if their answer is reasonable because they have been reasoning the whole time. Area models are very useful for modeling the chunking that takes place in using partial products.

Notice in Figure 5.12 that if you combine the chunks of area in certain ways, you can see the steps of the traditional algorithm for either orientation. The traditional algorithm computes each of these areas and adds them together in a way that is clever and compact, but not very transparent.

FIGURE 5.12

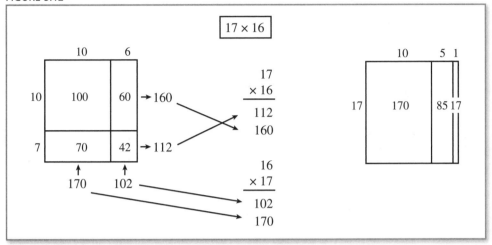

Maybe because using partial products is so transparent, with all of the steps manageable and maintaining magnitude, many reform elementary programs advocate partial products as the preferred strategy. Some teachers even teach it as another rote algorithm: break the numbers into place-value pieces, multiply the pieces together, and add all the parts. But rote application of a memorized procedure is not numeracy, nor is it the fastest, most efficient, or most sophisticated strategy for most multiplication problems. Note, for example, that in solving $12 \cdot 16$ without place-value chunking, we used only two chunks, and in solving $17 \cdot 16$ we used only three chunks. Just as the goal in addition and subtraction is for larger jumps on a number line, the search here is for larger chunks of arrays.

When students begin to multiply by reasoning in chunks, they will often begin by multiplying by 10 and then doubling. However, for some numbers, it can be more efficient to find multiples first and then scale up by 10. Remember that flexibility is key. For example, with $36 \cdot 42$, instead of multiplying by 10 and then doubling and doubling again to get $36 \cdot 40$, you might double 36 twice to get $4 \cdot 36 = 144$, then multiply that by 10 to get $36 \cdot 40$. The initial doubling also gives you $2 \cdot 36 = 72$, so now you have $36(40 + 2) = 1,440 + 72 = 1,512$. In other words, instead of multiplying by 10 and then doubling, start first with *multiples* of the factor and scale up by 10 or 100 to get where you need to go.

The Distributive Property of Multiplication over Subtraction

The distributive property of multiplication over subtraction can help solve many problems quickly and efficiently. For example, to find how many sticks of gum are in 19 packs that contain 17 sticks each, we could reason that 20 packs contain 340 sticks. Take away 1 pack of 17 sticks and you have 19 packs with $340 - 17 = 343 - 20 = 323$ sticks. This strategy could be written as $17 \cdot 19 = 17(20 - 1)$. Similarly, you could find $49 \cdot 17$ by first finding how many sticks are in 100 packs of 17 sticks each, 1,700 sticks. Since 100 packs have 1,700 sticks, 50 packs would have half of 1,700, or 850 sticks. We want 49 packs, so subtract the 17 sticks in 1 pack for $850 - 17 = 853 - 20 = 833$ sticks. This strategy could be written as $49 \cdot 17 = (50 - 1) \cdot 17$. This strategy can be called *over and under* because to find these products, you find a product that is just a little too much and subtract off what you don't need. See Figure 5.13 for the ratio table and array for these examples.

FIGURE 5.13

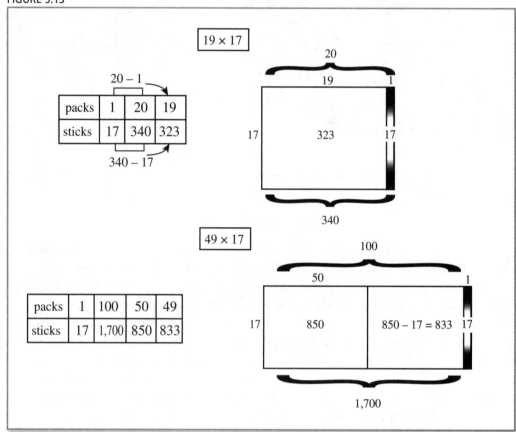

Division: A "Digit Approach"

Of the algorithms for the four operations, the one for division might be the most obscure. Many different mnemonics are taught, from "Dirty Monkeys Smell Bad" to "Dad, Mom, Sister, Brother" to "Dracula Must Suck Blood"—all referring to the steps of divide, multiply, subtract, and bring down. For example, to divide 1,188 by 12 (see Figure 5.14), first you divide, asking "How many times does 12 go into 1?" Then "How many times does 12 go into 11?" Finally, "How many times does 12 go into 118?"

FIGURE 5.14

$$\begin{array}{r} 9 \\ 12\overline{)1{,}188} \\ -108 \\ \hline 108 \end{array} \qquad \begin{array}{r} 99 \\ 12\overline{)1{,}188} \\ -108 \\ \hline 108 \\ -108 \end{array}$$

To answer this question, most students begin off to the side of the paper trying to find $12 \times$ lots of numbers until they get $12 \cdot 9 = 108$. Then, they need to subtract $118 - 108$ (often using a digit approach!) to find that $118 - 108 = 10$. Then they bring down the remaining 8, and so on. Because many students have little sense of the multiples of 12, their trial-and-error results are often haphazard and time-consuming. Also note how each step is digit oriented; the steps do not promote thinking about how 12 relates to 1,188. Students ignore the magnitudes in the problem and just use the digits. The strategies that follow will help students *understand* division, instead of simply manipulating digits.

Division Strategies

Quotative and Partitive Division

The division algorithm uses only one meaning of division: how many times does 4 go into 178? But there are two major situations in division, quotative (measurement or grouping) and partitive (sharing) division. Consider the following two problems:

There are 26 kids from the math team going on a field trip. How many vans do we need if 8 kids can ride in each van?

There are 26 kids from the math team going on a field trip. There are 8 vehicles available to carry the team. If the kids are split as evenly as possible, how many kids will ride in each vehicle?

The first problem is an example of *quotative* division: starting with the number in the group and being asked to find the number of groups. The second problem is an example of *partitive* division: starting with the number of groups and being asked to find the size of each group.

The standard division algorithm implies only quotative division. One way this plays out in higher math is that students use only quotative strategies, even when a partitive strategy is called for. Compare $298 \div 2$ and $298 \div 149$. If you think of these as quotative problems, you would think of them as "How many twos are in 298?" and "How many one hundred forty-nines are in 298?" But does that make sense for both problems? For the first problem, wouldn't it make more sense to divide 298 into 2 chunks?

What about $897 \div 3$? Which of these two approaches seems more efficient to you?

▶ Find how many threes are in 897.

▶ Think, "900 into 3 chunks is 300, so 1 less 3 in 897 means that each of those chunks is 1 less for 299."

Problems such as $2\overline{)68}$ and $3\overline{)75}$ are often used to teach the quotative long division steps, but students with a good grasp of the partitive meaning of division could more efficiently solve the problems by cutting 68 in half and seeing the three quarters in 75. Consider 5 ÷ 2.5. Is it more efficient to find how many 2.5s are in 5 or to cut 5 in 2.5 pieces? What we really need is for students to be flexible enough to use both solution strategies when they are appropriate.

Partial Quotients: Ratio Tables and the Distributive Property of Multiplication

Just as students can use a ratio table to record multiplication strategies to find the answers to multiplication problems, they can also use the same ratio table and the same multiplication strategies to *multiply* to find the answer to division problems. Remember our gum situation? How many packs should you get if there are 17 sticks in a pack and you need 374 sticks? Before reading on, find an answer for yourself.

Students who are versed in multiplication using ratio tables might naturally put this scenario into a ratio table as in Figure 5.15 and then begin by multiplying 17 by friendly numbers that get them close to 374. For example, you could reason that $10 \cdot 17 = 170$ and double that to get 20 packs for $20 \cdot 17 = 340$ sticks. That's only 34 away from the target of 374, so you just need 2 more packs, $20 + 2 = 22$ total packs.

A closely related strategy is to first double 17 and recognize that 34×10 is 340. These strategies can be written as $374 \div 17 = (340 + 34) \div 17$ or $^{374}/_{17} = \dfrac{(340 + 34)}{17} = {}^{340}/_{17} + {}^{34}/_{17}$. This strategy can be called *partial quotients* and uses the distributive property of multiplication over addition.

What if you needed 1,513 sticks—$1{,}513 \div 17$? Again, thinking in terms of packs and sticks, and using multiples of 10, you could reason that 100 packs is 1,700 sticks. That's too much, so get rid of 10 packs (170 sticks) for 1,530 sticks in 90 packs. That's only 17 sticks (1 pack) away; $1{,}530 - 17 = 1{,}513$, so you need 89 packs. Here we found $1{,}513 \div 17 = (1{,}700 - 170 - 17) \div 17$ or $^{1,513}/_{17} = \dfrac{(1{,}700 - 170 - 17)}{17} = {}^{1,700}/_{17} - {}^{170}/_{17} - {}^{17}/_{17}$. This is an *over and under* strategy—multiplying by too much and removing the extra—and uses the distributive property of multiplication over subtraction.

FIGURE 5.15

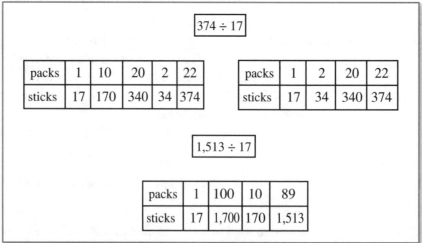

374 ÷ 17

packs	1	10	20	2	22
sticks	17	170	340	34	374

packs	1	2	20	22
sticks	17	34	340	374

1,513 ÷ 17

packs	1	100	10	89
sticks	17	1,700	170	1,513

64   BUILDING POWERFUL NUMERACY FOR MIDDLE AND HIGH SCHOOL STUDENTS

Notice that, for both of these examples, the ratio table encourages students to use their multiplication strategies to find the answer. The first problem actually uses the same partial quotients as the algorithm, but the second uses an over and under strategy to divide a four-digit number by a two-digit number in only three chunks. This strategy of going over and then subtracting off just a bit is not accessible with the standard algorithm. Think back to the first division problem in this chapter, 1,188 ÷ 12. How would you solve it using an over and under strategy? Figure 5.16 shows one example, a two-chunk over and under strategy for that problem.

FIGURE 5.16

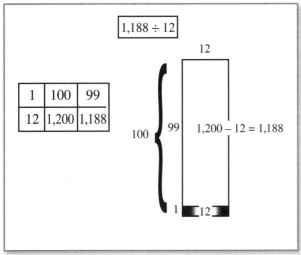

Thus, in two easy-to-manage steps, we have an answer for a problem that takes many nontransparent steps with the algorithm.

Constant Ratio

A powerful strategy in many division problems is to realize that $a \div b = \frac{a}{b}$ and determine if any common factors could be easily divided out, keeping the ratio constant and creating equivalent fractions. Often the result is easier to divide or may even lead directly to a solution. For instance, the problem 1,188 ÷ 12 simplifies to $1{,}188 \div 12 = \frac{1{,}188}{12} = \frac{594}{6} = \frac{297}{3} = 99$.

As secondary math teachers, we are very adept at simplifying fractions. But we don't always see that we could use this same approach to make division problems easier. Yet, this is often a great way to start a problem. In fact, in Ann Dowker's research in which she asked mathematicians to solve multiplication and division problems, the strategies used most often took advantage of nicer numbers (like those mentioned earlier in the discussion on multiplying strategies) or what she called *factorization* (which includes what I'm calling a *constant ratio* strategy) (Dowker 1992, 47).

For example, consider 642 ÷ 12. You can easily divide out a common factor of 2 to get $\frac{642}{12} = \frac{321}{6}$ and then a common factor of 3 to get $\frac{642}{12} = \frac{321}{6} = \frac{107}{2}$. Now just cut 107 in half to get the quotient, 642 ÷ 12 = 53.5. This constant ratio strategy does not help in all division problems, but if students have it in their repertoire, it can especially influence how they might solve many decimal division problems. Take, for example, 5.6 ÷ 0.7. Using this idea of equivalent fractions, we can reverse the process and introduce a common factor of 10, so $\dfrac{5.6 \cdot 10}{0.7 \cdot 10} = \dfrac{56}{7} = 8$. This constant ratio strategy is extremely important in generalizing fraction division as we'll see in Chapters 8 and 10.

Implications for Higher Mathematics

All of these numerical relationships, concepts, models, and strategies have implications for the higher mathematics that we teach. Armed with multiplication and division number sense, students are better prepared to reason and justify their thinking.

Understanding the Meanings of Division

Understanding the partitive meaning of division becomes crucial in higher math. Students will find the *quotient* meaning of fractions very difficult if they do not understand the partitive meaning of division (see Chapters 8 and 10). And, for another example, in finding the area under a curve in calculus, we often have to calculate $\dfrac{b - a}{n}$ when we partition a distance $b - a$ into n partitions. (For example, see the discussion of the Trapezoidal Rule later in this chapter and the graph in Figure 5.22.)

The Distributive Property of Multiplication with Variables

A very common error for algebra students is to distribute incorrectly. They might mistakenly note that $3(x + 2) = 3x + 2$ or that $(x + 2)(x + 1) = x^2 + 2$. In a geometric sense, they are missing parts of the rectangle, as shown in Figure 5.17. Teachers have used mnemonics such as FOIL (first, outside, inside, last) to help students to remember to "do it all." However, these mnemonics don't help students if they're trying to multiply anything other than two binomials.

FIGURE 5.17

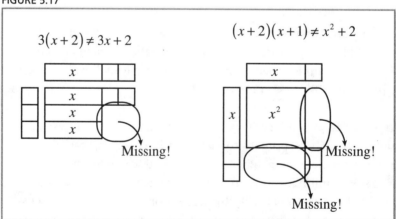

If students understand the distributive property with numbers, they will be able to apply it to polynomials with more terms. After they have had some practice modeling problems such as $(x^2 + 2x + 2)(x - 1)$ with concrete array models such as algebra tiles (the models in Figure 5.17), so that they better understand the parts involved, students can use an array approach to multiply without missing any parts. Figure 5.18 shows this approach. As the Common Core Standards state, "There is a world of difference between a student who can summon a mnemonic device to expand a product such as $(a + b)(x + y)$ and a student who can explain where the mnemonic comes from. The student who can explain the rule understands the mathematics, and may have a better chance to succeed at a less familiar task such as expanding $(a + b + c)(x + y)$" (Common Core State Standards Initiative 2011, 4).

FIGURE 5.18

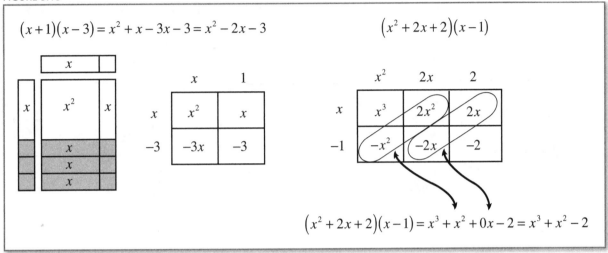

This approach can also be used to factor and divide polynomials. The factoring of polynomials is one of the main ideas of the Fundamental Theorem of Algebra, simply stated: that every polynomial P of degree n has n roots. Figure 5.19 shows how to factor a polynomial using the array approach.

FIGURE 5.19

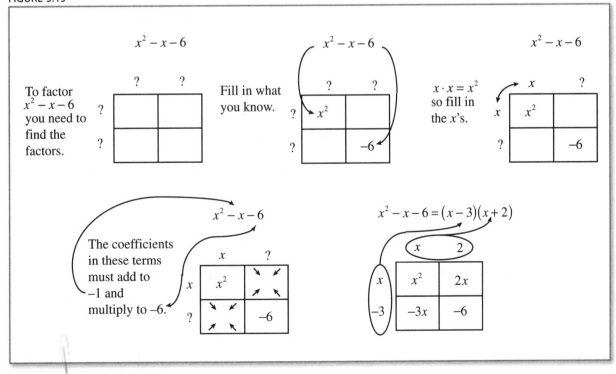

The traditional long division approach is even more obscure for polynomials than for numbers, because with polynomials there is the extra complication of subtracting negative terms. Figure 5.20 shows how an array approach can make division of polynomials more transparent.

FIGURE 5.20

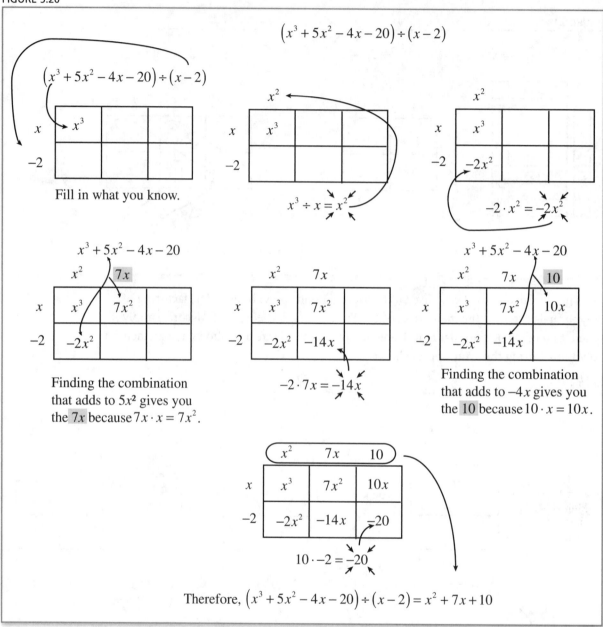

$$\left(x^3 + 5x^2 - 4x - 20\right) \div \left(x - 2\right)$$

$$\left(x^3 + 5x^2 - 4x - 20\right) \div \left(x - 2\right)$$

Fill in what you know.

$x^3 \div x = x^2$

$-2 \cdot x^2 = -2x^2$

$x^3 + 5x^2 - 4x - 20$

Finding the combination that adds to $5x^2$ gives you the $7x$ because $7x \cdot x = 7x^2$.

$-2 \cdot 7x = -14x$

$x^3 + 5x^2 - 4x - 20$

Finding the combination that adds to $-4x$ gives you the 10 because $10 \cdot x = 10x$.

$10 \cdot -2 = -20$

Therefore, $\left(x^3 + 5x^2 - 4x - 20\right) \div \left(x - 2\right) = x^2 + 7x + 10$

Array and Area Models in Geometry and Calculus

If students work with the area model to build multiplication and division concepts, their experience chunking and rearranging areas pays off when it comes to finding the area of other shapes. Virtually all of the common two-dimensional area formulas can be based on the area of a rectangle. In Figure 5.21, you see that the formulas for the area of a parallelogram, trapezoid, square, triangle, and even circle can be built from an understanding of the area of a rectangle. Connecting the formulas in this way drastically cuts the amount of rote memorization for students.

FIGURE 5.21

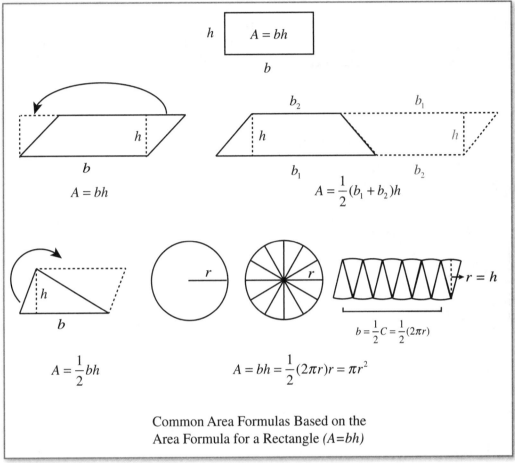

Common Area Formulas Based on the
Area Formula for a Rectangle *(A=bh)*

The underpinnings of integral calculus are all about chunking area and using calculus to find the limit of the sum of the areas of an infinite number of infinitely small pieces. The Fundamental Theorem of Calculus allows students to calculate the definite integral, which is the area under the curve. Some functions require a numerical method, such as the Trapezoidal Rule that uses *n* trapezoids to approximate the area under the curve. All of these concepts are based on chunking area, as shown in Figure 5.22.

FIGURE 5.22

Approximating Area Under a Curve with Increasingly Smaller Rectangles

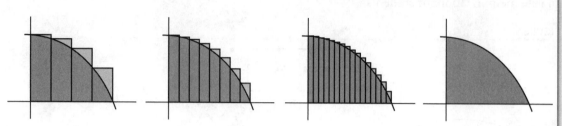

The Definite Integral

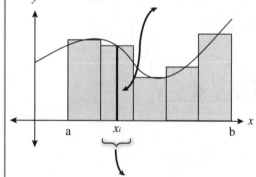

height of rectangle $= f(x_i)$

width of rectangle $=\Delta x$

Area of a rectangle = (height) (width)

Area under the curve $= \int_a^b f(x)\,dx$

height   width

The Trapezoidal Rule

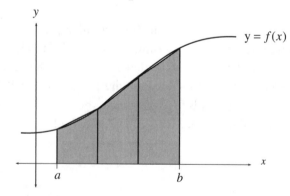

$y = f(x)$

$$\int_a^b f(x)\,dx \approx \frac{b-a}{2n}\left[f(x_0) + 2f(x_1) + \ldots + 2f(x_{n-1}) + f(x_n)\right]$$

When students have constructed an understanding of area, we can then develop their understanding of volume as the area of the base (B) times the height of the solid (H) by having students chunk layers of volume. This approach works for right rectangular prisms, cylinders, and other similar figures. Then the volume of a pyramid or cone is ⅓ of the volume of the respective prism or cylinder, as shown in Figure 5.23.

FIGURE 5.23

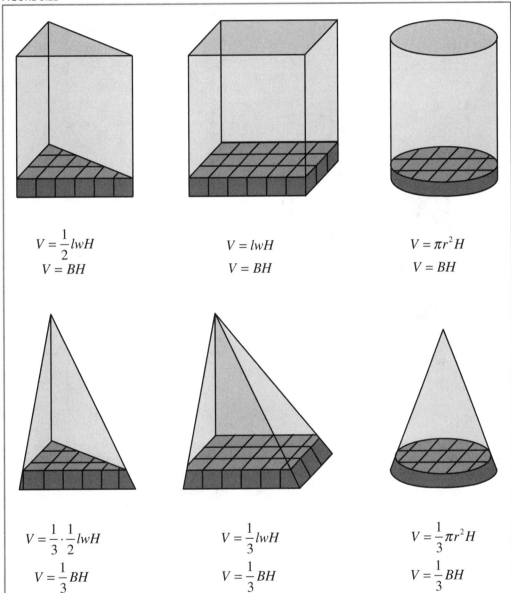

$$V = \frac{1}{2}lwH$$
$$V = BH$$

$$V = lwH$$
$$V = BH$$

$$V = \pi r^2 H$$
$$V = BH$$

$$V = \frac{1}{3} \cdot \frac{1}{2}lwH$$
$$V = \frac{1}{3}BH$$

$$V = \frac{1}{3}lwH$$
$$V = \frac{1}{3}BH$$

$$V = \frac{1}{3}\pi r^2 H$$
$$V = \frac{1}{3}BH$$

This same approach underlies methods of finding volume through calculus. The formula in Figure 5.24 is based on the idea of finding the volume of a solid by using calculus to add up the volumes of infinitely small layers of the solid. So, you need to find the area of the base of each layer, multiply that area times the height of the layer to get the volume of the layer, and then use calculus to add up all of the infinitely small volumes to get the volume of the solid.

FIGURE 5.24

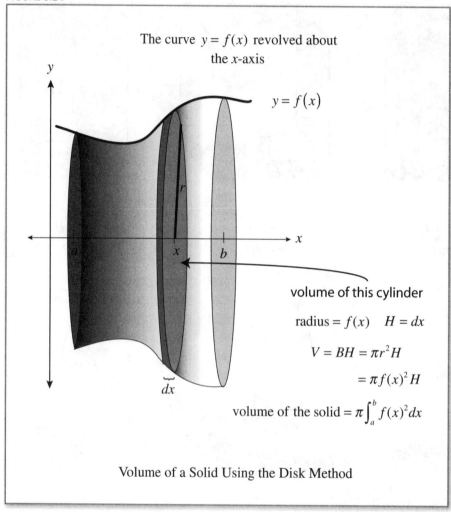

The curve $y = f(x)$ revolved about the x-axis

$y = f(x)$

volume of this cylinder

radius $= f(x)$ $H = dx$

$V = BH = \pi r^2 H$

$= \pi f(x)^2 H$

volume of the solid $= \pi \int_a^b f(x)^2 dx$

Volume of a Solid Using the Disk Method

In Chapters 6 and 7, we'll look at how using problem strings and other short lessons can help our secondary students construct these multiplication and division strategies as they construct multiplicative and proportional reasoning.

Six **6** ⊞ :....

Multiplication

Teaching students to understand the mathematics rather than to perform the cal-culations by rote memory will truly empower them toward the confidence needed to succeed in math.

NUMERACY WORKSHOP PARTICIPANT

Recently I had a brief conversation with a nationally prominent math educator and writer. She chided me gently about my view of the traditional algorithms. "Pam, you know that much of the time we just want kids to be able to get an answer quickly and efficiently."

I responded, "True, but are the algorithms always or even usually the quickest or the most efficient? What is 99 plus anything? What is 99 times anything?"

"Oh," she looked at me thoughtfully. "Is *that* what you mean?"

In this chapter, you'll find strings and activities to help students construct the major multiplication strategies using the open array and ratio table.

Using Proportional Reasoning

Let's enter a middle school classroom to see one way of helping students build proportional reasoning with the ratio table, working toward understanding "99 times anything." The string shown in Figure 6.1 is the basis for this lesson.

FIGURE 6.1

$$2 \cdot 27$$
$$4 \cdot 27$$
$$8 \cdot 27$$
$$10 \cdot 27$$
$$9 \cdot 27$$
$$100 \cdot 27$$
$$99 \cdot 27$$

Pam, the teacher, begins, "Today for our string, we're going to consider a box full of 27 widgets. How many widgets would you have if you had 2 boxes? Amira?"

"That's easy—just double to get 54," answers Amira.

Pam records *2* and *54* in a ratio table with arrows to model the strategy (see Figure 6.2). "What if you have 4 boxes? How many widgets?"

FIGURE 6.2

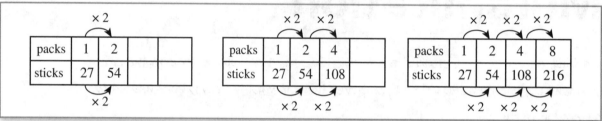

"4 boxes is 108," suggests Sebastian.

Pam records (*4, 108*) in the ratio table and continues, "What if I have 8 boxes? Can we double again?"

"Yeah, that one's not too bad either. That's 216," says LaNan.

"What arithmetic problem did you just do?" asks Pam as she records (*8, 216*). Some students recognize that they have found $8 \cdot 27$. The teacher follows up with, "How did you do it?"

"Doubled and doubled and doubled," answers Sebastian.

To nudge students toward recording their thinking mathematically, Pam models what the students have just done. "So if I wanted to multiply 8 times 27, I could just double, double, and double again? Does that always work? Why?" Pam pauses to let students consider the question. Pushing toward understanding of the associative property, she continues, "Let's write down what you just said. You doubled 27 so I'll write $2 \cdot 27$. Then you doubled that, so now we have $2(2 \cdot 27)$. Doubling once more gives $2(2(2 \cdot 27))$, which we can rewrite as $(2 \cdot 2 \cdot 2) \cdot 27$, which is equal to $8 \cdot 27$."

Pam then presents the next problem, 10 boxes of 27, which the students know quickly. She records their answer in the ratio table: (*10, 270*). "OK, so how about 9 boxes?" Since both (*8, 216*) (*10, 270*) are in the table, students can work from either $8 \cdot 27$ or $10 \cdot 27$.

"I added 27 to $8 \cdot 27$ so that's 243," says Jose.

"I subtracted one 27 from 270 and got 243 too," adds Cameron.

Pam records (*9, 243*) in the table (Figure 6.3), and then asks for the number of widgets in 100 boxes. She records the answer: *2,700*.

FIGURE 6.3

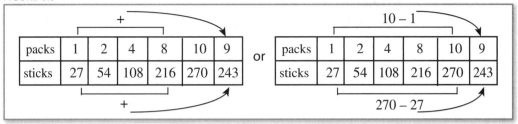

"Fantastic. Here's our last problem. How many widgets do you have if you have 99 boxes?" she continues.

"I know—2,699!" LaNan blurts out.

"Wait," says Jose, "you can't just subtract 1 from 2,700. It's boxes, not widgets. I mean, it's widgets not boxes. Oh, it's hard to explain."

"Who can help explain what's going on?" asks Pam. Questions such as these encourage students to work as a community of learners, where ideas are suggested and defended.

"100 boxes have 2,700 widgets, but you want 99 boxes, right?" asks Sebastian. "So, you have to take away a whole box, not just 1 widget."

LaNan corrects her earlier mistake. "So 2,700 minus 27 is 2,673, because you have to take away a whole box."

Pam records their result in a ratio table, as shown in Figure 6.4.

FIGURE 6.4

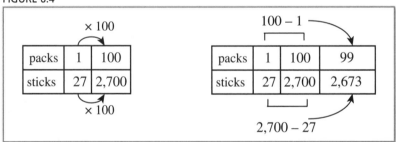

The teacher nudges the students toward generalizing the method. "Nice thinking everyone. Now I want to get a little general. What is 99 times anything? Think about it for a minute, and then discuss it with your partner, please."

After some discussion, the teacher calls on a student who answers, "99 times anything is 100 times that thing and then take 1 of them away." The teacher records this on the board as $99 \cdot a = (100 - 1) \cdot a = (100 \cdot a) - (1 \cdot a) = 100a - a$.

These students are practicing both multiplicative thinking and proportional reasoning and then generalizing relationships using the distributive property. By keeping the problem in the context of widgets in boxes, the students reason about what operations they can use. Double the number of boxes, then you must double the number of widgets. Subtract a box, subtract the widgets. With this concrete image that students can visualize, they can begin to generalize strategies to attack many multiplication problems. This string also sets the stage for students to work with more complicated ratios and proportions (see Chapter 8 for more discussion of these topics).

An Algebra Ending: Direct Variation

In a class where students are learning about rates, direct variation, graphing, and lines, the algebra string from Figure 6.1 might end in an exchange like the following between Abby and her algebra class. After getting to the "99 times anything" point in the string, Abby asks her class to consider the numbers in the table as ordered pairs.

Students graph the ordered pairs and are interested to see that the graph looks linear (see Figure 6.5). As they investigate the line, they find that the rate of change of the line is 27. Abby digs for connections and reasons. Students respond:

"There are 27 widgets in each box," says Adain.

"Well, 54 ÷ 2 is 27, and 108 ÷ 4 is 27," offers Samantha.

"And 2,700 ÷ 100 is 27," adds Jose.

"For each entry, there were always 27 widgets in each box, so when you divide the total number of widgets by the number of boxes, you'll always get 27 widgets per box," suggests Christopher.

Abby records this as $\frac{2700}{100} = \frac{270}{10} = \frac{108}{4} = \frac{54}{2} = \frac{27}{1} = 27 = \frac{y}{x}$, as she says, "Every y divided by its corresponding x is 27, so if $y \div x$ is 27, the equation of the line is . . . ?"

Chuey answers, "The line is $y = 27x$."

"Is the origin on this line? Why does your answer make sense in the problem situation?" asks Abby.

"If you have 0 boxes, then you don't have any widgets, so yes, it makes sense that $(0, 0)$ is on the line," answers Claire.

FIGURE 6.5

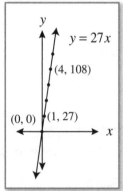

These students are learning proportional reasoning while constructing multiplicative relationships. This reasoning can then lead to discussions of direct variation with added insight about the qualities of a proportional linear function, including that these ratios are all equivalent to the rate of change of the line. These concepts are all related, and we can use these relationships to strengthen students' understandings.

Doubling and Halving

All of the strings in Figure 6.6 can be used to construct numeracy while at the same time advancing the mathematics at hand. They use the associative property to double and halve with the array model.

FIGURE 6.6

Doubling and Halving		
Middle School	Algebra	Geometry
$3 \cdot 8$	$6 \cdot 8$	$15 \cdot 18$
$6 \cdot 4$	$12 \cdot 8$	$30 \cdot 9$
$8 \cdot 6$	$24 \cdot 4$	$45 \cdot 6$
$4 \cdot 12$	$6 \cdot 16$	$90 \cdot 3$
$16 \cdot 3$	$3 \cdot 32$	$135 \cdot 2$
$2 \cdot 24$	$9 \cdot 5$	$5 \cdot 54$
$6 \cdot 8$	$3 \cdot 15$	$10 \cdot 27$
$2 \cdot 2 \cdot 2 \cdot 2 \cdot 3$	$1 \cdot 45$	Area formulas based on
Find more equivalent problems?	$a \cdot b = a \cdot \left(\frac{1}{c} \cdot c\right) \cdot b = \left(a \cdot \frac{1}{c}\right) \cdot (c \cdot b)$	moving areas around

The open array can be a helpful model to develop the doubling/halving strategy and the associative property. You might start a doubling/halving string by asking students to sketch and record the dimensions and areas of several related rectangular arrays, such as $3 \cdot 8, 6 \cdot 4$, and $8 \cdot 6$. Ask students to sketch one at a time, and as you record their sketches, line up the appropriate dimensions as shown in Figure 6.7. What do you notice about the relationship between the rectangles? Elicit responses from students about what they notice. Their answers may include statements such as:

"The first two have the same area."

"The last one has double the area of the other two."

"If you double the 3, you get 6 (pointing to the 3 of $3 \cdot 8$ and the 6 of $6 \cdot 4$. and the other side is half (pointing to the 4 of the $6 \cdot 4$ and the 8 of the $3 \cdot 8$)."

"The bigger rectangle has one side doubled and the area doubled."

With the next problem, $4 \cdot 12$, students will notice that you've done it again: when you double one side and halve the other, the area stays the same (see Figure 6.7). Have pairs of students use grid paper to show what is happening. Some students may cut out both arrays and overlay them, while others may cut one array in half and move the pieces to demonstrate the equivalent areas.

FIGURE 6.7

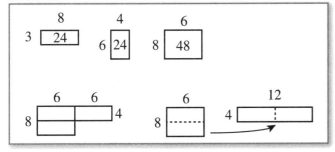

Continue the string with three more problems: $16 \cdot 3, 2 \cdot 24$, and $6 \cdot 8$. Have students discuss the relationships between the different problems and the arrays that model them, sometimes doubling one dimension to double the area and other times doubling and halving dimensions to get an equivalent area. The representation of these problems using arrays helps build students' conceptual and spatial understanding of the multiplication problems they are doing. By constructing these relationships, students will now be inclined to use them by doubling and halving in more difficult multiplication problems.

A Middle School Ending: The Fundamental Theorem of Arithmetic

At the end of such a double/half string, Amy, a middle school teacher, could continue in different ways. Since the orientations of the arrays were continually shifting, Amy could seize the moment to emphasize the commutative property, but she has another focus in mind for this middle school class: the Fundamental Theorem of Arithmetic. Her last problem is $2 \cdot 2 \cdot 2 \cdot 2 \cdot 3$.

After students work for a minute, Amy asks, "What did you get and what does this problem have to do with this whole problem string? After you have had a bit to think, when you are ready, turn to your partner and discuss your ideas."

Students discuss their thoughts with their partners and then Amy brings them back together, "Who wants to start?"

"You're just moving factors around," says Toni.

"Yeah, 8×6 is just the first 3 twos times the last 2 and the 3," adds Melik. Amy records this as $8 \cdot 6 = (2 \cdot 2 \cdot 2)(2 \cdot 3)$.

"And for 4×12, just move the parentheses again," suggests Jose. Amy records this as $4 \cdot 12 = (2 \cdot 2)(2 \cdot 2 \cdot 3)$.

Amy and her students continue modeling the last three problems: $16 \cdot 3 = (2 \cdot 2 \cdot 2 \cdot 2)(3)$, $2 \cdot 24 = 2(2 \cdot 2 \cdot 2 \cdot 3)$, and $6 \cdot 8 = (2 \cdot 3)(2 \cdot 2 \cdot 2)$.

Amy ends the string by asking, "Did we get them all? For these factors, did we already do all of the problems? We have the string of problems on the board. Can you find any other equivalent problems?"

These students are working with factors and the associative and commutative properties. They are justifying their ideas with mathematical properties. They are dealing with the prime factorization of numbers in an interesting and intriguing way. And besides being good factor work, helping students really understand prime factorization, this is also a helpful multiplication strategy. Consider the problem $6 \cdot 35$. Factor that into $6 \cdot 35 = 3 \cdot 2 \cdot 5 \cdot 7$. Now reassociate to get $3 \cdot (2 \cdot 5) \cdot 7 = 21 \cdot 10$, which is easy to compute mentally.

Consider $42 \cdot 35$. What can you do with it? $42 \cdot 35 = (21 \cdot 2)(5 \cdot 7) = 21 \cdot 10 \cdot 7$. Now, is $21 \cdot 7 \cdot 10$ easier to compute than $42 \cdot 35$? What about messing with the factors a little more? Then you might have $42 \cdot 35 = (21 \cdot 2)(5 \cdot 7) = 3 \cdot 7 \cdot 10 \cdot 7 = 3 \cdot 49 \cdot 10$. And 3×49 is simply $150 - 3 = 147$. Thus, $3 \cdot 49 \cdot 10 = 147 \cdot 10 = 1,470$. This approach uses an understanding of factors, prime factorization, and associative and commutative properties in both multiplication and subtraction.

An Algebra Ending: Multiplicative Identity and Inverse

Starting from the same arrays shown in Figure 6.7, an algebra string might proceed similarly to the following one from Abby's algebra class. Students flexibly relate the problems to each other. Abby then continues with two more problems: $9 \cdot 5$ and $3 \cdot 15$. The following discussion ensues.

"This time, you didn't double and halve, you tripled and thirded!" exclaims Ashley.

"Can you do that?" asks Abby, chuckling at the use of *thirded*. "What does Ashley mean?"

"You take the 9-by-5 array and instead of cutting it in half, cut it into 3 equal parts, then line those up. Now you have a 3 by 15," suggests Matthew.

"Does that work? Are the products, the areas, the same?" pushes Abby. "That was a great explanation geometrically, but I'd also like to look at what's going on numerically. Where is the triple and where is the third?"

Abby and her class go on to discuss the multiplicative identity and inverse for rational number multiplication, that is, that $(1/a) \cdot a = 1 = a (1/a)$. This shows up in doubling and halving, as in $12 \cdot 8 = 12 \cdot 1 \cdot 8 = 12 (2 \cdot \frac{1}{2}) \cdot 8 = (12 \cdot 2) \cdot (\frac{1}{2} \cdot 8) = 24 \cdot 4$. One can also triple and divide by 3 because $(\frac{1}{3}) \cdot 3 = 1 = 3 \cdot (\frac{1}{3})$ as in $9 \cdot 5 = (9 \cdot \frac{1}{3})(3 \cdot 5) = 3 \cdot 15$.

Abby's students also noticed, comparing $24 \cdot 4$ to $6 \cdot 16$, that you could quadruple and divide by 4. Abby ended the discussion by modeling the general case, that $a \cdot b = a (1) b = a (c \cdot 1/c) \cdot b = (a \cdot c)(1/c \cdot b)$. More than just building numeracy, these students are seeing the connections between numeric properties and algebraic properties—that things that hold true for numbers can be modeled with variables and equations.

The Associative Property in a Geometry Class

Consider the geometry string in Figure 6.6. This string can help students connect a growing understanding about doubling and halving with angle measures. Notice that many of the numbers are common angle measures: 30, 45, and 90. As you proceed through the string, use angle diagrams as well as array models to show the doubling and halving. Both arrays and angles represent continuous quantities that can be difficult for students to make sense of. By using a problem string with numbers that lend themselves to common angle measures, you can help build numeracy while at the same time reinforcing current geometric concepts.

Chunking: The Distributive Property

The problem strings in Figure 6.8 are built around "chunking" multiplication problems to build toward the distributive property of multiplication over addition. They encourage students to construct mental numerical relationships that they then generalize to algebraic expressions.

FIGURE 6.8

Middle School	Algebra	Algebra 2
$9 \cdot 10$	$6 \cdot 20$	$3 \cdot 80$
$9 \cdot 4$	$6 \cdot 7$	$3 \cdot 3$
$9 \cdot 14$	$6 \cdot 27$	$3 \cdot 83$
$10 \cdot 11$	$10 \cdot 23$	$23 \cdot 2$
$7 \cdot 11$	$2 \cdot 23$	$23 \cdot 10$
$17 \cdot 11$	$12 \cdot 23$	$23 \cdot 12$
$12 \cdot 16$	$14 \cdot 12$	$15 \cdot 18$
$a(x + b) = ax + ab$	$(a + b)(c + d) = ac + ad + bc + bd$ $(ax + b)(cx + d) = acx^2 + bcx +$ $adx + bd = acx^2 + (bc + ad)x + bd$	$(2x - 1)(x^2 + x - 3)$

The array is useful to model the problems in these strings. Let's enter Amy's middle school classroom as students are working with a multiplication chunking strategy.

"Let's get warmed up with a few easy problems. First, what is 9×10?" begins Amy. Even though this initial problem is easy, it will build quickly into important ideas.

As the students answer 90, Amy draws a 9-by-10 array and labels the inside as *90*. She does the same with the next problem, $9 \cdot 4$. Then she asks for $9 \cdot 14$. Students discuss how they can move the 9×4 array over next to the 9×10 array to get a 9×14 array. Thus the area of the 9×14 array is $9(10 + 4) = 9 \cdot 10 + 9 \cdot 4 = 90 + 36 = 126$ (see Figure 6.9).

Similarly, Amy presents the next set of three problems, $10 \cdot 11$, $7 \cdot 11$, and $17 \cdot 11$. She models each with an array, combining the first two arrays to get the third array as students suggest.

"Do you realize that you multiplied a two-digit number by a two-digit number in two steps?" asks Amy. "How? Talk to me about what's going on here."

"When you break the 17 into 10 and 7, it's easy to multiply those parts and then just stick the chunks together. 110 and 77 is 187," suggests Paul.

"Are there any other ways to break the 17 that would also make the problem easy?" asks Amy.

After some think time, Trak answers, "Since it's 11, you could do 9 times 11 and 8 times 11. That's just 99 and 88." He smiles big, "And now we have a 99 plus anything problem. It's 187."

FIGURE 6.9

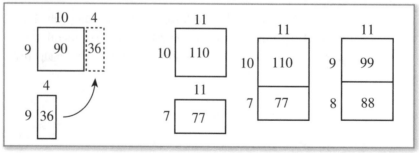

"So, with that in mind, this idea of partitioning the factors to make easy-to-find chunks, let's try 12 × 16. Try to do it in just two chunks," instructs Amy as she sends them off to work.

As the class discusses each strategy that students find, Amy labels them. One strategy is to break up the 12 into 10 and 2: $(10 + 2) \cdot 16 = 10 \cdot 16 + 2 \cdot 16 = 160 + 32 = 192$. Another strategy is to break up the 16 into 10 and 6: $12(10 + 6) = 12 \cdot 10 + 12 \cdot 6 = 120 + 72 = 192$. Still another is to break either the 12 or 16 in half: $(6 + 6) \cdot 16 = 6 \cdot 16 + 6 \cdot 16 = 96 + 96 = 192$ or $12(8 + 8) = 12 \cdot 8 + 12 \cdot 8 = 96 + 96 = 192$ (see Figure 6.10).

FIGURE 6.10

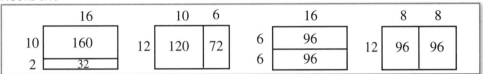

After these strategies are on the board, the class discusses which is easier to compute mentally. They compare and make generalizations about which they think will be most efficient. Amy wants to represent this symbolically. Because the students have been partitioning one of the factors, she writes $(a + b) \cdot c = a \cdot c + b \cdot c$ and $a(b + c) = a \cdot b + a \cdot c$. They discuss how these symbols relate to what they have been doing and how it influences how they will do problems such as simplifying $3(x + 2)$ and factoring $10x + 20$. Her students are constructing mental numerical relationships that they then generalize to algebraic expressions.

Over and Under

What would a string look like to promote the distributive property of multiplication over subtraction? Let's say you are currently working with quadratics. If you have spent five to ten minutes for a few days starting class with a chunking string like those in Figure 6.11 you could next write an over and under string to help students gain more insight into the distributive property, specifically with distributing a negative number.

FIGURE 6.11

Over and Under Strings: Distributive Property of Multiplication over Subtraction		
Middle School	**Algebra**	**All Levels**
$7 \cdot 60$	$9 \cdot 70$	$499 \cdot 1,000$
$7 \cdot 59$	$9 \cdot 69$	$499 \cdot 999$
$12 \cdot 30$	$40 \cdot 13$	$60 \cdot 40$
$12 \cdot 29$	$39 \cdot 13$	$61 \cdot 39$
$20 \cdot 13$	$12 \cdot 60$	
$18 \cdot 13$	$12 \cdot 58$	
$48 \cdot 12$	$29 \cdot 12$	
$a(x - b) = ax - ab$	$(a - b)(c + d) = ac + ad - bc - bd$	

To write such a string, consider your students, the problems you've given them previously, and numbers that will stretch them but also allow all your students to access the problems. These strings work well as a series of paired problems, where the first helps elicit a strategy to solve the second. Choose a starter problem, like 9 · 70, that is easy for your students but will lead to the more difficult 9 · 69.

To make sure that students are clear about what to subtract when, vary the order of the factors, which changes the orientation of the arrays. Consider, for example, 40 · 13 leading to 39 · 13. Figure 6.12 shows that the arrays have changed orientation from the first two problems, and therefore the partial arrays are oriented differently. Notice also that this ups the difficulty because both 40 and 13 are two-digit numbers, making the multiplication more difficult than the first problems but still manageable. Therefore, students can solve a much more difficult two-digit-by-two-digit problem (13 · 39) with only two chunks: begin with 40 · 13 and subtract one 13.

For the next set of paired problems, continue using two-digit by two-digit multiplication, with a difference of two groups instead of one between the problems (as in 12 · 60 and 12 · 58). Make the last problem a singleton, like 29 · 12; students will need to make their own helper problem.

As always, when you facilitate this string with students, you may need to adjust the numbers if they are too difficult or too easy. If students have not constructed the understanding you are looking for, you may want to add in an additional set of paired problems before giving students the last problem. If your students struggle with the changing orientation of the arrays, you could add in another set of paired problems that change the orientation to continue that discussion. You may need to continue a string on a second day, depending on how long your discussions continue. And in all cases, take note of how the string goes to help you decide on tomorrow's string.

FIGURE 6.12

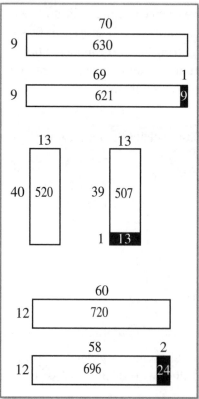

BUILDING POWERFUL NUMERACY FOR MIDDLE AND HIGH SCHOOL STUDENTS

The middle school string in Figure 6.11 includes easier numbers and ends with students examining the distributive property of multiplication over subtraction with variables with a constant times a binomial. The "all levels" string gets at a slightly different notion: when multiplying a little over and under, you must to be careful not to remove too much. The array is helpful to show what can happen when students inadvertently remove both a row and a column at the same time. The first helper problem, $499 \times 1,000$, sets the stage for 499×999. After finding $499 \times 1,000 = 499,000$, students remove one column of 499 to get $499 \times 999 = 499(1,000 - 1) = 499,000 - 499$, leading to the answer 498,501. The next helper problem, 60×40, is purposely set up to cause disequilibrium for students when they consider its partner, 61×39. To get to the array for 61×39, some students will add a row of 40 to and subtract a column of 60 from the 60×40 array (as in Figure 6.13), because they correctly reason that $61 \times 39 = (60 + 1)(40 - 1)$. However, if they are not careful, they will miscalculate by deciding that they can simply take the product $60 \times 40 = 2,400$ and add 40 and subtract 60: $2,400 + 40 - 60 = 2,380$. Meanwhile, other students have correctly found that $61 \times 39 = 2,379$. The two answers are off by 1! This disequilibrium prompts students to use arrays to find that 1 "missing" unit square and has proven to be extremely helpful in nudging students to really understand the array model.

FIGURE 6.13

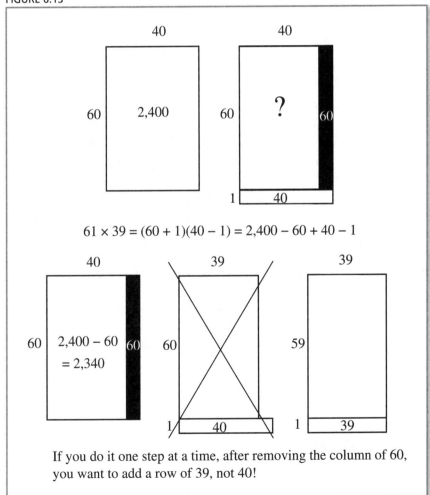

$61 \times 39 = (60 + 1)(40 - 1) = 2,400 - 60 + 40 - 1$

If you do it one step at a time, after removing the column of 60, you want to add a row of 39, not 40!

This over and under strategy—multiplying by a bit too much and removing the excess—gives access to a whole class of multiplication problems in which one factor is near a multiple of 10, 100, and so on. For example, 99 times anything draws on multiplying by 100 and removing the extra group. But also, 39 times n can be found by removing 1 group from $40n$ (which can be found by doubling twice and multiplying by 10).

5 Is Half of 10

We stressed doubling in the addition chapter, in part, because reversing the doubling reasoning is important for finding halves in multiplication. Besides the already helpful doubling/halving strategy, it is extremely useful in many problems where you could use the 5 is half of 10 strategy. See Figure 6.14 for example strings. Notice that these strings start with three related problems, followed by other problems for which students have to make their own helper problems.

FIGURE 6.14

5 Is Half of 10 Strings		
$28 \cdot 10$	$10 \cdot 52$	$84 \cdot 10$
$28 \cdot 5$	$5 \cdot 52$	$84 \cdot 5$
$15 \cdot 28$	$15 \cdot 52$	$84 \cdot 100$
$42 \cdot 15$	$150 \cdot 52$	$84 \cdot 95$
$42 \cdot 16$	$145 \cdot 52$	$84 \cdot 51$
	$81 \cdot 149$	$84 \cdot 49$

In the first string, after students find 15 groups of 28 with helper problems, they then find 15 groups of 42 and end by adding 1 more group of 42 for $42 \cdot 16$. In the second string, students use the patterns they are constructing to find 150 groups of 52. Since they already have 5 groups of $52 = 260$, they can just remove those 5 groups to get 145 groups of 52. Then they have to make their own helper problems for $81 \cdot 149$ by first finding $100 \cdot 81 = 8,100$ and then finding half: $50 \cdot 81 = 8,100 \div 2 = 4,050$. So $81 \cdot 150 = 8,100 + 4,050 = 12,150$. So, $81 \cdot 149 = 12,150 - 81 = 12,069$. In the last string, students use $10 \cdot 84$ to find $5 \cdot 84$, and then subtract that from $100 \cdot 84$ to find $95 \cdot 84$. You can then proceed to $50 \cdot 84$ and then work up and down for $51 \cdot 84$ and $49 \cdot 84$.

This 5 is half of 10 strategy also gives access to another class of problems, in which one factor is close to 5, 50, 500, and so on. This uses the associative property: $48 \cdot 5$ can be written as $48 \cdot 5 = 48 (10 \div 2) = (48 \cdot 10) \div 2$. Likewise, $664 \cdot 50 = 664(100 \div 2) = (664 \cdot 100) \div 2$. Once students begin to play with this strategy, they may begin to rearrange the order, using the commutative property to find the half first and then multiply by the 10, 100, and so on. For example, for $664 \cdot 50$, instead of first multiplying by 100 and then halving, you could halve first, and then multiply: $664 \cdot 50 = 664(100 \div 2) = (664 \div 2) \cdot 100$. This is easier for some problems than multiplying first.

Comparing Strategies

As with the other operations, it's important for students to have the understanding and flexibility to choose strategies that are appropriate for different multiplication problems.

After you do strings toward the associative property (doubling/halving, 5 is half of 10), the distributive property of multiplication over addition (chunking) and over subtraction (over and under), you could follow up by comparing these strategies as follows.

Consider several problems where one factor is 68. When is it more efficient to find big, friendly chunks? When is it more efficient to go just a little over or a little under? When is it necessary to multiply all of the parts?

99 · 68

To start to find 99 · 68, you could think in terms of the ratio 1:68 and then work to find the equivalent ratio 99:?. Fill in what you know in the ratio table and show your thinking with arrows and brackets as in Figure 6.15. You can use an over and under strategy: first multiply by 100, 68 · 100 = 6,800, and then take off 1 group of 68, for 6,800 − 68 = 6,732.

FIGURE 6.15

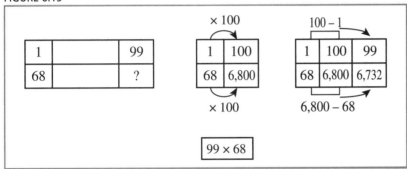

49 · 68, 51 · 68

In these situations, you can combine 5 is half of 10 with over and under. You could start by finding 100 · 68 = 6,800, and then find half: 50 · 68 = 3,400. Then, all that remains is to subtract (for 49 · 68) or add (for 51 · 68) 1 group of 68, for respective answers of 49 · 68 = 3,332 and 51 · 68 = 3,468 (see Figure 6.16). You could also use doubling/halving for these problems. For 49 · 68, you could consider 98 · 34, which equals 3,400 − 68. For 51 · 68, you get 102 · 34, which is even easier: 3,400 + 68.

FIGURE 6.16

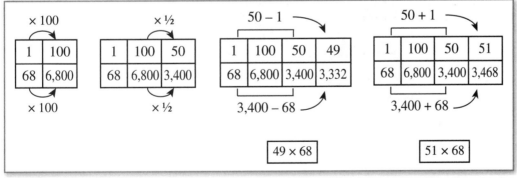

$74 \cdot 68, 76 \cdot 68$

Starting again from $50 \cdot 68 = 3{,}400$, you can find half to get $25 \cdot 68 = 1{,}700$. Combining these gives $75 \cdot 68 = (50 + 25) \cdot 68 = 3{,}400 + 1{,}700 = 5{,}100$. Then, $76 \cdot 68$ and $74 \cdot 68$ are just 1 more and 1 fewer group of 68. See Figure 6.17 for how this looks in a ratio table.

FIGURE 6.17

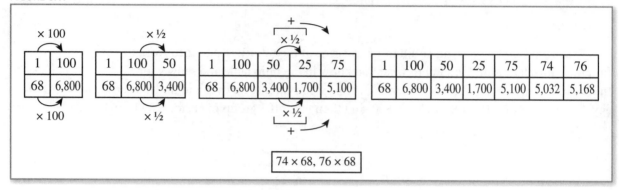

Toward $72 \cdot 68$

With a problem like $72 \cdot 68$, students may decide that the best strategy is to multiply all of the parts. These numbers are so middling that they don't lend themselves to easy chunks, an over and under strategy, or 5 is half of 10 (because neither factor is close to 5 or 50). Note that in this partial product strategy, the magnitudes are maintained, the strategy is transparent, and the sum of the chunks is easy to compute. Figure 6.18 also shows how this strategy relates to higher math—in this case, multiplying two binomials.

FIGURE 6.18

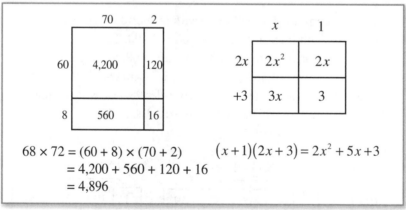

Consider the four following problems. Which strategy or strategies would you use for each problem? Then see the sample student responses that follow.

a. $499 \cdot 46$

b. $22 \cdot 301$

c. $75 \cdot 12$

d. $150 \cdot 18$

For 499 · 46, a student explained, "I found 1,000 · 46 = 46,000. Half of that is 500 · 46 = 23,000. 1 less 46 is 23,000 − 46 = 22,954."

For 22 · 301, a student said, "I first did 2 · 301 = 602, so 20 · 301 = 6,020. Add 2 more three hundred ones and that is 6,622." Another student described, "First, I found 3 · 22 = 66. So 300 · 22 = 6,600. Add 1 more 22 for 6,622."

For 75 · 12, one student said, "I found 100 times 12, that's 1,200. Half of that is 50 · 12 = 600. Half again is 25 · 12 = 300. So (25 + 50) · 12 = 900," and another said, "10 times 75 is 750. Add 2 more seventy-fives, 150, and get 900."

For 150 · 18, one student explained, "I did 100 times 18, 1,800. Half of that is 50 · 18 = 900. Add those together and that's 2,700."

Clarifying Understanding

If you find that some of your students are trying to memorize rotely and consequently misapply these multiplication strategies, use the activities that follow to help your students understand the differences between the operations and their different strategies.

As Close as It Gets

As you saw in Chapter 3, "As Close as It Gets" exercises help you encourage your students to develop the kind of understanding of numerical relationships that you want them to have. Be sure to have students discuss their reasoning for each problem. When students look at 86 · 9, they may reason that 86 · 10 is 860, so 86 · 9 is a bit less than that. The closest answer is 800. For the next problem, students might know that 10 · 3 = 30 and reason that the answer to 11 · 3.1 must be a bit higher. For the last problem, students might say that 100 · 39 is 3,900, which is pretty close to 4,000.

FIGURE 6.19

As Close as It Gets					
86 · 9		11 · 3.1		103.2 · 39	
a) 700	b) 800	a) 33	b) 300	a) 40	b) 400
c) 900	d) 1,000	c) 311	d) 0.30	c) 4,000	d) 40,000

Relational Thinking

Since your students have been using give and take with addition and give and give and take and take with subtraction, they may be tempted to try all of these strategies with multiplication. Are the following equivalent to 21 · 79?

▸ 22 · 80 (give and give)

▸ 20 · 78 (take and take)

▸ 20 · 80 (give and take)

It may be obvious to you that they are not, but students who have just memorized the strategies without understanding the relationships may confuse the strategies, not realizing that "take 1 from the 21 and give it to the 79" works in addition, but not in multiplication.

You can use the relational thinking activities in Figure 6.20 to help you identify any such misconceptions and help resolve them. Have students discuss why they choose which numbers belong in the blanks. Model students' thinking to help them evaluate their answers. For example, if they suggest that $21 \cdot 99$ is equal to $20 \cdot 100$, you might draw a 20×100 array and ask students to try to move the area around to see if they can get a 21×99 array. You could also introduce a context such as having 99 cases where each case contains 21 oranges. Would finding 100 cases of 20 oranges help? Why or why not?

If students think that $39 \cdot 79 = 40 \cdot 80$ is true, you might have them draw the two arrays superimposed and ask what it means that one encompasses the other. You might also suggest a context, such as ordering boxes of pencils. If you order 39 boxes of 79 pencils, would you get the same number of pencils as if you ordered 40 boxes of 80 pencils?

FIGURE 6.20

Relational Thinking

Fill in the blank:

$36 \cdot 99 = 36 \cdot (\underline{\hspace{1cm}} - 1)$

$49 \cdot 42 = (\underline{\hspace{1cm}} \cdot 42) - (\underline{\hspace{1cm}} \cdot 42)$

True or false? Why?

$21 \cdot 99 = 20 \cdot 100$

$39 \cdot 79 = 40 \cdot 80$

Recall the question at the beginning of the chapter: "What is 99 times anything?" How might students apply that answer to "What is 999 times anything?" How might you solve $999 \cdot 887$? How about $499 \cdot 887$? This kind of multiplicative thinking exemplifies the numerical power that we can build in our students and ourselves. Students can use this powerful sense of multiplication to divide, as we'll see in the next chapter.

seven 7

Division

I have learned how to explain my "mental math." I hadn't realized how hard it was to explain, in words, the steps that I do to solve a problem in my head. It is much easier to understand the numbers when you can "see" them.

NUMERACY WORKSHOP PARTICIPANT

Of the four arithmetic operations, division is often the most obscure for students. Because the division strategies in this chapter are based on multiplication strategies, make sure that you have done enough multiplication work with your students before you tackle the division strings and activities in this chapter. If you find students getting more frustrated than intrigued, consider doing more multiplication work and then returning to division. Thinking and reasoning about division is hard work, and students may be tempted to revert to memorized rules. Remember to emphasize using relationships to compute in transparent ways.

Quotative and Partitive Division

One way to help your students use both quotative and partitive division flexibly is to use the array model for division. The array connects the two meanings of division because it contains both in the same picture. For example, the array in Figure 7.1 can model $62 \div 2$ as either 62 cut in half (2 rows of 31) or "How many twos are in 62?" (31 columns of 2). As students work through the strings in this chapter, there will be many opportunities for them to grapple with when to use which division interpretation as they solve problems.

FIGURE 7.1

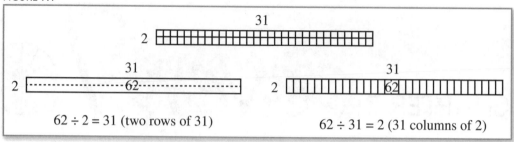

$62 \div 2 = 31$ (two rows of 31) $62 \div 31 = 2$ (31 columns of 2)

As students use the array model, gaining flexibility with both meanings, they begin to learn that they can use those multiplication strategies in a ratio table to solve any division problem, regardless of context. You will see this transition as we move through this chapter.

Connecting Multiplication and Division

Using arrays to model division entails helping students think about what the numbers in a division problem represent on an array. Whereas multiplication questions provide the dimensions and ask for the area, division questions provide the area and one dimension and ask for the other dimension. This may not be clear to students at first, especially how to actually draw the array that represents a division problem. The multiply, then divide strings in Figure 7.2 can help.

FIGURE 7.2

Multiply, Then Divide Strings		
Partial Products ⇒ Partial Quotients	5 Is Half of 10	Over and Under
21 · 3	54 · 10	14 · 100
21 · 20	54 · 5	14 · 2
21 · 23	54 · 15	14 · 98
63 ÷ 21	540 ÷ 54	1,400 ÷ 14
420 ÷ 21	270 ÷ 54	28 ÷ 14
483 ÷ 21	810 ÷ 54	1,372 ÷ 14
308 ÷ 14	990 ÷ 66	378 ÷ 42

In these strings, the first three problems are related multiplication problems. The next three problems are related division problems that *undo* the first three problems. These strings may seem a bit obvious, but you may find it surprising that many students do not initially notice the connection and even those who do often have to think about how to use that connection.

You could begin the first string in Figure 7.2 by modeling the first three problems with open arrays, one at a time, as students solve each problem. Ask a student to reiterate where each number belongs on the array: the factors as the dimensions and the product as the area (see Figure 7.3).

FIGURE 7.3

21·3
21·20
21·23
63 ÷ 21
420 ÷ 21
483 ÷ 21
308 ÷ 14

```
        21
    3 [  63  ]
        21
   20 [  420  ]
```

```
        21
    3 [··· 63 ···]
   20 [   420    ]
```

How would you model the next problem in the string, 63 ÷ 21? Let's join Amy in her middle school class as she gives students this problem and students respond with the answer 3.

"I want to model this problem on an array. Where would the numbers go? What do they mean?" Amy asks.

"The 63 is the area and the 21 is one of the dimensions," says Charity.

"So, I'll put the 21 up here and the 63 where the area goes," says Amy, drawing the array as shown in Figure 7.4.

FIGURE 7.4

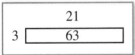

"Then, what question is the division problem 63 ÷ 21 asking?" asks Amy.

"Well, 21 by what is 63?" suggests Jackson.

"Or, what by 21 is 63?" adds Taren. "So, since 21 times 3 is 63, the other side is 3." Amy models the result as shown in Figure 7.5.

FIGURE 7.5

```
        21
    3 [  63  ]
```

"Super! Let's model the next problem on an array also: 420 ÷ 21. What would that look like?" asks Amy.

She asks a couple of students to display their arrays with the document camera. One has put the 21 across the top and the other has put the 21 along the side (as shown in Figure 7.6). The class decides that both are correct and Amy explains that for consistency's sake, she'll always write the divisor across the top. Her reason for this choice is that placing the divisor along the side on an unfinished array can appear like the traditional division algorithm notation and Amy doesn't want to inadvertently make that subliminal suggestion. Instead, she wants to encourage them to continue thinking and reasoning about division.

FIGURE 7.6

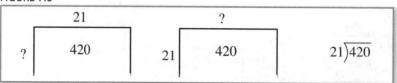

"So, what is the answer to 420 ÷ 21?" asks Amy. She has a couple of students explain their strategies, and they agree that the answer is 20. Amy fills in the array (Figure 7.7).

FIGURE 7.7

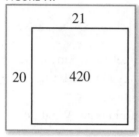

Amy then has students work on the next problem, 483 ÷ 21. A couple of students have noticed the relationship between the string's multiplication problems and these division problems.

"Well, at first we did the problem 21 · 23 = 483, so it must be that 483 ÷ 21 is 23," says Melik.

"You are using the relationship between multiplication and division. If you know the multiplication sentence, then you can use it to find the division answer," says Amy as she records that on the board (see Figure 7.8).

"I used the two arrays that we already had. Since 63 ÷ 21 is 3 and 420 ÷ 21 is 20, then I added them together to get 483 ÷ 21 is 20 + 3 = 23," says Angel.

FIGURE 7.8

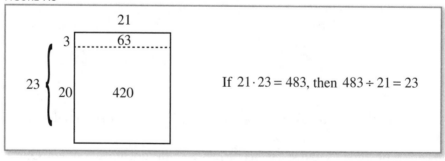

"Great work! Let's think about what we just did. We used some helper problems to find the answer to a division question. Some of you used the multiplication problems and some of you used the division problems. Turn to your partner and make sure you understand both strategies," instructs Amy.

After some partner discussion, Amy gives them the last problem in the string, "So, let's say that I don't give you any helper problems, just a division problem like 308 ÷ 14. Can you make up your own helper problems?" Students work and then Amy asks some students to share their strategies. Their models are shown in Figure 7.9.

FIGURE 7.9

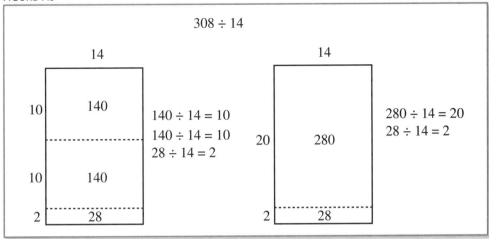

$308 \div 14$

$140 \div 14 = 10$
$140 \div 14 = 10$
$28 \div 14 = 2$

$280 \div 14 = 20$
$28 \div 14 = 2$

This multiply, then divide string takes a set of chunking multiplication problems and links them to a set of division problems. Students apply their growing multiplication sense to division. The last problem, $308 \div 14$, requires students to create their own helper problems. Students learn that when they solve a division problem, they can use their number sense to find helper problems to build up to the dividend. During this process, they remain aware of the magnitudes in the problem and they can defend their choices using arrays. As they continue to do the strings in the rest of the chapter, they will become more efficient and sophisticated in their choices.

The second string in Figure 7.2 is similar but with bigger numbers. Notice that the multiplication problems draw on the 5 is half of 10 strategy, which could also be used for the last division problem. The third string begins with an over and under multiplication problem, a strategy that can also apply to the last problem. These three multiply, then divide strings all foreshadow major division strategies by connecting their multiplication counterparts to division problems that involve the same relationships. These division strategies are considered in more detail later in this chapter.

Another activity to help students relate multiplication and division is to use arrays to model several strategies for the same problem. Consider the three arrays in Figure 7.10. Each models a different strategy for the same problem. Notice that several of the numbers are missing. Give students all three arrays at the same time, have them fill in the blanks, and ask them what one problem all the arrays represent. Filling in the blanks requires both multiplication and division. Figuring out what problem all the arrays represent requires analysis. Now we are ripe to ask: "Which strategy do you like best for this problem and why?" The answer is less important than the discussion. What is it about that strategy that works for these numbers? What is it about these numbers that lends to this strategy? What numbers would lend themselves to one of the other strategies? How?

FIGURE 7.10

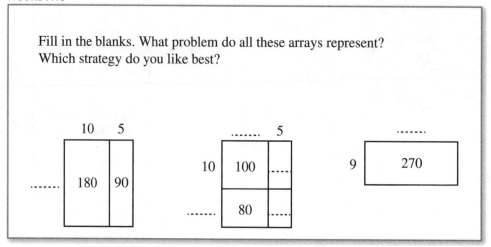

Fill in the blanks. What problem do all these arrays represent? Which strategy do you like best?

Partial Quotients

Figure 7.11 gives some problem strings to develop students' understanding and use of partial quotients. These strings are similar to the second half of the multiply, then divide strings used earlier. The first three problems are related; you can use the first two as helpers to solve the third. The next three problems are similarly related. The last problem requires that students find their own helper problems.

To write a partial quotient string, you want to find two division problems where the answer is fairly obvious, such as 99 ÷ 9 and 9 ÷ 9, which can be combined to make a problem that is not so obvious—in this case, 108 ÷ 9. Notice that all three problems have the same divisor. In this example, the larger 99 problem is first, then the smaller 9 problem. For the next three related problems, you could switch that order. (It doesn't matter which order you do first; the important thing is to give students the chance to work with both orders.) Depending on your students, you could use a two-digit divisor. Start these three with an easy problem, such as 22 ÷ 22. Now write the next problem to build on that relationship, perhaps 220 ÷ 22. The final problem of the set combines the two: 242 ÷ 22. The last problem is a singleton, where students will have to write their own helper problems. You'll want to choose a problem such that after students choose an obvious chunk, like 80 ÷ 8 = 10, the difference is also an obvious chunk, like 24 ÷ 8 = 3. So in this case, the problem would be 104 ÷ 8. Notice that for all of the problems in this string, the addition of the chunks is fairly straightforward.

The next partial product strings you write could use bigger or less comfortable numbers. You could make the addition of the chunks more difficult (as in the string 170 ÷ 17, 51 ÷ 17, and 221 ÷ 17). You could also use paired problems rather than sets of three, as in the last string in Figure 7.11. In this case, students are given only one helper problem, so they have to find the missing chunk on their own.

FIGURE 7.11

Partial Quotients—Chunking Strategy		
Middle School	**Algebra**	**Precalculus**
$99 \div 9$	$18 \div 9$	$400 \div 5$
$9 \div 9$	$180 \div 9$	$440 \div 5$
$108 \div 9$	$198 \div 9$	$220 \div 22$
$22 \div 22$	$260 \div 13$	$264 \div 22$
$220 \div 22$	$39 \div 13$	$280 \div 14$
$242 \div 22$	$299 \div 13$	$308 \div 14$
$104 \div 8$	$198 \div 6$	$372 \div 31$
	factor:	$(x^3 + 2x^2 - 17x + 6) \div (x - 3)$
	$2x^2 - 5x - 3$	

An Algebra Ending

After working through the division problems in the algebra string in Figure 7.11, Abby decides to connect the string to the class' work with factoring quadratics. She begins this discussion by asking students to summarize part of their work in this string of problems.

Abby asks, "Could someone describe how you are using arrays in this string?"

Hunter answers, "Division problems give you the area and one dimension. You have to find the other dimension."

"How does that connect to our work with factoring quadratics? Let's say you're factoring $2x^2 - 5x - 3$. How is that the same and how is it different?" asks Abby.

"When you factor you only get the area—you have to find both of the dimensions," says Houston.

"Talk me through your thinking for this problem, $2x^2 - 5x - 3$," says Abby. RheAnn volunteers and explains her thinking with arrays, as shown in Figure 7.12.

FIGURE 7.12

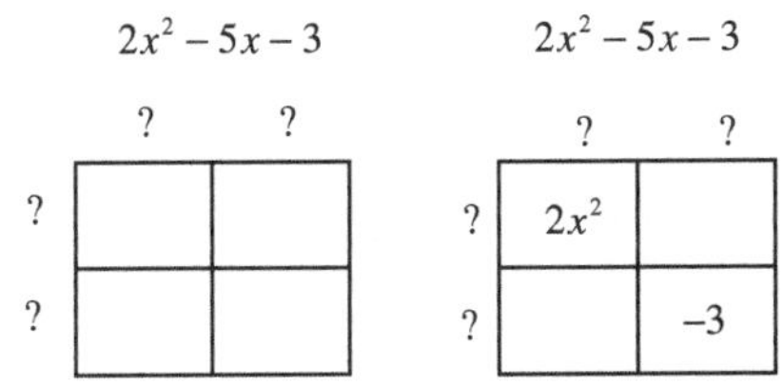

"Yeah, you put the $2x^2$ and the -3 in first. Then you have to figure out how to chunk the $-5x$ to go into the other boxes."

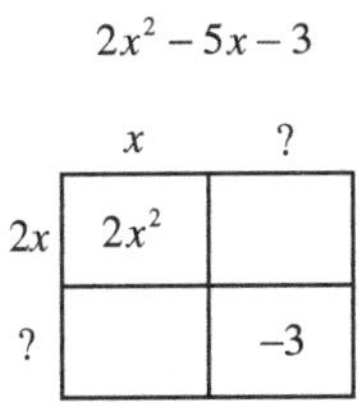

"Since you know you have $2x^2$, then one side will have x and the other side will have $2x$."

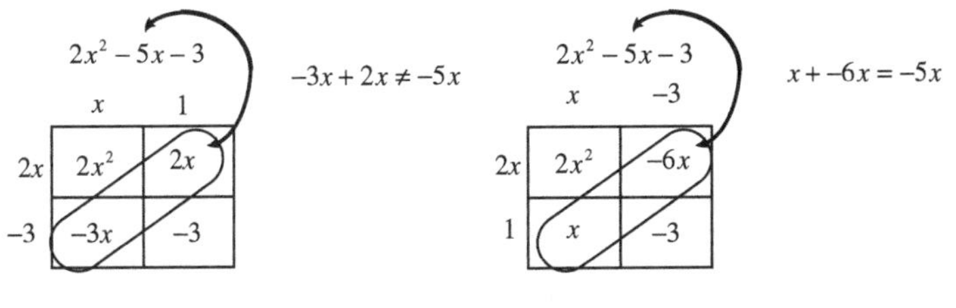

"Now, it's kinda trial and error. I try to find factors that multiply to -3 first. So, if you put -3 on the left, then 1 goes on the top. But then you'd have $-3x$ and $2x$. They don't add to $-5x$. So switch the -3 to the top and the 1 to the left and it works."

"So, I see all of these x's and numbers. What's the answer?" asks Abby.

"The factors are the answer, $(2x + 1)(x - 3)$," answers Gabi.

A Precalculus Ending

After working through a similar string in his precalculus class, Rick extends the lesson to polynomial long division. He asks the class to consider $(x^3 + 2x^2 - 17x + 6) \div (x - 3)$. They have a similar conversation, except now they are given both the area and one dimension.

"I like this better than factoring," suggests Melik. "When you give us one of the factors, it all just falls out. We don't have to guess and check to find the factors."

"What do you mean, it all just falls out?" asks Rick. "Talk me through this problem." Melik models his thinking as shown in Figure 7.13.

FIGURE 7.13

$(x^3 + 2x^2 - 17x + 6) \div (x - 3)$ Array: x, -3 down the side; x^3 in first inside box. Second array adds x^2 on top.	"All you do is put the x^3 in the first box on the inside. Put the $(x - 3)$ down the side. That forces an x^2 on the top."
Arrays with x^2 on top, x^3 and $-3x^2$ filled in; second array shows $5x^2$ added with circle. Must add to $2x^2$	"Now just multiply the -3 and the x^2 to get $-3x^2$. Since the original polynomial has $2x^2$, you put $5x^2$ because $-3x^2 + 5x^2 = 2x^2$."
Arrays with x^2, $5x$ on top; x^3, $5x^2$, $-3x^2$ filled; second adds $-15x$ with circle. Must add to $-17x^2$	"And you just keep going like that. You know that $5x$ has to be the factor on top, which then forces the $-15x$."
Arrays with x^2, $5x$, -2 on top; x^3, $5x^2$, $-2x$, $-3x^2$, $-15x$, and finally 6 filled in.	"That $-15x$ must combine with something to make $-17x$, so then fill in $-2x$. So, you can now fill in the last term on the top, -2. Since $-2 \cdot -3 = 6$, you're done."

"What do you mean that since $-2 \cdot -3 = 6$, you're done? What if you got there and that last product did not equal the constant in the polynomial?" asks Rick.

"Then you have a remainder," answers Cameron

These students are applying the multiplication and division sense they have built and their understanding of the array model to the division of polynomials.

Over and Under

Using the distributive property of multiplication, students can use the over and under strategy to find quotients that are just a little over or under landmark quotients. The strings in Figure 7.14 are one way to approach this strategy.

FIGURE 7.14

Over and Under Strategy		
160 ÷ 8	120 ÷ 12	560 ÷ 56
168 ÷ 8	240 ÷ 12	504 ÷ 56
176 ÷ 8	228 ÷ 12	616 ÷ 56
152 ÷ 8	252 ÷ 12	1,120 ÷ 56
144 ÷ 8	360 ÷ 12	1,176 ÷ 56
240 ÷ 8	348 ÷ 12	1,064 ÷ 56
232 ÷ 8	384 ÷ 12	1,680 ÷ 56

You may want to set the first string in a context if your students have not had enough experience yet using the ratio table as a tool. You could use 8 yogurt cups in a box, or any other context that makes sense to your students.

The first problem, 160 ÷ 8, prompts students to ask, "What can I do to 8 to get to 160?" Record student strategies in the table (see Figure 7.15).

FIGURE 7.15

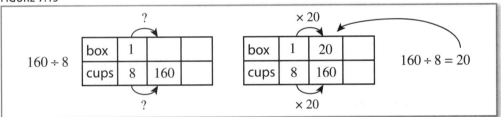

The next two problems, 168 ÷ 8 and 176 ÷ 8, can be solved by adding 1 more box of 8 cups, as shown in Figure 7.16.

FIGURE 7.16

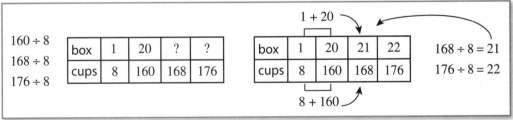

The next problems, 152 ÷ 8 and 144 ÷ 8, can be found by subtracting 1 more box of 8 cups each, shown in Figure 7.17.

FIGURE 7.17

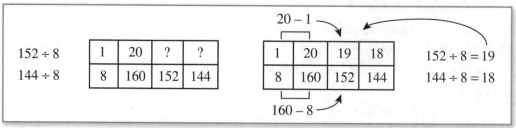

The last two problems (shown in Figure 7.18) are paired. Once you find that 240 ÷ 8 = 30, then you can just subtract 1 box of 8 cups for 232 ÷ 8 = 29.

FIGURE 7.18

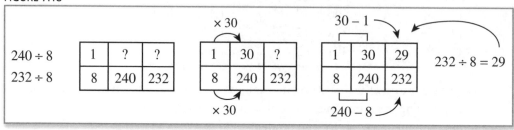

The problems in this string could also have been modeled with arrays. When you deliver over and under problem strings, vary the model that you use. The advantage of the array model is that it clearly shows the chunks you use, while the ratio table gives a more step-by-step record of the process.

The other two strings in Figure 7.14 offer the same kind of over and under string but with increasingly difficult numbers. Each string uses the same divisor in all the problems to explore finding one more group and one fewer group than landmark multiples. This encourages students to begin looking to use landmarks that are close to the target and adding or subtracting off the excess group or groups. The under process is similar to the traditional algorithm, but the over process is not. For example, in the last string, students can solve 504 ÷ 56 by overshooting to find 560 ÷ 56 = 10, then simply removing one group of 56 to get 504 ÷ 56 = 9. This overshooting process is not accessible with the division algorithm, but is often extremely convenient for many problems and real-life situations.

5 Is Half of 10 Strings

You can use strings like those in Figure 7.19 to give students experience using the 5 is half of 10 strategy for division. This strategy makes use of multiples of 10 and 5, 100 and 50, and so on. Then you can go over or under to add or subtract enough to get the quotient you need.

FIGURE 7.19

5 Is Half of 10 Strategy		
120 ÷ 12	280 ÷ 28	550 ÷ 55
60 ÷ 12	140 ÷ 28	275 ÷ 55
180 ÷ 12	420 ÷ 28	825 ÷ 55
180 ÷ 18	360 ÷ 36	1,440 ÷ 144
90 ÷ 18	180 ÷ 36	720 ÷ 144
270 ÷ 18	540 ÷ 36	2,160 ÷ 144
240 ÷ 16	660 ÷ 44	12,600 ÷ 84

After having done a 5 is half of 10 string like those in Figure 7.19 the day before, I asked sixth-grade students to solve some problems cold. One of the students, Melia, explained her strategy to solve 270 ÷ 18. She said, "I knew that 10 times 18 is 180. And since with angles and stuff, I knew that 5 times 18 is 90. So the answer is 15." She used the connection between angles (straight angle of 180° ÷ 2 = 90° angle) to find the answer to a multiplication problem, 5 times 18, to solve a division problem. The array in Figure 7.20 shows the pieces she used, and the ratio table model shows her thinking step by step.

FIGURE 7.20

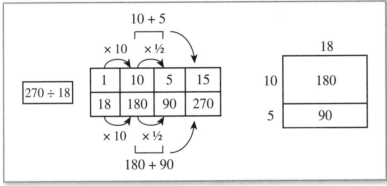

Constant Ratio Strategy

As Amy, a middle school teacher, plans her next strings, she has the constant ratio strategy for division as her goal. She knows that along with that strategy come big ideas about area and dimensions, fraction notation, common factors, equivalence, and proportional reasoning. There is a good chance that her students have experience with simplifying fractions, but she doesn't want to just *tell* them that when they see a division problem, they can treat it like simplifying a fraction. First, she wants to build ideas about division, and then connect those ideas to fraction notation. She uses the strings shown in Figure 7.21 over a period of several days.

FIGURE 7.21

Constant Ratio Strategy		
40 ÷ 2	75 ÷ 3	60 ÷ 12
80 ÷ 4	150 ÷ 6	30 ÷ 6
160 ÷ 8	150 ÷ 3	15 ÷ 3
320 ÷ 16	300 ÷ 12	48 ÷ 8
160 ÷ 16	300 ÷ 6	24 ÷ 4
320 ÷ 8	600 ÷ 24	12 ÷ 2
640 ÷ 32	1,200 ÷ 24	504 ÷ 84
	600 ÷ 12	288 ÷ 36

Amy starts the first day's string by reminding students of one of their favorite multiplication strategies, doubling and halving. She asks a student to briefly reiterate why that strategy works with arrays.

"When you double one dimension and halve the other, the area stays the same," explains Essence. "So when you double one factor and halve the other, the product stays the same."

"Great! Today, let's explore the same idea for division," Amy gives the first three problems, 40 ÷ 2, 80 ÷ 4, and 160 ÷ 8, one at a time. Students sketch and label appropriate arrays, shown in Figure 7.22. Since the answers to all three problems are the same, 20, a discussion ensues about why. Students comment:

"You're doubling the rectangle."

"If you keep one dimension the same but double the area, the other dimension doubles."

"You're doubling one dimension, so the area is twice as much."

Amy draws dotted lines in the arrays and arrows between the problems to show the relationship.

FIGURE 7.22

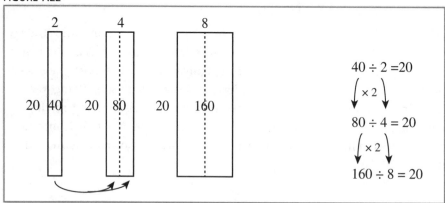

"So, are you doubling and halving, like with multiplication?" asks Amy.
"No, you're doubling and doubling," says Che.
"Let's keep that idea in mind with the rest of the string," suggests Amy.

The string continues with 320 ÷ 16, 160 ÷ 16, and 320 ÷ 8, with students comparing and discussing the results in terms of areas and dimensions. The string ends with 640 ÷ 32. Several students notice the double relationship with the earlier problem, 320 ÷ 16.

"So, since you double doubled 320 ÷ 16 to get 640 ÷ 32, the answer should be the same, so it's still 20," says Angelica.

After Amy ensures that students have drawn and discussed appropriate arrays, she tells students that they'll come back to this idea in the next few days.

The next day, she does the 75 ÷ 3 string. This string is less pointed toward the constant ratio strategy, but gives students needed experience making sense of the relationships involved in doubling the area and the dimensions (dividend and divisor). Since the string is built on 75 ÷ 3 = 25, money will likely enter the conversation in a helpful way. Not only are students developing a spatial sense of what's happening, but they are also working with problems that are both partitive (75 ÷ 3) and quotative (300 ÷ 12). As students chunk 75 into 3 quarters, they get better at chunking 150 into 6 quarters, which leads to chunking 300 into 12 quarters. This builds proportional reasoning and is important in really understanding equivalent ratios and fractions.

The next day, Amy does the 60 ÷ 12 string, which more directly leads to the constant ratio strategy. The first three problems, 60 ÷ 12, 30 ÷ 6, and 15 ÷ 3, are equivalent, as shown in the arrays in Figure 7.23. The missing dimension is 5 in each case. As students finish the problems, Amy writes 60 ÷ 12 = $^{60}\!/_{12}$ on the board and asks students to discuss the fraction notation.

"How does this relate to what we are doing?" asks Amy, pointing to the $^{60}\!/_{12}$.

"Oh!" exclaimed Craig, "They are the same." Amy asks what he means. "The problems, $^{60}\!/_{12}$, $^{30}\!/_{6}$, $^{15}\!/_{3}$, they are all equivalent ratios," explains Craig. Amy records this equivalence next to the arrays.

FIGURE 7.23

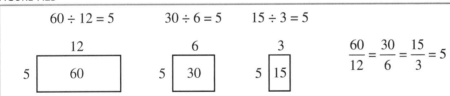

$$60 ÷ 12 = 5 \qquad 30 ÷ 6 = 5 \qquad 15 ÷ 3 = 5$$

$$\frac{60}{12} = \frac{30}{6} = \frac{15}{3} = 5$$

If you halve the area and one dimension, the other dimension stays the same.

Amy knows that her students have seen fraction notation before, but Amy wants to connect it with what they have been learning in division, especially with arrays. She knows that some students may have only a part-whole definition of fractions and may see $^{60}\!/_{12}$ only as 60 out of 12 or sixty-twelfths. To help clarify, she asks, "Where are the dimensions and the area in the fractions and why?"

The students discuss that the fraction bar can mean "divided by" and that the dividend, or area, is the numerator, and the divisor, or dimension, is the denominator. Amy follows with the next three related problems, giving the students more experience. The last two problems, given without helper problems, give the students a chance to use the relationships they have been constructing. For example, for 504 ÷ 84, students can find equivalent ratios by dividing out common factors to get $^{504}\!/_{84} = {}^{252}\!/_{42} = {}^{126}\!/_{21} = {}^{42}\!/_7 = 6$. Similarly, for the last problem, $288 \div 36$, $^{288}\!/_{36} = {}^{144}\!/_{18} = {}^{72}\!/_9 = 8$.

Students are connecting this work with equivalent ratios to division problems and they can now add equivalent ratios to the repertoire of division strategies.

Comparing Strategies

Consider these four problems. Which strategy or strategies would you use for each problem? Then compare your answers to the sample student responses that follow.

> a. $2,376 \div 24$
>
> b. $240 \div 16$
>
> c. $147 \div 21$
>
> d. $686 \div 14$

For $2,376 \div 24$, Celeste says, "I just went a little over. I know that 100 times 24 is 2,400. Then subtract one 24, $2,400 - 24 = 2,376$, so the answer is 99."

For $240 \div 16$, Marco says, "They both have factors of 2, so I simplified and found that $^{240}\!/_{16} = {}^{120}\!/_8 = {}^{60}\!/_4 = 15$." Kaitlyn says, "I know that 10×16 is 160. Half of that gives me 5 times 16 is 80, so the answer is 15."

For $147 \div 21$, Dan says, "Simplify by 3 to $\dfrac{49 \cdot 3}{7 \cdot 3} = \dfrac{49}{7}$ so the answer is 7." Danielle says, "I know that $^{210}\!/_{21} = 10$, so $^{105}\!/_{21} = 5$. I just need 2 more twenty-ones to get 147, so the answer is 7."

For $686 \div 14$, Abby says, "I found 100 times 14, that's 1,400. Divide that in half for $50 \cdot 14 = 700$. That's one 14 too much, so the answer's 49." She shows her work in the ratio table in Figure 7.24.

FIGURE 7.24

1	100	50	49
14	1,400	700	686

Clarifying Understanding

As students work with division, you can use the activities that follow to help students understand place value and apply the division strategies appropriately.

As Close as It Gets

The "As Close as It Gets" problems in Figure 7.25 use decimals, not to work with decimal multiplication, but to help students think about multiplying by "about 10." For $100.2 \cdot 9.9$, students could reason that "about 100" $\times$ "about 10" should be "about 1,000." If students mention moving the decimal point, make sure to emphasize the reasoning that 10 one hundreds equals 1,000. For $3.2 \div 11$, students could reason that "about 3" $\div$ "about 10" is close to $^3\!/_{10}$, or 0.3. They could also reason that $\$3 \div 10$ can be found by finding $^1\!/_{10}$ three times, or $^{\$1.00}\!/_{10} + {}^{\$1.00}\!/_{10} + {}^{\$1.00}\!/_{10} = \$0.30$. We want students to know that dividing by 10 results in a place-value shift, where the quotient is one-tenth of the dividend. We want students to be able to justify their thinking, rather than rotely moving decimal points.

FIGURE 7.25

As Close as It Gets		
$100.2 \cdot 9.9$	$3.2 \div 11$	$51 \div 9.9$
a) 0.1 b) 1	a) 0.032 b) 0.32	a) 0.5 b) 5
c) 10 d) 1,000	c) 3.2 d) 32.11	c) 50 d) 51

Relational Thinking

The problems in the relational thinking exercises given in Figure 7.26 give a bit of a different look to division by using fraction notation.

FIGURE 7.26

Relational Thinking

Fill in the blank:

$$\frac{403}{13} = \frac{390}{13} + \frac{\quad}{13}$$

$$\frac{198}{22} = \frac{220}{22} + \frac{\quad}{22}$$

True or false? Why?

$$\frac{240}{12} = \frac{240}{10} + \frac{240}{2}$$

$$\frac{326}{34} = \frac{320}{32} + \frac{6}{2}$$

The fraction notation is another way to help students clarify that in division, you can chunk the dividend but not the divisor to make the problem into manageable chunks. (For instance, when given a problem like $403 \div 13$, you can split up the dividend, 403, into easy-to-handle parts like 390 and 13, both of which are divisible by 13. For $198 \div 22$, you can use the fact that $198 = 220 - 22$.) Students who understand fraction addition may be able to apply that understanding to help them understand which number you can split up and why. Students who have been using the distributive property of multiplication may be inclined to try to distribute division by partitioning the divisor. You cannot distribute division over addition: $240 \div 12 = 240(10 + 2) \neq 240 \div 10 + 240 \div 2$. By writing these problems in fraction notation, students can see that you cannot add $^{240}\!/_{10} + {}^{240}\!/_{2}$ to get $^{240}\!/_{12}$.

Another way to help students make sense of this is to ask them to sketch the arrays for $240 \div 12, 240 \div 10$, and $240 \div 2$ (see Figure 7.27). The two arrays for $240 \div 10$ and $240 \div 2$ do not combine in any way to make the original $240 \div 12$. By discussing these relational thinking problems, students clarify their understanding of what numbers they can chunk when solving division problems.

FIGURE 7.27

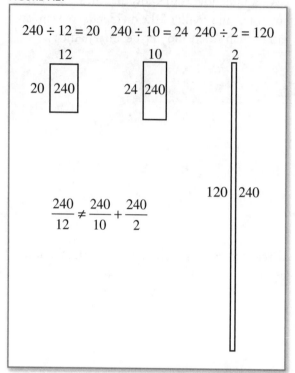

In this chapter, you have seen students use several division strategies with whole numbers. Students look to the numbers first before deciding on a strategy. They use connections between division and fractions to make some division problems easier. These strategies will be linked to decimals and fractions in Chapter 8, where students learn to be even more efficient and sophisticated with division.

CHAPTER 8 *eight* **8**

Decimals, Fractions, and Percents: Models and Strategies

I can add, subtract, multiply, or divide anything without a calculator (quickly) and teach my students how to do the same.

NUMERACY WORKSHOP PARTICIPANT

In this chapter, you'll find discussion of the major models and strategies for decimals, fractions, and percents. Chapters 9 and 10 will continue with examples of how to help your students operate on these rational numbers. Please note that this is not intended to be an exhaustive or complete treatment of rational number concepts and computation. These chapters can help when your students come to you with incomplete understanding or rote use of the operations. They can help you understand some of the strategies that students may bring to your class. Though you may not have time to reteach everything in its entirety, you can still help your students take advantage of some major models and strategies that will pay off for them in your course, in higher mathematics, and in life.

Decimals

"Is this where I move the decimal or where I line up the decimals?" I heard this question often when decimal questions came up in my classes. Many students clearly had only a digit approach to decimal operations. The algorithms, so cleverly compact, obscure the place-value shifts that occur when you multiply by a number a tenth or hundredth of its related whole number (i.e., 3.2 is $\frac{1}{10}$ of 32). You've already seen some major place-value ideas and strategies that make operations with whole numbers more transparent. Similar strategies can help with decimals.

Students need experience choosing friendly numbers for decimals. Just as 10 and multiples of 10 and money amounts (5, 25, 75, etc.) are friendly for whole numbers, tenths, multiples of tenths and hundredths, and money amounts (0.25, 0.5, 0.75, etc.) are friendly for decimals. Give students practice with adding and subtracting these friendly numbers and quickly move to the major strategies: give and take for addition; difference versus removal and constant difference for subtraction. Give students experience multiplying and dividing by tenths and hundredths and then use strings to develop the strategies of partial products, chunking, over and under, and doubling/halving for multiplication and partial quotients, over and under, and constant ratio for division. Students soon learn that they can use their whole number strategies with decimals, using place-value understanding to adjust the place value as necessary. Through the rest of the book, we'll continually examine place value and the effects of multiplying or dividing by powers of ten. Students can use these patterns to justify place-value shifts, instead of just "moving the decimal point."

At the same time, students' understanding of decimals can help them with whole number operations. For example, consider the problem $26 \cdot 84$. To find $26 \cdot 84$, you could first find $25 \cdot 84$ by finding $0.25 \cdot 84 = \frac{1}{4} \cdot 84 = 21$, and then adjusting the place value. Since 25 is 100×0.25, the answer to $25 \cdot 84$ is 100 times greater, or 2,100. Now you just need one more 84, so $26 \cdot 84 = 2,100 + 84 = 2,184$.

Rational Numbers

Rational numbers and their operations are very important to numeracy. As you saw in Chapter 5, mathematicians given multiplication and division problems frequently used fractional strategies to solve them (Dowker 1992, 52). Unfortunately, many elementary students come with only a limited understanding of the meaning of fractions. They may have a procedural sense of finding equivalent fractions and a collection of fraction operation rules, but for many students, the operations have little meaning and are often mixed up and combined.

Throughout the rest of the book, you'll find the following five interpretations of rational numbers, based on those given by Susan Lamon (2005, 226) in *Teaching Fractions and Ratios for Understanding*:

- ► Part-whole comparison ($\frac{4}{5}$ = "4 parts out of 5 equal parts")
- ► Measurement ($\frac{4}{5}$ = "four one-fifth units" or "the location of $\frac{4}{5}$ on the number line")
- ► Operator ($\frac{4}{5}$ = "four-fifths of something")
- ► Quotient ($\frac{4}{5}$ = "$4 \div 5$")
- ► Ratio ($\frac{4}{5}$ = "the ratio of 4 to 5")

All of these meanings are important, and students need experience to construct the separate notions and their interconnectedness. Unfortunately, many students think of rational numbers as fractions with only the part-whole meaning.

Of all of the interpretations, the concept of ratio might be the one that brings the most confusion. In textbooks, it is often isolated in obvious "solve this proportion" problems. But students need the ratio meaning when we develop fraction division, for the study of rates of change, including slope, and many more topics in higher math. Why is the ratio meaning confusing?

The greatest difference between ratios and the other interpretations of rational numbers is in the way they combine through arithmetic operations. The other interpretations of rational numbers are all different conceptually, but they are indistinguishable once they are written symbolically. They add, subtract, multiply, and divide according to the same rules. However, we do not operate on ratios in the same way that we do on fractions. (Lamon 2005, 229)

We saw this earlier in our work with ratio tables. Recall the ratio of 1 gum pack to 17 sticks that we used in multiplication and division of whole numbers. To find the number in 3 packs, we could add 1:17 and 2:34 to get 3:51. Writing this in fraction notation, $\frac{1}{17}$ + $\frac{2}{34}$ = $\frac{3}{51}$, is correct for ratios (though, by convention, not generally done), but not for all of the other meanings of fractions. We need to help students understand all of the meanings, their similarities and differences, and when each meaning is helpful.

One reason for all of the ratio table work with whole number multiplication and division in Chapters 5 to 7 is as Lamon suggests: "Students who studied ratios and rates as their primary interpretation of rational numbers developed a very strong notion of equivalence classes and of proportionality in general. They easily switched between ratio and part-whole comparisons and had no trouble with fraction addition and subtraction. Most of them developed their own ways of thinking about multiplication and division" (Lamon 2005, 230).

The Quotient Meaning of Fractions and Equivalence

The strings in Figure 8.1 can help students develop their understanding of the quotient meaning of fractions, an important part of developing rational number equivalence. Students are familiar with the idea of sharing money fairly among people, especially when the share is greater than 1: share $200 with 16 people, and they each get $12.50. These strings help students develop this understanding for quotients less than 1. Even though the strings are about fractional equivalence, all of these strings will use decimals to help in the development.

FIGURE 8.1

Fractions Are Quotients		
$5 ÷ 10	$10 ÷ 5	$3 ÷ 5
$2 ÷ 10	$5 ÷ 5	$6 ÷ 5
$4 ÷ 10	$2 ÷ 5	$6 ÷ 10
$1 ÷ 10	$4 ÷ 5	$2 ÷ 3
$6 ÷ 10	$1 ÷ 5	$2 ÷ 6
$8 ÷ 10	$3 ÷ 5	$6 ÷ 9
$3 ÷ 10	$0.50 ÷ 5	$3 ÷ 4

The first string is the foundation for the other two strings and works toward connecting division by 10 to a place-value shift and the meaning of one-tenth. For the first problem, $5 ÷ 10, ask students what their share is if they divide $5 among 10 people. Each share is $0.50, so $5 ÷ 10 = 0.5 = $\frac{5}{10}$ = 0.5. For $2 shared among 10 people, the share is

$0.20, so $^2/_{10} = 0.2$, and so on. As students work through each problem, encourage them to talk about the connections they find, possibly including:

- When you divide by 10, the number gets smaller.
- That's why we call 0.1 "one-tenth"—because it is $1 \div 10$, $^1/_{10}$!
- 2×10 is 20. The digit 2 shifts to the left because it is 2 tens. So for $2 \div 10$, the digit 2 shifts to the right to represent two-tenths.

The second string works toward generalizing the quotient meaning of division. To deliver this string, keep the language about fair sharing. For the problem $\$2 \div 5$, for example, you might hear students use strategies like the following:

- Since there are 200¢ in \$2, and $200 \div 5$ is 40, so \$0.40.
- I know $\$1 \div 5$ is \$0.20, so since it's \$2, I doubled the \$0.20 to get \$0.40.
- $20 \div 5$ is 4, so $\$2 \div 5$ has to be 10 times smaller, \$0.40.

Model the equivalence for students by writing $\$2 \div 5 = \$0.40$ per person $= ^2/_5$ of a dollar per person.

As you work through the remaining problems, encourage students to discuss that for positive numbers a, b, it is true that $a \div b = ^a/_b$ even if $a < b$, and therefore the share is a fraction between 0 and 1. (We'll restrict to positive numbers for ease in notation.) This is a powerful idea, that a fraction can represent a quotient. We can use it to build ideas about equivalence.

Now that we have the basis of connecting fair sharing division problems with their fraction look, the last string in Figure 8.1 continues building fractions as quotients as it plays with equivalence. What happens to the share if you share twice as much money with the same number of people? What if you share the same amount of money with twice as many people? After you deliver each problem as a fair sharing division problem, write the fractions and discuss the equivalences.

- Compare $\$3 \div 5$ people, $^3/_5$, to $\$6 \div 5$ people: $^6/_5$. Which way do I get more money? Does that mean that $^6/_5 > ^3/_5$ or $^3/_5 > ^6/_5$? Why?
- Now compare those two scenarios with $\$6 \div 10$ people. Are any of these situations equivalent—do I get the same amount of money? Does $^3/_5 = ^6/_{10}$? Why? What does it mean that both the numerator and the denominator scaled up from $^3/_5$ to $^6/_{10}$? What does it mean that only the numerator scaled up from $^3/_5$ to $^6/_5$?

Connecting Fractions and Decimals

We can capitalize on our students' experience with money to help them make sense of both fractions and decimals and the connections between them. Facility with fraction-decimal equivalents can help students sort out fraction equivalence. For example, students already know that \$0.50 is half a dollar, so $0.5 = ^1/_2$, and that a quarter is \$0.25, so $0.25 = ^1/_4$. With that, they should be able to find the decimal equivalent of $^1/_8$ using the relationship that $^1/_8$ is half of $^1/_4$, so $^1/_8 = ^1/_2$ of $^1/_4 = ^1/_2$ of $0.25 = 0.125$. You can support this reasoning using a ratio table, as shown in Figure 8.2. The figure also shows two ways to find the decimal equivalent of $^3/_5$.

FIGURE 8.2

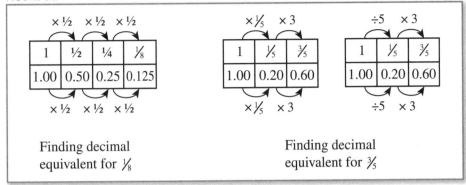

Finding decimal
equivalent for ⅛

Finding decimal
equivalent for ⅗

To convert ³⁄₂₀ to a decimal, students can reason that ³⁄₂₀ is 3 one-twentieths. They can find ¹⁄₂₀ by asking "What is a dollar divided by 20?" Since there are 20 nickels in a dollar, $1.00 ÷ 10 = $0.05 and 3 nickels is $0.15, hence ³⁄₂₀ = 3(¹⁄₂₀) = 3(0.05) = 0.15 (see Figure 8.3). Through the rest of the book, we'll use decimals and fractions interchangeably to fit the needs of the conversation.

FIGURE 8.3

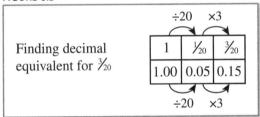

Finding decimal
equivalent for ³⁄₂₀

Equivalent Fractions: The Double Number Line Model

Students need experience with many different situations to support understanding that quantities and symbols that look very different can represent equivalent rational numbers. One way to do this is a variation on the open number line, the double number line. As with the open number line, we put numbers that are helpful for a particular problem on the double number line. But, because fractions are relations, we put related numbers on both the top and bottom of the line to show those relationships. This process can help develop the *operator* and *measurement* meanings of fractions.

Figure 8.4 shows how to use the double number line to reason in finding equivalent fractions for ⅕. The context for these examples is finding ⅕ of the length of a race; each uses a different total length, and so involves finding a different equivalent fraction. As students try to decide where to put the ⅕ on the top, they visualize the length being cut into 5 fifths. They then cut the course length of 10 into the corresponding 5 pieces to get ⅕ of 10; since 10 ÷ 5 = 2, each chunk is 2 miles. The act of partitioning the number line into 5 equal chunks helps students visualize how to partition the course length into 5 equivalent chunks.

FIGURE 8.4

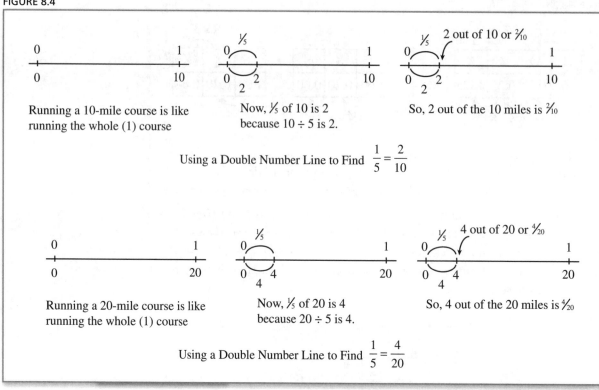

Running a 10-mile course is like running the whole (1) course

Now, $\frac{1}{5}$ of 10 is 2 because $10 \div 5$ is 2.

So, 2 out of the 10 miles is $\frac{2}{10}$

Using a Double Number Line to Find $\frac{1}{5} = \frac{2}{10}$

Running a 20-mile course is like running the whole (1) course

Now, $\frac{1}{5}$ of 20 is 4 because $20 \div 5$ is 4.

So, 4 out of the 20 miles is $\frac{4}{20}$

Using a Double Number Line to Find $\frac{1}{5} = \frac{4}{20}$

The same model can be used to help students make sense of comparing fractions, like $\frac{2}{5}$ and $\frac{3}{7}$. To compare $\frac{2}{5}$ and $\frac{3}{7}$, students could first choose a "nice" racecourse length of 70 and then use the double number line in Figure 8.5. They could first find an equivalent for $\frac{1}{5}$ by chunking the 70 into 5 chunks to find $\frac{1}{5}$ of 70 = 14, so an equivalent fraction to $\frac{1}{5}$ is $\frac{14}{70}$. To find an equivalent fraction for $\frac{2}{5}$, double the $\frac{14}{70}$ to get $\frac{28}{70}$.

FIGURE 8.5

To find an equivalent fraction for $\frac{2}{5}$, find $\frac{1}{5}$ of 70 = $\frac{14}{70}$ and double for $\frac{28}{70}$

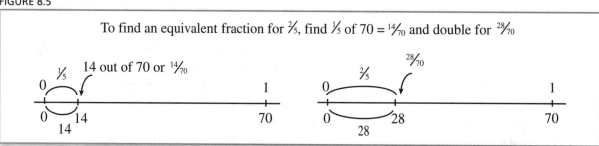

To find an equivalent fraction for $\frac{3}{7}$, a student could similarly find $\frac{1}{7}$ by chunking the 70 into 7 equal chunks ($\frac{1}{7}$ of 70 = 10) and multiply by 3 to get $\frac{30}{70}$, as shown in Figure 8.6. Then, putting these on the same number line, the comparison is obvious: $\frac{28}{70} < \frac{30}{70}$, so $\frac{2}{5} < \frac{3}{7}$ (shown in Figure 8.7).

FIGURE 8.6

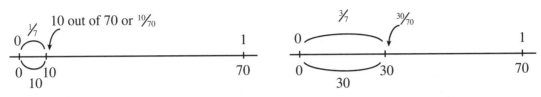

To find an equivalent fraction for $\frac{3}{7}$, find $\frac{1}{7}$ of 70 = $\frac{10}{70}$ and multiply times 3 for $\frac{30}{70}$

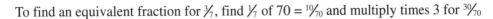

FIGURE 8.7

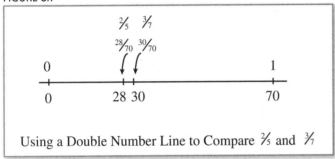

Using a Double Number Line to Compare $\frac{2}{5}$ and $\frac{3}{7}$

The double number line model helps students construct both the operator and measurement meanings of fractions. As students find $\frac{1}{7}$ of 70 and then scale up to find 3 times that for $\frac{3}{7}$ of 70, they are developing the operator meaning. Algebraically, this relationship can be generalized as $a \cdot \frac{1}{b} = \frac{a}{b}$. A multiple, a, of a unit fraction, $\frac{1}{b}$, is the common fraction, $\frac{a}{b}$. Using measurement on the double number line, we can establish the position of the underlying rational number on the number line. With a unit of length 1, the nonnegative rational number $\frac{a}{b}$ is a intervals of length $\frac{1}{b}$ from 0, as shown in Figure 8.8. In a strict sense, this represents a measurement from 0, and we refer to the rational number as a point on the number line.

FIGURE 8.8

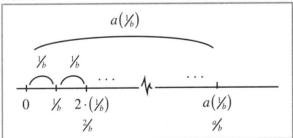

Fraction Addition and Subtraction

In order for students to be successful with addition and subtraction of fractions, they must understand equivalent fractions. A colleague, Garland Linkenhoger, once said to me, "If students truly understand fraction equivalence, the operations take care of themselves." Instead of memorizing rule after rule about what to do with fractions, students can reason through addition and subtraction problems using equivalence.

We want students to have a sense for the *magnitude* of a fraction in equivalent forms—simultaneously seeing ¾ as a fraction between 0 and 1, a fraction halfway between ½ and 1, 0.75, 75%, ½ + ¼, half of 1.5, double ⅜, 3 out of 4, 3 ÷ 4, the ratio of 3:4, the point ¾ of a unit from 0, the point ¼ of a unit back from 1, 45 minutes (out of an hour), $0.75, 75¢, and so on. This flexibility enables students to see, or at least sense, an equivalent form that will be useful in the problem at hand.

This simultaneity of thought is complex and takes time and experience to develop. How do we build such multidimensional thought, such connected images, what Lamon calls "rational number personalities" (2005, 26)? We could try investigating equivalent fractions to find out why they are equivalent, and we could create different equivalent fractions. But students need a *reason* to find equivalencies; they need questions that demand equivalencies in order to solve. Addition and subtraction problems provide that reason. Students need to find equivalencies in order to add and subtract fractions. As students work through and discuss addition and subtraction problems and compare the equivalent fractions they use to solve them, they focus on equivalence.

To build this strong sense of fraction equivalence, we can engage students in addition and subtraction strings based on models, such as clocks and money, for which students can readily find and compare equivalencies. We'll consider such strings in Chapter 9. The focus is not on finding a procedure to add and subtract fractions. Instead, we want students to think, "What are all the ways I can see these numbers? Which equivalent ways are more or most helpful here? Why are they equivalent?" Once students can easily find and use equivalent fractions, they can add and subtract fractions as they do whole numbers: by looking to the numbers and deciding on a strategy.

Fraction Multiplication

The array model makes multiplication of fractions very accessible. To find the product of two unit fractions, like ⅕ · ¼ we can find ¼ of a rectangle using one dimension and find ⅕ of the rectangle using the other dimension. The solution is the area of the piece that is ¼ the length of the rectangle in one dimension and ⅕ of the length of the rectangle in the other dimension, as shown in Figure 8.9.

FIGURE 8.9

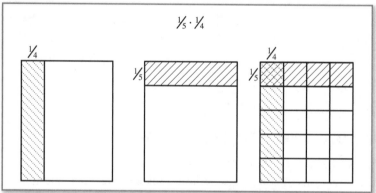

The product of nonunit fractions can be found similarly, as shown in Figure 8.10 For example, ⅖ · ¾ can be thought of as ⅖ of ¾ of the array. In other words, ⅖ · ¾ is the area of an inner array formed by $\frac{2}{5}$ of one dimension of the outer array and $\frac{3}{4}$ of the other dimension of the outer array. To find the product, you could find $\frac{3}{4}$ of a rectangle using one dimension and then find $\frac{2}{5}$ of that $\frac{3}{4}$. This results in a 2-by-3 inner array out of a 4-by-5 outer array, for $\frac{6}{20}$. So $\frac{a}{b} \cdot \frac{c}{d} = \frac{ac}{bd}$, where a and c are the dimensions of the inner array and b and d are the dimensions of the outer array.

FIGURE 8.10

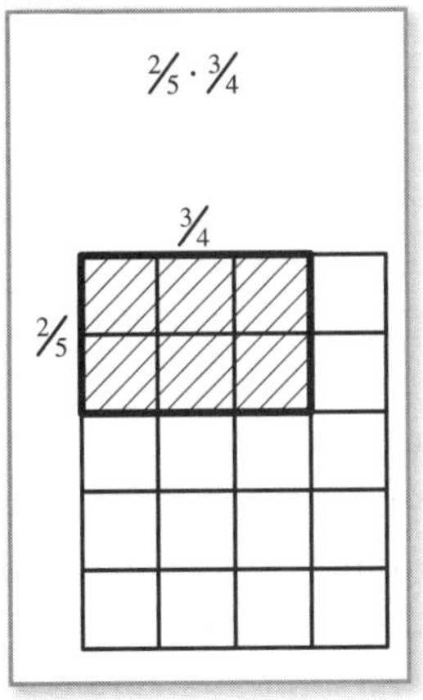

Once students grasp the array model for fraction multiplication, they can investigate the equivalence when the numerators or denominators in the factors trade places. The result is just a rotation of the inner rectangle, as shown in Figure 8.11. Thus the product remains the same. Often the swapping places strategy can result in an easier problem, such as $\frac{2}{5} \cdot \frac{3}{4} = \frac{2}{4} \cdot \frac{3}{5} = \frac{1}{2} \cdot \frac{3}{5}$. And $\frac{1}{2} \cdot \frac{3}{5}$ is easy to find—it's just $\frac{1}{2}$ of $\frac{3}{5}$, or $\frac{1.5}{5} = \frac{3}{10}$. This strategy is helpful when the numerators and denominators have common factors. For instance, both $\frac{3}{7} \cdot \frac{14}{6} = \frac{3}{6} \cdot \frac{14}{7} = \frac{1}{2} \cdot 2$ and $\frac{3}{7} \cdot \frac{14}{6} = \frac{14}{7} \cdot \frac{3}{6} = 2 \cdot \frac{1}{2}$ use the commutative property to make the result easy to solve.

FIGURE 8.11

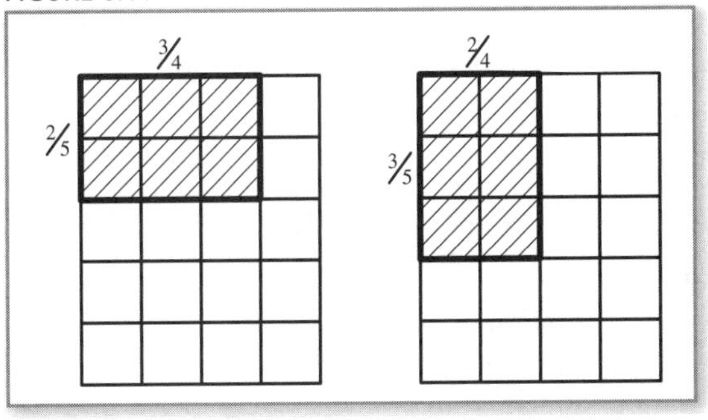

Another strategy is to use doubling and halving and related strategies that take advantage of the associative property. For example, to find $7\frac{1}{2} \cdot 16$, you can use doubling/halving to get $15 \cdot 8$. With $3\frac{1}{3} \cdot 9$, you can multiply and divide by 3 to get $10 \cdot 3$. When doubling or tripling mixed numbers, students must remember to distribute; this can be a valuable reminder, strengthening their sense of the distributive property.

Fraction Division

For fraction division to make sense, students must develop proportional reasoning. The ability to scale up and down multiplicatively in these situations is critical to understanding fraction division in both quotative and partitive situations.

Division with Common Denominators

Students may take a quotative approach to dividing by fractions. For example, for $\frac{1}{2} \div \frac{1}{4}$ we can ask, "How many one-fourths are in $\frac{1}{2}$?" Since there are 2 one-fourths in $\frac{1}{2}$, $\frac{1}{2} \div \frac{1}{4}$ = 2. As students do more problems like this, many begin thinking in terms of common denominators. In other words, to find how many eighths are in $\frac{3}{4}$, $\frac{3}{4} \div \frac{1}{8}$, they can think of $\frac{3}{4}$ in terms of eighths: $\frac{3}{4} \div \frac{1}{8} = \frac{6}{8} \div \frac{1}{8}$. The question then becomes, "How many one-eighths are in six-eighths?" This leads to the answer 6: $\frac{3}{4} \div \frac{1}{8} = \frac{6}{8} \div \frac{1}{8} = 6$. When the divisor is not a unit fraction, as in $\frac{3}{4} \div \frac{3}{8}$, they can still find a common denominator, $\frac{3}{4} \div \frac{3}{8} = \frac{6}{8} \div \frac{3}{8}$ and ask how many three-eighths are in six-eighths—$\frac{3}{4} \div \frac{3}{8} = \frac{6}{8} \div \frac{3}{8} = 2$. Students begin to construct the generalization that once you have common denominators, you can just divide the numerators. When students are confident with problems that yield whole number answers, then they can extend their reasoning to understand that $\frac{5}{3} \div \frac{2}{3}$ can be answered by dividing the numerators, $5 \div 2$, so $\frac{5}{3} \div \frac{2}{3} = 5 \div 2 = \frac{5}{2}$. With all of this understanding, students can generalize that to find an answer to any fraction division problem, find a common denominator and then divide numerators. While this may be surprising to those of us who memorized "invert and multiply," students with a strong sense of equivalence can often just *see* the equivalence and then the division follows naturally.

The Constant Ratio Strategy

Recall the constant ratio strategy with whole number division, where we solved problems by keeping the ratio constant. Consider this partitive problem: It took 2 cups of grated cheese to make $\frac{1}{3}$ of a pizza. How many cups of cheese will it take to make a whole pizza? We can record strategies to solve this problem in a ratio table, as shown in Figure 8.12.

FIGURE 8.12

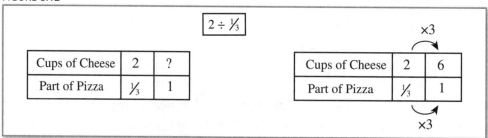

In effect, by finding the number of cups of cheese to make 1 pizza, we changed the problem into an equivalent problem where the divisor is 1, $2 \div \frac{1}{3} = 6 \div 1 = 6$. We multiplied both the dividend and the divisor by 3 to keep the ratio constant. Figure 8.13 shows how this strategy works for two more complicated problems:

FIGURE 8.13

If $\frac{1}{4}$ of a cup of cheese made $\frac{1}{5}$ of a pizza, how much cheese would be needed for a whole pizza?

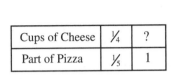

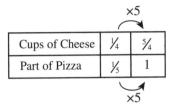

$\boxed{\frac{1}{4} \div \frac{1}{5}}$

Cups of Cheese	$\frac{1}{4}$	?
Part of Pizza	$\frac{1}{5}$	1

×5

Cups of Cheese	$\frac{1}{4}$	$\frac{5}{4}$
Part of Pizza	$\frac{1}{5}$	1

×5

If it took $\frac{3}{4}$ of a cup of cheese to make $\frac{2}{5}$ of a pizza, how much cheese do we need to make a whole pizza?

$\boxed{\frac{3}{4} \div \frac{2}{5}}$

Cups of Cheese	$\frac{3}{4}$	?
Part of Pizza	$\frac{2}{5}$	1

$\times \frac{5}{2}$

Cups of Cheese	$\frac{3}{4}$	$\frac{15}{8}$
Part of Pizza	$\frac{2}{5}$	1

$\times \frac{5}{2}$

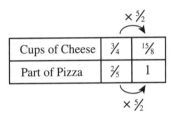

With this last problem, the solution is represented as $\frac{3}{4} \div \frac{2}{5} = (\frac{3}{4})(\frac{5}{2}) \div (\frac{2}{5})(\frac{5}{2}) = \frac{15}{8} \div 1$. You can see the traditional "invert and multiply" algorithm in this representation. The ratio table model allows us and students to reason *why* this method works!

Percents

Percents are ratios in which the second number is 100. They are not absolute numbers, but refer to proportional amounts. Students today have tons of experience with percents, thanks to progress bars found on electronic devices that show time remaining on downloads, battery life, and so on (see Figure 8.14). Because these gauges often show both percent and absolute numbers, students gain experience with these percents and their meanings.

FIGURE 8.14

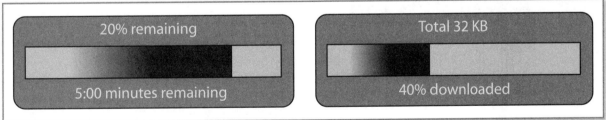

A percent bar model based on these gauges can be a helpful model for students to figure percent problems by finding friendly percents and scaling up and down. The percent bar model is similar to the double number line because students can label what they know and use the bar as a model to act on.

Problem Strings for Percents

The strings in Figure 8.15 provide students with experience with percent problems where the unknowns are in all positions: the start value, the percent, and the result. Use the percent bar to model and compare student strategies.

The problems in the start unknown strings (Figure 8.15) ask students to find different percents of the same number. This is like the quotient meaning of rational numbers— 50% of 40 is equivalent to ½ of 40. Encourage students to flexibly use fractions or decimals as they work on these problems. Students can also add smaller percentages to find the greater ones. For example, once students find 5% of 40 = 2 and 1% of 40 = 0.4, they can add those together to find 6% of 40 = 2.4. Encourage students to be flexible and to try to find clever strategies.

FIGURE 8.15

Start Unknown	Percent Unknown	Result Unknown
_____ is 100% of 40.	10 is what percent of 20?	3 is 100% of _____.
_____ is 200% of 40.	5 is what percent of 20?	3 is 50% of _____.
_____ is 50% of 40.	15 is what percent of 20?	3 is 25% of _____.
_____ is 25% of 40.	2 is what percent of 20?	3 is 10% of _____.
_____ is 10% of 40.	3 is what percent of 20?	3 is 1% of _____.
_____ is 5% of 40.	5 is what percent of 50?	3 is 12% of _____.
_____ is 1% of 40.	15 is what percent of 50?	6 is 50% of _____.
_____ is 6% of 40.	2 is what percent of 50?	12 is 50% of _____.
_____ is 0.5% of 40.	17 is what percent of 50?	3 is 50% of _____.
_____ is 13.5% of 40.	39 is what percent of 40?	6 is 25% of _____.

Figure 8.16 shows a percent bar model of one strategy for finding 91% of 20.

FIGURE 8.16

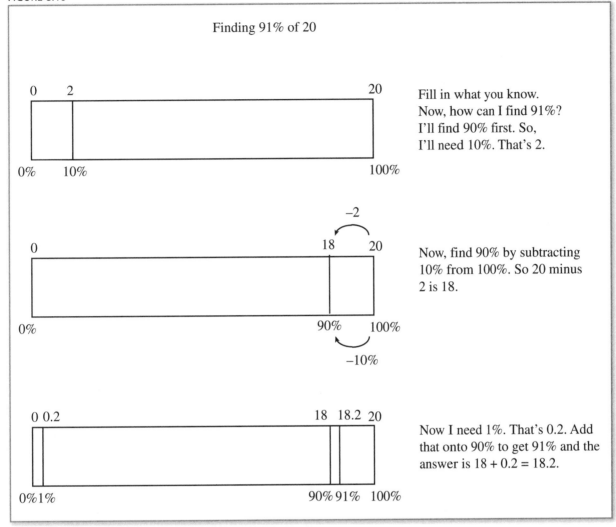

Finding 91% of 20

Fill in what you know.
Now, how can I find 91%?
I'll find 90% first. So,
I'll need 10%. That's 2.

Now, find 90% by subtracting
10% from 100%. So 20 minus
2 is 18.

Now I need 1%. That's 0.2. Add
that onto 90% to get 91% and the
answer is 18 + 0.2 = 18.2.

The problems in the percent unknown string in Figure 8.15 ask students to find the relationship between two numbers. Just as students could add percents together in the last string, here they can add the start numbers. For instance, once students reason that 10 is 50% of 20 (because 10 is half of 20) and 5 is 25% of 20 (because 5 is ¼ of 20), then 15 (5 + 10 = 15) is 75% (50% + 25% = 75%) of 20.

Figure 8.17 shows a bar model for one strategy for finding the answer to the last problem.

FIGURE 8.17

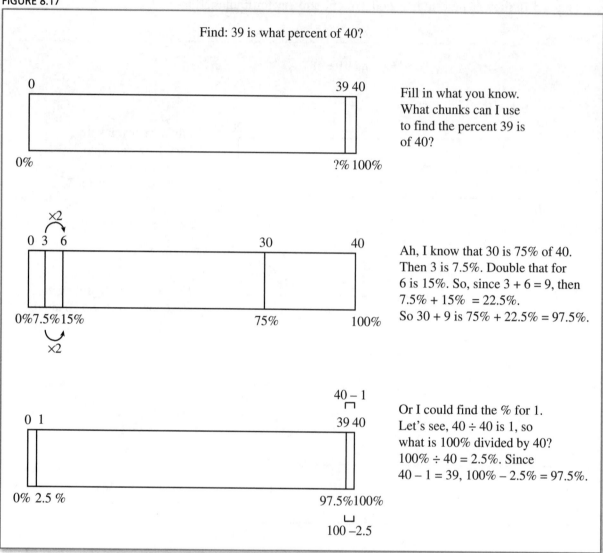

Find: 39 is what percent of 40?

Fill in what you know. What chunks can I use to find the percent 39 is of 40?

Ah, I know that 30 is 75% of 40. Then 3 is 7.5%. Double that for 6 is 15%. So, since 3 + 6 = 9, then 7.5% + 15% = 22.5%. So 30 + 9 is 75% + 22.5% = 97.5%.

Or I could find the % for 1. Let's see, 40 ÷ 40 is 1, so what is 100% divided by 40? 100% ÷ 40 = 2.5%. Since 40 − 1 = 39, 100% − 2.5% = 97.5%.

With the result unknown string in Figure 8.15, use the percent bar to help students decide how to proceed. After they have filled in what they know, ask "How can you get from the given percent to 100%?" In the first few problems of each string, that's fairly easy. For the question "3 is 25% of what number?" students can reason that if you multiply 25% by 4, you get 100%. Therefore you must also multiply 3 by 4 to get 12, so 3 is 25% of 12.

When the given percent does not divide evenly into 100%, then you need to be more creative. In the problem "8 is 16% of what number?" 16% does not divide evenly into 100%. But you can scale down from 16% to 4% and then back up again to 100%, as shown in Figure 8.18.

FIGURE 8.18

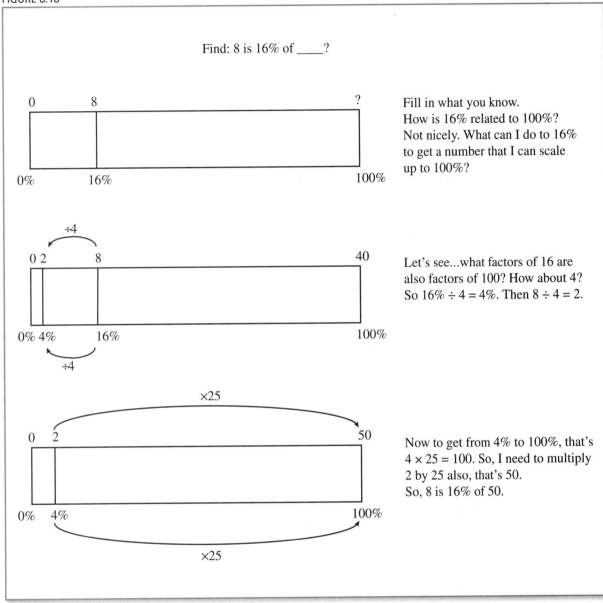

Find: 8 is 16% of ____?

Fill in what you know.
How is 16% related to 100%?
Not nicely. What can I do to 16%
to get a number that I can scale
up to 100%?

Let's see...what factors of 16 are
also factors of 100? How about 4?
So 16% ÷ 4 = 4%. Then 8 ÷ 4 = 2.

Now to get from 4% to 100%, that's
4 × 25 = 100. So, I need to multiply
2 by 25 also, that's 50.
So, 8 is 16% of 50.

With the experience from these strings, students can tackle virtually any of the typical percent problems. Figure 8.19 shows how the percent bar can help a student visualize and solve even an ugly problem, like 14.2 is 23.7% of ____?

FIGURE 8.19

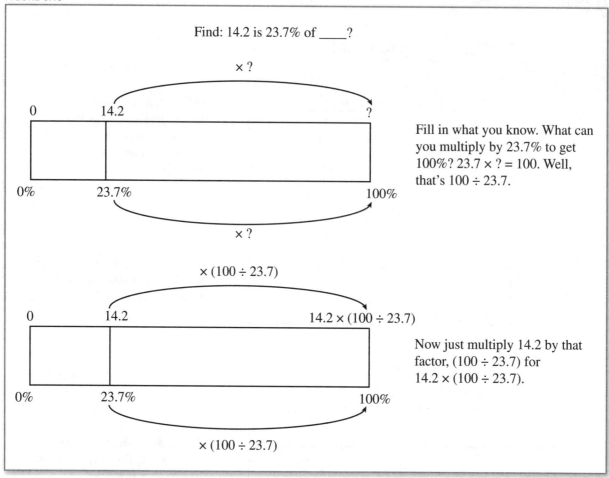

Find: 14.2 is 23.7% of ____?

Fill in what you know. What can you multiply by 23.7% to get 100%? 23.7 × ? = 100. Well, that's 100 ÷ 23.7.

Now just multiply 14.2 by that factor, (100 ÷ 23.7) for 14.2 × (100 ÷ 23.7).

Using Fractions and Decimals in Whole Number Operations

As students grapple with both decimal and fraction operations, you can support the power of interchanging whole numbers, decimals, and fractions in all sorts of problems. These are the strategies Dowker (1992) calls "fractional relationships." Consider this problem that came from my son's sixth-grade teacher, who claimed it "wouldn't work" with strategies other than the traditional algorithm: 76 · 36. This is exactly the kind of problem to use with sixth graders' budding decimal and fraction understanding to bring it all together. To find 76 · 36, first find 75 · 36 by finding ¾ of 36, 0.75 · 36 = ¾ · 36 = 27 and then adjusting the place value, 75 · 36 = 2,700. Now you just need one more 36, so 76 · 36 = 2,736.

We must take computation seriously, and we want students to be able to compute efficiently. And students who have this kind of understanding can do just that. It's important for secondary teachers to build their own numeracy and mathematical thinking as well, so they can improve, not supplant, students' developing strategies.

Implications for Higher Mathematics

Developing Proportional Reasoning

Susan Lamon estimates that over 90% of adults do not reason proportionally (Lamon 2005, 10). We want to actively promote a progression from counting strategies to additive thinking to multiplicative thinking and proportional reasoning. In many textbooks, students get a token treatment of ratios and proportions by looking at a few examples and then quickly being taught a nontransparent rule to cross multiply and divide. Because they have jumped so quickly to a rule, many do not gain the sense of ratio that accompanies a proportional situation. They are not learning to reason proportionally. But, proportional reasoning is vitally important to the K–12 curriculum (Lesh, Post, and Behr 1988).

What is proportional reasoning? Lamon suggests that proportional reasoning "is reasoning up and down in situations in which there exists an invariant (constant) relationship between two quantities that are linked and varying together. As the word *reasoning* implies, it requires argumentation and explanation beyond the use of symbols" (Lamon 2005, 3). Just as multiplication demands that students consider the group and the number in the group simultaneously, proportional reasoning demands dealing with the relationships of a ratio to a ratio. Proportional reasoning is key for students' understanding of later applications such as algebra, calculus, and many scientific topics such as force and mechanical advantage.

Solving Proportions

Traditionally students have been taught to cross multiply and divide to solve a proportion, $a/b = c/d$. Because of the look of the proportion, students have inadvertently mixed this rule with other fraction rules. In my high school classroom, it seemed "cross multiply and divide" was the favorite rule; students cross multiplied and divided to add, subtract, multiply, and divide fractions and rational expressions. Sometimes they would mix it with other rules and find common denominators, then cross multiply, and then invert and "cancel" everything. If it weren't so frustrating, it would be very humorous.

In contrast, students who have used ratio tables to multiply and divide in situations with constant rates are accustomed to these proportional situations. Students who have used the constant ratio strategy in ratio tables have scaled up and down to find equivalent ratios. They are prepared to transition to using ratio tables to model other proportional situations. Consider how the examples in Figure 8.20 extend students' previous ratio table work. Even though we aren't using fractions explicitly, the concept of ratio embodied in these tables helps students see these problems as the proportional situations that they are.

FIGURE 8.20

The ratio of pink rose bushes to yellow rose bushes is 3:4.
How many yellow rose bushes are there if there are 36 pink rose bushes?

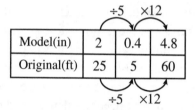

Number of Pink	3	36
Number of Yellow	4	?

		×12
Number of Pink	3	36
Number of Yellow	4	48
		×12

Renae is building a doll house where the scale is 2 inches:25 feet.
How long is the doll house if the original is 60 feet long?

Model(in)	2	?
Original(ft)	25	60

		÷5	×12
Model(in)	2	0.4	4.8
Original(ft)	25	5	60
		÷5	×12

Geometry: Similar Figures

Students can use ratio tables to solve the proportions in typical similar-figure problems, like finding missing side lengths (see Figure 8.21). Notice that since students are thinking in terms of ratios and proportions, they are not seeing these problems as fraction operation problems.

FIGURE 8.21

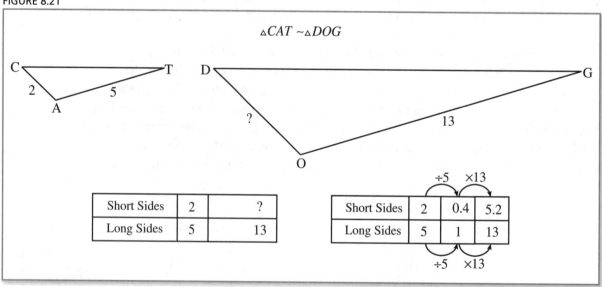

$\triangle CAT \sim \triangle DOG$

Short Sides	2	?
Long Sides	5	13

		÷5	×13
Short Sides	2	0.4	5.2
Long Sides	5	1	13
		÷5	×13

Direct and Inverse Variation

With this background in fractions and ratios, students are better prepared to understand and work with proportional relations. From a transformation perspective, the function rule of direct variation, $y = kx$, is a vertical stretch of the linear parent function, $y = x$, by a factor of k. Students will continue working with linear functions through high school math. And because students have been reasoning with equivalent fractions, they have experience with quantities that are related in such a way that when one increases, the other decreases. For example, when the denominator of a unit fraction increases, the value of the unit fraction decreases. This understanding helps prepare students to deal with inverse variation, where $y = {}^k\!/_x$.

Rate of Change

Students are also better prepared to deal with the concept of rate of change, and particularly slope. If students have a shallow sense of ratio, they do not tend to see a rate of 2 as a ratio of 2 to 1 (e.g., 2 miles per 1 hour or 2 feet per 1 second). Slope, commonly summarized as "rise over run," is actually "the ratio of rise to run," or the ratio of the difference in the y-values to the difference in the x-values, slope $= {}^{\Delta y}\!/_{\Delta x}$. This understanding also applies to the wider study of rates in physics and calculus.

Rational Expressions

If students are well grounded in equivalent fractions and can reason through the operations, their work with rational expressions and rational equations can build on that understanding. They will be less likely to confuse the procedures appropriate to the different operations in these expressions. Students with constructed relationships of equivalent fractions will be less inclined to "cancel" everything. The constant ratio strategy will help students better understand the multiplicative relationships that allow them to divide out common factors.

If students firmly understand equivalent fractions, and thus what it really means to find a common denominator, then adding and subtracting rational expressions will follow more naturally. They can even use a ratio table to find the common denominator of a rational expression, as in Figure 8.22.

FIGURE 8.22

$$\frac{x}{2(x+2)} + \frac{x^2}{(x+2)(x-1)}$$

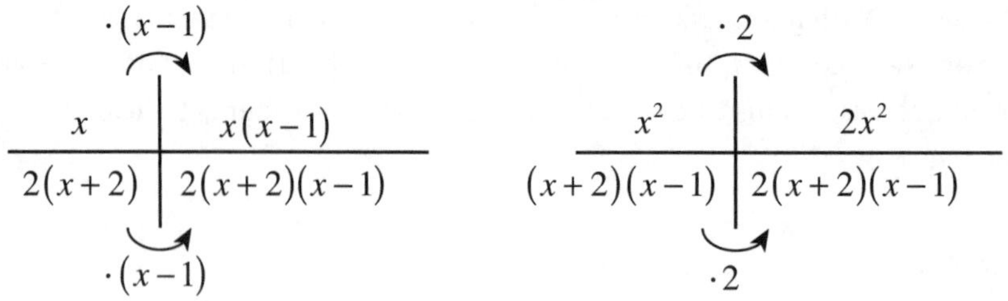

$$\overset{\cdot(x-1)}{\frown}$$

$$\frac{x}{2(x+2)} \;\bigg|\; \frac{x(x-1)}{2(x+2)(x-1)}$$

$$\underset{\cdot(x-1)}{\smile}$$

$$\overset{\cdot 2}{\frown}$$

$$\frac{x^2}{(x+2)(x-1)} \;\bigg|\; \frac{2x^2}{2(x+2)(x-1)}$$

$$\underset{\cdot 2}{\smile}$$

$$\frac{x(x-1)}{2(x+2)(x-1)} + \frac{2x^2}{2(x+2)(x-1)} = \frac{x(x-1)+2x^2}{2(x+2)(x-1)}$$

When students need to multiply rational expressions, they can draw on their sense of constant ratio and use that knowledge to divide out common factors. When students need to divide rational expressions (as in Figure 8.23), they can draw on their understanding of fraction division to know why to invert and multiply: you are making the divisor 1!

FIGURE 8.23

$$\frac{x}{x^2+x-2} \div \frac{x^2}{x-1} = \left(\frac{x}{x^2+x-2}\right) \cdot \left(\frac{x-1}{x^2}\right) \div \frac{x^2}{x-1} \cdot \left(\frac{x-1}{x^2}\right)$$

$$= \left(\frac{x}{x^2+x-2}\right) \cdot \left(\frac{x-1}{x^2}\right) \div 1$$

Developing a deep understanding of rational numbers and how to operate on them takes time and careful construction. While this book cannot give a full treatment of rational number concepts and computation, the remaining chapters give you problem strings and activities to guide you in helping your students construct the most important strategies.

nine **9**

Decimals and Fractions: Addition and Subtraction

My view of teaching fraction operations has changed completely. I've realized the value in conceptualizing that adding fractions requires the same-sized pieces, not just finding an LCD [least common denominator]. If they can just understand that they just need to find the size of the piece, it's not necessary to get the least common denominator, but actually any common denominator. The concepts behind the rules are far more important than the rules themselves.

NUMERACY WORKSHOP PARTICIPANT

In this chapter, you'll find problem strings and activities to help students with strategies for decimal and fraction addition and subtraction. By using these strings and activities, you'll also build the important concepts of fraction equivalence and place value for decimals. You'll strengthen students' facility with the multiple meanings of fractions, especially those of fractions as operators, fractions as quotients, and fractions as measures.

Decimal Addition

When working with addition and subtraction of decimals, students with less place-value understanding may need time and experience adding smaller chunks that make sense to them. You can juxtapose those less efficient small-jump strategies with others using larger jumps. As you work through the problems, highlight students who use money to help make sense of place value. Money is helpful because students have a wealth of experience from which to draw. Vary your use of decimal names, using tenths and money interchangeably. For example, for 3.8, you could say three point eight (the common "shorthand"), three and eight-tenths, and three dollars and eighty cents. This helps students get a feel for the equivalence and also for when one interpretation might be more helpful.

The get to a friendly number string in Figure 9.1 is similar to the get to a friendly number strings for whole numbers in Chapter 3. The first four problems are in pairs, where the first problem is easy because the addends sum to a whole number, as in $14.8 + 0.2 = 15$. The next problem builds on that helper problem, suggesting that when encountering a problem like $14.8 + 0.3$, you can add $14.8 + 0.2$ first to get 15 and then tack on the remaining 0.1 for 15.1. The next two problems are given without helper problems. You may see students using familiar whole number strategies, such as doubles.

FIGURE 9.1

Get to a Friendly Number
$14.8 + 0.2$
$14.8 + 0.3$
$7.96 + 0.04$
$7.96 + 0.05$
$3.76 + 1.25$
$0.12 + 5.89$

The give and take string (Figure 9.2) is similar to the whole number give and take strings in Chapter 3. These problems each have numbers that lend themselves to giving and taking because at least one number is close to a whole number. Give just a little, and the problem turns into the easier addition of a whole number and a decimal. The string is designed so that problems deal with different place values to give students experience navigating numbers of all sizes. When leading this string, juxtapose students' strategies to encourage them to make bigger jumps. For the problem $2.97 + 1.54$, you might start with a student's strategy of splitting the numbers into place-value parts and then bringing the chunks back together. You might compare this strategy with another in which a student starts with the 2.97 and adds 1 to get 3.97, then adds 0.10 to get 4.07, then adds 0.40 to get 4.47, and then adds the remaining 0.04 to get 4.51. Make sure to bring in a student who starts with the 2.97, adds 0.03 to get 3.00, and then adds what's left, $3 + 1.51 = 4.51$. These three strategies are modeled in Figure 9.2. By juxtaposing these strategies, you can help students increase their sense of place value and begin to look for ways to chunk the numbers more efficiently.

FIGURE 9.2

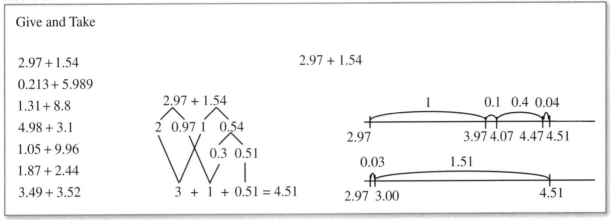

Give and Take

2.97 + 1.54

0.213 + 5.989

1.31 + 8.8

4.98 + 3.1

1.05 + 9.96

1.87 + 2.44

3.49 + 3.52

Decimal Subtraction

With decimal subtraction, you could start with a subtract to a friendly number string, shown in Figure 9.3. As with the addition string in Figure 9.1, the first four problems are in pairs, where the first of each pair is an easy problem. For example, 19.3 − 0.3 subtracts readily to 19. This sets up the next problem, 19.3 − 0.4; students can start by subtracting 0.3 to get to 19 and then remove the remaining 0.1. The next pair is similar. To find 2.014 − 0.027, first find 2.014 − 0.014 = 2 and then remove the remaining 0.013 to find 2 − 0.013 = 1.987. The last three problems are given without support.

FIGURE 9.3

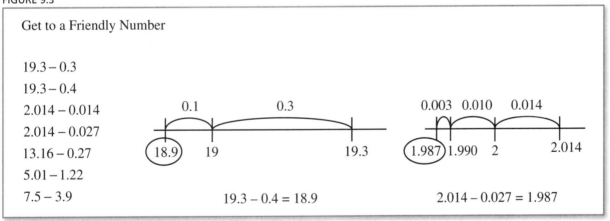

Get to a Friendly Number

19.3 − 0.3

19.3 − 0.4

2.014 − 0.014

2.014 − 0.027

13.16 − 0.27

5.01 − 1.22

7.5 − 3.9

If your students need more work differentiating between finding the difference and removing, you could use strings like the one shown in Figure 9.4. For 9.11 − 0.99, students could first remove 0.11 and then the remaining 0.88. For 1,000 − 978.9, they might find it more efficient to find the difference by counting up.

FIGURE 9.4

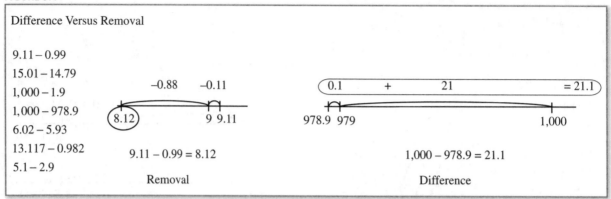

Difference Versus Removal

9.11 – 0.99
15.01 – 14.79
1,000 – 1.9
1,000 – 978.9
6.02 – 5.93
13.117 – 0.982
5.1 – 2.9

9.11 – 0.99 = 8.12

Removal

1,000 – 978.9 = 21.1

Difference

If your students need more work with the constant difference strategy, strings like the one in Figure 9.5 can help. The first four problems are paired; the first problem in each pair is easy to solve and the second problem is equivalent to the first. When you lead this string, model the differences on the number line so that students can see that the distance remains constant for problems like $80.9 - 40$ and $80.2 - 39.3$. The last three problems are given without helper problems. Encourage students to discuss where to shift the difference to make the problems easier.

FIGURE 9.5

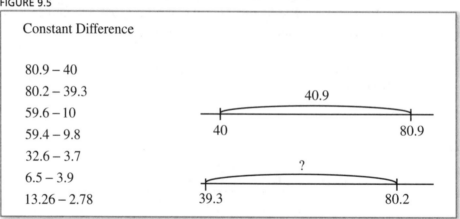

Constant Difference

80.9 – 40
80.2 – 39.3
59.6 – 10
59.4 – 9.8
32.6 – 3.7
6.5 – 3.9
13.26 – 2.78

Comparing Strategies: Decimals

Use these problems to compare strategies and encourage students to defend their strategy choices based on the numbers in each problem. Which strategy would you use for each of these problems?

    a. 35.602 + 2.187

    b. 2.53 + 2.48

    c. 237.36 + 4.95

    d. 13.16 – 12.89

    e. 3.014 – 0.021

    f. 2.347 – 2.013

For 35.602 + 2.187, Sebastian said, "I just lined them up, because I didn't have to carry—it was easy."

For 2.53 + 2.48, Janae said, "I used doubles, because 2.5 doubled is 5, so you just have 1 penny extra, so 5.01."

For 237.36 + 4.95, Jerome said, "Just give a nickel to $4.95 to get $5. So 237.36 and 5 is 242.36, but you have to get rid of the extra nickel, so 242.31."

For 13.16 − 12.89, Talia said, "Since the numbers are so close together, I found the difference. Starting on 12.89, add 11¢ to get $13. Then you just need 16¢ more. So 0.11 + 0.16 is 0.27." Juan said, "I shifted the distance to make the 12.89 nicer. So I added 0.11 to both to get 13.27 − 13 = 0.27."

For 3.014 − 0.021, Stone said, "Since the numbers are so far apart, I just subtracted. I started with 3.014 and took away 0.014 to land on 3. Then I still had to remove 0.007, so 3 − 0.007 is 2.993. Minh said, "I moved the difference 3.014 − 0.021 by adding 0.979 to both. That gave me 3.993 − 1. And that's easy, just 2.993."

For 2.347 − 2.013, Hahn said, "Since you don't have to borrow, I just lined them up and subtracted, so 0.334."

Fraction Addition and Subtraction

For addition and subtraction of fractions, we'll use four models: money, the clock, the double number line, and the ratio table. Each has distinct advantages. Students have experience with money and clocks and can use commonly held ideas with those models to help make connections. Money helps with fractions that have denominators that are factors of 100, including 5, 10, 20, and 25. The clock helps students work with fractions with denominators that are factors of 60, such as 3, 6, and 12. The double number line and ratio table are more general and can work with any denominator. You will find strings that deal with money, strings that deal with the clock, and then strings that generalize to all denominators using the double number line and ratio table. Flexibly relating and connecting fractions and decimals are an important part of this process.

Fraction Addition and Subtraction with the Money Model

We continue to take advantage of our secondary students' experience with money to add fractions. Here's a look at part of a fraction addition with money string in a middle school class. The teacher, Amy, starts by listing several fractions one at a time and having students identify an equivalent money amount for each one (based on $1 as the whole). For example, for ⅕, students say that there are 5 chunks of 20¢ in a dollar, so ⅕ = $0.20. Since there are 4 quarters in a dollar, ¼ = $0.25, and so on: ½ = $0.50, ⅒ = $0.10, 1/20 = $0.05, 1/25 = $0.04. Then she asks students to find ½ + ¼.

Tshar offers, "That's like 50¢ and 25¢, which is 75¢."

Amy asks, "How can I write 75¢?"

Tshar answers "Like 0.75 or like the fraction ¾."

"How do you know that 75¢ can be written as the fraction ¾?" asks Amy.

"Well, it's like there's 3 coins that are called *quarters*. One quarter is 25¢ but it is also the fraction ¼. So 3 quarters is 3 over 4," answers Belin.

Amy asks, "3 over 4? What does that mean?" Amy knows it is common to say *over* but that the word is not helpful in understanding fractions.

"3 out of 4 quarters is ¾," answers Tim. Tania adds that 3 one-quarters is ¾. Amy writes down ½ + ¼ = 0.75 = ¾.

The string continues with students using money equivalents to find sums for ¾ + ½ and ¾ + ¾. When Amy asks students for ¹⁄₁₀ + ½, students suggest that the answer is like 0.10 + 0.50 = 0.60. Amy asks for a fraction equivalent for 0.60 and the students offer ⁶⁰⁄₁₀₀ and ⁶⁄₁₀. One student, Rowan, suggests ³⁄₅.

"Where did you get ³⁄₅, Rowan?" asks Amy.

"First I just simplified ⁶⁄₁₀ but now I can see that 60¢ is like 3 groups of 20¢. So that's like 3 one-fifths, so ³⁄₅," explains Rowan.

Amy knows that not all of her students followed his explanation, but they'll be doing more strings with fifths and twentieths soon, so she concentrates on the denominators in today's string: 2, 4, and 10. "Great connection. We'll do some more with fifths soon. The next question is 1¼ + ¹⁄₁₀." Amy includes mixed number questions in the string because she wants students to be comfortable dealing with all forms of fractions.

Cedric looks confused, "So, I know it's 35¢, but I am not sure how to write that as a fraction."

Tshar offers, "35¢ is like 35 out of a dollar, so you can write it ³⁵⁄₁₀₀. But don't forget the 1 from the problem, so the answer is 1³⁵⁄₁₀₀."

Ashley adds, "5¢ is a nickel and 35¢ is 7 nickels. Since there are 20 nickels in a dollar, then ³⁵⁄₁₀₀ = ⁷⁄₂₀."

The string ends with a similar problem, 2¾ + 3³⁄₁₀. Many students use a splitting strategy. They add the units 2 and 3 to get 5, and then add the fractions ¾ and ³⁄₁₀ by adding 75¢ to 30¢ for 1⁵⁄₁₀₀ or 1¹⁄₂₀, making the total 6¹⁄₂₀. Before moving on, Amy asks if anyone solved 2¾ + 3³⁄₁₀ by keeping the 2¾ whole.

Russell answered, "I started with $2 and 75¢. I took a quarter from the $3 and 30¢. So now I had $3 + $3.05, so that is $6.05 or 6⁵⁄₁₀₀."

Both the splitting strategy and Russell's give and take strategy (shown in Figure 9.6) are useful. It's important that students have both strategies in their repertoire and can look at a problem in multiple ways, all the while searching for efficiency, sophistication, and even elegance.

FIGURE 9.6

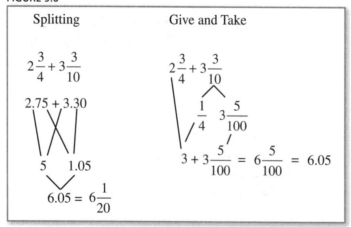

Amy plans to do more money strings over the next few days, both with addition and subtraction, and with more denominators, like ¼, ⅒, ¹⁄₂₅, and ¹⁄₁₀₀. It is important to note that we gain more with these strings than adding and subtracting fractions. Students use both fraction and decimal equivalents, making sense of when to think in fractions and when to think in decimals. They are strengthening their concept of fraction equivalence and of decimal to fraction conversion. Once students really understand finding equivalent fractions, then addition and subtraction of fractions just follows naturally.

Figure 9.7 lists strings for fraction addition using money. Notice that many of the problems deal with unit fractions. After students gain facility with unit fractions, you could do more strings with fractions with numerators greater than 1. Students will need time to sort out that ⅕ ≠ 0.05 and ¹⁄₂₀ ≠ 0.20, but that ⅕ = 0.2 and ¹⁄₂₀ = 0.05. Their part-whole fraction reasoning can help; they can find the decimal equivalent to ¹⁄₂₀ by reasoning that there are 20 nickels in a dollar, so 1 out of those 20 nickels equals 5¢ out of 100¢, or 0.05. This also helps them understand the idea of a fraction as an operator: what does it mean to say ¹⁄₂₀ of a dollar?

The first string concentrates on chunks of dollars that are easy, because they are coins like quarters (¼) and dimes (⅒). The second string brings in nickels (¹⁄₂₀) and 20¢ chunks (⅕). The last string brings in pennies (¹⁄₁₀₀) and harder money chunks of 4¢ (¹⁄₂₅) and 2¢ (¹⁄₅₀). Since these latter amounts are not coins, they nudge students to apply what they have been doing with the familiar coins to the unfamiliar amounts, while still using familiar factors of 100 as denominators.

FIGURE 9.7

Fraction Addition with Money		
Money, Unit Fractions, Dimes, Quarters	**Money, Unit Fractions, 20¢, Nickels**	**Harder Money— Equivalence**
$\frac{1}{2} + \frac{1}{4}$	$\frac{1}{2} + \frac{1}{5}$	$\frac{1}{25} + \frac{1}{2}$
$\frac{3}{4} + \frac{1}{2}$	$\frac{1}{5} + \frac{1}{10}$	$\frac{1}{4} + \frac{5}{25}$
$\frac{3}{4} + \frac{3}{4}$	$\frac{3}{10} + \frac{2}{5}$	$\frac{1}{100} + \frac{3}{25}$
$\frac{1}{10} + \frac{1}{2}$	$1\frac{1}{4} + \frac{4}{5}$	$\frac{1}{10} + \frac{9}{100}$
$1\frac{1}{4} + \frac{1}{10}$	$\frac{1}{20} + \frac{1}{10}$	$\frac{3}{50} + \frac{3}{100}$
$2\frac{3}{4} + 3\frac{3}{10}$	$2\frac{2}{5} + 1\frac{1}{20}$	$\frac{1}{20} + \frac{1}{25}$

The subtraction strings in Figure 9.8 are built similarly, moving from easy coins to less familiar amounts. In the second string, you'll find that the problems are set up to encourage students to stay in mixed numbers when appropriate. For example, the first problem suggests to just subtract 1, 2¼ − 1, and sets the stage for the next problem, 2¼ − 1½, where students can first subtract the 1 and then deal with subtracting the ½. This is intended to help students look to the numbers first, rather than rotely converting mixed numbers to improper fractions when they don't need to.

FIGURE 9.8

Fraction Subtraction with Money		
Money, Unit Fractions, Dimes, Quarters	Money, Unit Fractions, 20¢, Nickels	Harder Money— Equivalence
$\frac{1}{2} - \frac{1}{4}$	$2\frac{1}{4} - 1$	$\frac{1}{2} - \frac{1}{25}$
$\frac{3}{4} - \frac{1}{2}$	$2\frac{1}{4} - 1\frac{1}{2}$	$\frac{3}{5} - \frac{2}{5}$
$\frac{1}{2} - \frac{1}{10}$	$5\frac{1}{2} - 3\frac{3}{4}$	$\frac{1}{5} - \frac{1}{100}$
$\frac{3}{4} - \frac{1}{10}$	$10\frac{1}{10} - 9\frac{1}{5}$	$\frac{1}{10} - \frac{19}{100}$
$1\frac{1}{4} - \frac{1}{2}$	$\frac{3}{5} - \frac{1}{20}$	$\frac{1}{50} - \frac{1}{100}$
$2\frac{1}{2} - 1\frac{1}{10}$	$\frac{3}{4} - \frac{2}{5}$	$\frac{3}{20} - \frac{3}{25}$

Fraction Addition and Subtraction with the Clock Model

A clock is another concrete model related to student experience that helps students work with the factors of 60 as denominators as they continue to build their understanding of fraction equivalence, addition, and subtraction. You could begin working with clock strings by listing some fractional equivalencies based on the clock: ½ is like 30 minutes out of 60 minutes, or $^{30}/_{60}$. It is also like 6 of the 12 five-minute chunks, $^{6}/_{12}$, and like 3 of the 6 ten-minute chunks, $^{3}/_{6}$ (see Figure 9.9). Notice that in these examples, the unit shifts from minutes, to five-minute chunks, to ten-minute chunks, and all of these are units within the unit of the entire hour. This requires unitizing. The clock model gives an opportunity for students to sort out these complex fraction relationships, strengthen their concept of fraction equivalence, and build addition and subtraction facility at the same time. To lead clock fraction strings, you may want to have some predrawn circles handy.

FIGURE 9.9

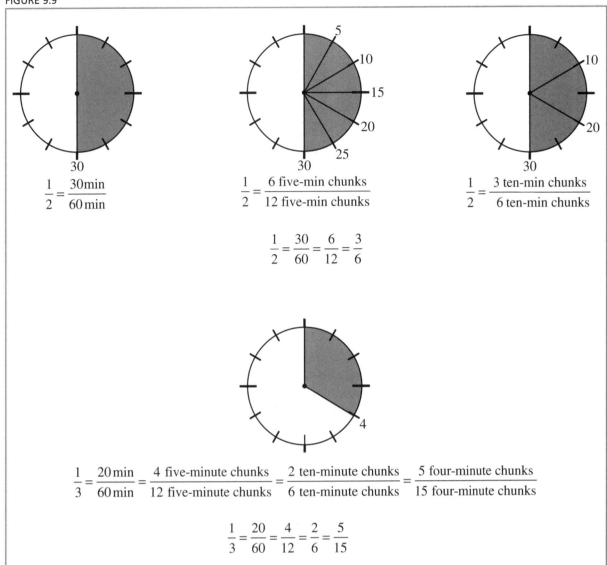

$$\frac{1}{2} = \frac{30\,\text{min}}{60\,\text{min}}$$

$$\frac{1}{2} = \frac{6 \text{ five-min chunks}}{12 \text{ five-min chunks}}$$

$$\frac{1}{2} = \frac{3 \text{ ten-min chunks}}{6 \text{ ten-min chunks}}$$

$$\frac{1}{2} = \frac{30}{60} = \frac{6}{12} = \frac{3}{6}$$

$$\frac{1}{3} = \frac{20\,\text{min}}{60\,\text{min}} = \frac{4 \text{ five-minute chunks}}{12 \text{ five-minute chunks}} = \frac{2 \text{ ten-minute chunks}}{6 \text{ ten-minute chunks}} = \frac{5 \text{ four-minute chunks}}{15 \text{ four-minute chunks}}$$

$$\frac{1}{3} = \frac{20}{60} = \frac{4}{12} = \frac{2}{6} = \frac{5}{15}$$

Fraction Addition Using a Clock Model Let's join Abby in her algebra class. A few days before, Abby and her students had listed several equivalent fractions on a clock and had done some addition strings with easy clock fractions. Abby begins today with the third string in Figure 9.10, starting with ½ + ⅒. This is an easy problem with money, so Abby knows students will be successful; they can use that success to help back up their reasoning with the clock model. After the students work on the problem, Abby asks them to share.

"So, I have half an hour and ⅒ of a hour. 60 minutes divided by 10 is 6 minutes. So there are 10 six-minute chunks in an hour. So ⅒ of an hour is 6 minutes. That's like 30 minutes and 6 minutes, so ³⁶⁄₆₀," says Justin.

"You can simplify that to ⁶⁄₁₀, because for ³⁶⁄₆₀ there are 6 six-minute chunks out of 10 six-minute chunks," adds Levi.

"You could also say that it's $\frac{3}{5}$ because 12 times 3 is 36 so there are 3 twelve-minute chunks out of 5 twelve-minute chunks," suggests Talia.

Abby writes $\frac{1}{2} + \frac{1}{10} = \frac{36}{60} = \frac{6}{10} = \frac{3}{5}$ and then gives the next problem, $\frac{1}{15} + \frac{1}{4}$. Before you read on, figure this out using the clock. What are the relationships involved?

Students work a bit and the following discussion ensues. Eddie starts, "I think that $\frac{1}{15}$ is like 4 minutes, so it's $\frac{4}{60}$. One-quarter of an hour is 15 minutes. So $\frac{4}{60}$ and $\frac{15}{60}$ is $\frac{19}{60}$." Abby writes $\frac{1}{15} + \frac{1}{4} = \frac{4}{60} + \frac{15}{60} = \frac{19}{60}$.

Some of the students notice a relationship. Matt says, "It's like the numbers are switching places. There are fours and fifteens everywhere."

"That's because 4 times 15 is 60. And you're adding $\frac{1}{15}$ and $\frac{1}{4}$," adds Zach. "So when you divide 60 by 15 to find out $\frac{1}{15}$ of 60, you get 4 minutes. When you divide 60 by 4 to get $\frac{1}{4}$ of 60, you get 15 minutes."

"Great noticings!" says Abby. As they finish the string, she'll continue to bring out similar relationships. For example, in the problem $\frac{5}{6} + \frac{1}{10}$, $\frac{1}{6}$ of 60 is 10 minutes and $\frac{1}{10}$ of 60 is 6 minutes. This will lead nicely into today's algebra lesson exploring the function $y = \frac{a}{x}$ where students will continue to see such relationships among the points on that function. Because $y = \frac{a}{x}$, $xy = a$, and so there are points (x, y) and (y, x) that both lie on the graph of the function.

This kind of fraction work builds student intuition about common denominators. They realize that to add fractions, they need to add the same kind of pieces. They also build the idea that the common denominator can be the multiple of the two denominators. The first string in Figure 9.10 uses unit fractions that are big chunks on a clock, which are easy to visualize. The second string uses common fractions, and the third string uses smaller chunks that are typically more difficult to visualize, like groups of 6 minutes ($\frac{1}{10}$) or 3 minutes ($\frac{1}{20}$).

FIGURE 9.10

Addition on a Clock		
Unit Fractions—Equivalence	Common Fractions—Equivalence	Harder Clock Fractions—Equivalence
$\frac{1}{2} + \frac{1}{3}$	$\frac{1}{6} + \frac{1}{12}$	$\frac{1}{2} + \frac{1}{10}$
$\frac{1}{3} + \frac{1}{4}$	$\frac{1}{12} + \frac{1}{4}$	$\frac{1}{15} + \frac{1}{4}$
$\frac{1}{2} + \frac{1}{4}$	$\frac{2}{3} + \frac{1}{12}$	$\frac{5}{6} + \frac{1}{10}$
$\frac{1}{3} + \frac{1}{6}$	$\frac{5}{12} + \frac{5}{6}$	$\frac{1}{20} + \frac{2}{3}$
$\frac{1}{6} + \frac{1}{2}$	$\frac{3}{4} + \frac{1}{6}$	$\frac{1}{30} + \frac{1}{5} + \frac{1}{60}$
$\frac{1}{4} + \frac{1}{6}$	$\frac{1}{4} + \frac{7}{12}$	$\frac{2}{15} + \frac{1}{30}$

Fraction Subtraction Using a Clock Model You can model both the finding the difference and removal strategies on adjacent clocks to compare and talk about which strategy is most useful for which problems. The strings in Figure 9.11 can help with this.

FIGURE 9.11

Subtraction on a Clock		
Difference	**Removal**	**Difference or Removal— Equivalence, Harder Fractions**
$\frac{1}{2} - \frac{1}{3}$	$\frac{11}{12} - \frac{1}{6}$	$\frac{1}{2} - \frac{1}{10}$
$\frac{5}{6} - \frac{1}{2}$	$\frac{5}{6} - \frac{1}{12}$	$\frac{1}{4} - \frac{1}{15}$
$\frac{2}{3} - \frac{1}{2}$	$1\frac{1}{4} - \frac{1}{3}$	$\frac{1}{6} - \frac{1}{10}$
$\frac{11}{12} - \frac{5}{6}$	$\frac{3}{4} - \frac{1}{12}$	$\frac{1}{3} - \frac{1}{20}$
$\frac{3}{4} - \frac{1}{3}$	$\frac{7}{12} - \frac{1}{6}$	$\frac{1}{5} - \frac{1}{12}$
$\frac{7}{12} - \frac{1}{4}$	$\frac{5}{6} - \frac{1}{4}$	$\frac{1}{2} - \frac{1}{30}$

For example, to solve ½ − ⅓, students may choose to shade in ½ of a clock and ⅓ of a second clock and look at the difference between the two, as shown in Figure 9.12. They could find the difference by noticing that the ½ overlaps the ⅓ by 2 five-minute chunks, so 2 out of 12 five-minute chunks is ²⁄₁₂, or that they overlap by 1 ten-minute chunk, so 1 out of 6 ten-minute chunks is ⅙.

FIGURE 9.12

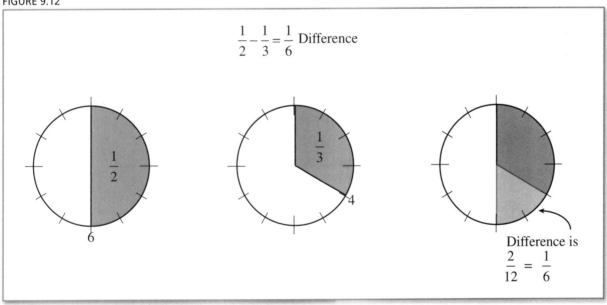

$$\frac{1}{2} - \frac{1}{3} = \frac{1}{6} \text{ Difference}$$

Difference is
$$\frac{2}{12} = \frac{1}{6}$$

Students might choose, however, to remove ⅓ from ½. Students shade in ½ of a clock and then remove ⅓ from that ½, as shown in Figure 9.13. They find the difference by noticing what is left once they take away the ⅓. This time the 2 five-minute chunks or 1 ten-minute chunk is what is left, and the answer is $\frac{2}{12} = \frac{1}{6}$.

FIGURE 9.13

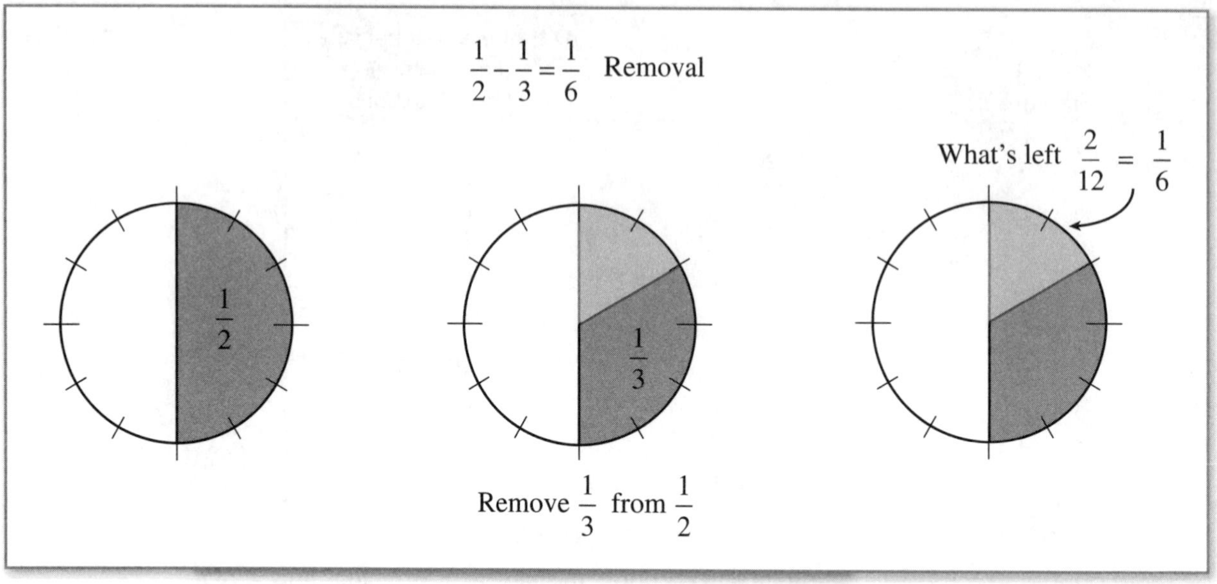

1/2 − 1/3 = 1/6 Removal
What's left 2/12 = 1/6
1/2
1/3
Remove 1/3 from 1/2

The last string in Figure 9.11 works with harder denominators for a clock, like 10 (six-minute chunk) and 15 (four-minute chunk), because we don't usually think in terms of six- or four-minute chunks of time. Students gain more experience finding equivalent fractions and choosing whether to remove or to find the difference. Figure 9.14 shows a difference strategy for $\frac{5}{6} - \frac{1}{2}$ and a removal strategy for $\frac{11}{12} - \frac{1}{6}$. Throughout, encourage students to reason and justify their thinking.

FIGURE 9.14

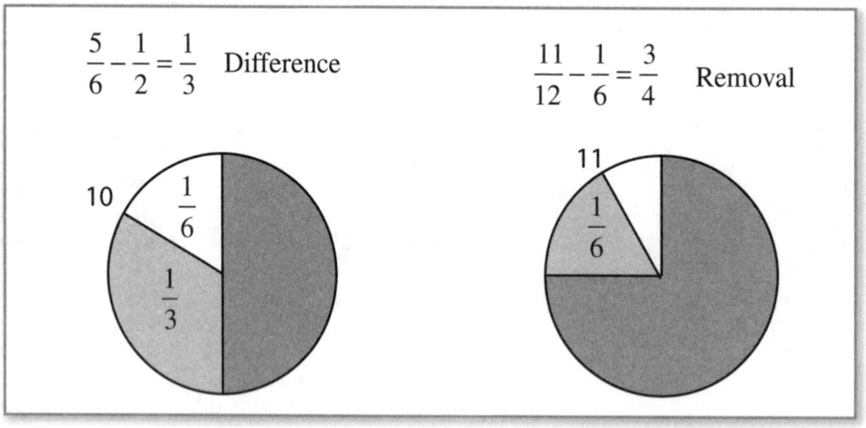

5/6 − 1/2 = 1/3 Difference
11/12 − 1/6 = 3/4 Removal
10
1/6
1/3
11
1/6

Fraction Addition and Subtraction with the Double Number Line

After students have done money and clock fraction strings, do some problems with them where they can choose the model. The first string in Figure 9.15 gives students the opportunity to decide which model works best for each problem. Some of the problems have denominators like 5 and 10 that point to the money model, while other problems have denominators of 3 and 4, for which a clock model might be easier. Some have denominators that work for either model, such as $\frac{3}{4} - \frac{1}{20}$.

FIGURE 9.15

Double Number Line Strings		
Choose Your Model	**Choose Your Denominator**	**Choose Your Denominator**
$\frac{1}{4} + \frac{2}{3}$	$\frac{1}{5} + \frac{1}{7}$	$\frac{1}{2} + \frac{1}{3} + \frac{1}{4}$
$\frac{5}{6} - \frac{1}{3}$	$\frac{2}{7} + \frac{3}{5}$	$\frac{1}{5} + \frac{1}{10} + \frac{1}{100}$
$\frac{2}{3} + \frac{1}{6}$	$\frac{1}{3} - \frac{1}{8}$	$\frac{1}{5} + \frac{1}{6} + \frac{1}{2}$
$\frac{1}{5} + \frac{3}{10}$	$\frac{2}{3} - \frac{3}{8}$	$\frac{1}{5} + \frac{1}{7} + \frac{1}{2}$
$\frac{3}{4} - \frac{1}{20}$	$\frac{1}{4} + \frac{1}{9}$	$\frac{1}{24} + \frac{1}{12} + \frac{1}{6}$
$\frac{1}{2} + \frac{31}{60}$	$\frac{3}{4} + \frac{2}{9}$	
$\frac{51}{100} - \frac{1}{4}$	$\frac{2}{5} - \frac{1}{15}$	

The other two strings in Figure 9.15 have denominators that do not fit well with either a money or clock model, like 7, 8, and 9. For these problems, you could introduce a measurement context, like a race course. Let's join Rick in his algebra 2 class as he leads a choose your denominator string. The students have already identified that the $\frac{1}{7}$ in the first problem does not work easily with either a money or a clock model. Rick sets up a new context: running a course through a neighborhood park.

"To warm up, I walked $\frac{1}{5}$ of the course and then I ran $\frac{1}{7}$ of the course. So, the question is, how much of the course did I complete? You can make up any length you want for the course. Think about a course length that works well with $\frac{1}{5}$ and $\frac{1}{7}$." After students work, Rick models strategies on the board. One student suggests that 35 is a good length because $5 \times 7 = 35$. Rick models the strategy by drawing a line to represent the course and marking the beginning and ending of the course (Figure 9.16).

FIGURE 9.16

Rick then asks a student, Abrianna, how much of the course he walked to warm up. She answers, "You walked 7 km because $\frac{1}{5}$ of 35 is 7." As she is talking, Rick models a jump of ⅕ on the top of the number line, and then labels that same-sized jump on the bottom of the number line with the 7 (Figure 9.17).

FIGURE 9.17

"And you ran 5 km because ⅐ of 35 is 5," continues Abrianna.

Rick draws a jump of ⅐ on the top and an equivalent jump of 5 on the bottom. "So how much of the course did I finish that day?" asks Rick.

"Well, since you went 12 km, that's 12 out of the 35 km, so ¹²⁄₃₅," finishes Abrianna.

Rick marks that on the double number line (Figure 9.18) and asks, "Any comments or questions for Abrianna?"

FIGURE 9.18

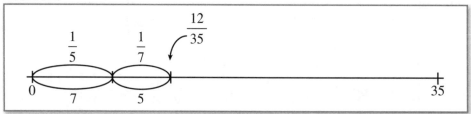

"I did it another way. I used 70, not 35," says Jeremy.

Since the conversation is not just about adding fractions but also equivalence, Rick wants to compare other course lengths and welcomes Jeremy's strategy, even though it does not use the lowest common denominator. Jeremy explains, "I used 70 because I knew that 7 times 10 is 70. I also knew since 70 ends in 0, that 5 would divide into it. So ⅕ of 70 is 14 and ⅐ of 70 is 10. So you went 24 out of 70 km."

Rick models this on the board (Figure 9.19) and asks, "So, are these equivalent answers? Is ¹²⁄₃₅ equivalent to ²⁴⁄₇₀?"

FIGURE 9.19

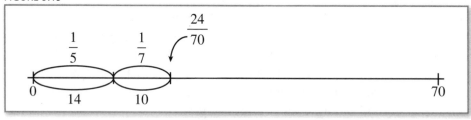

Cameron answers, "Yes. It's like the course is twice as long so you have to run twice as far."

Paulina adds, "You multiply both 12 and 35 by 2, and you get ²⁴⁄₇₀. They both are twice as long." This is proportional reasoning—if you double the scale of the course, you double the distance you cover.

The string continues with ²/₇ + ³/₅, where students deal with common fractions by doubling the ¹/₇ of the course to find ²/₇ and tripling the ¹/₅ to find ³/₅. Next in the string are two paired problems for subtraction, where Rick continues his running context. He asks, "So, what if I ran ¹/₃ of the course and then walked back ¹/₈ of the course? How much of the course did I still need to walk back to get to the beginning?"

Trevor volunteers, "I used a 24-km course. So you ran ¹/₃ of 24, and that's 8. And then you walked back ¹/₈ of 24, that's 3. So you are at the 5 km point. You still have 5 out of 24 km to go, so ⁵/₂₄." Rick models Trevor's answer on the number line, as shown in Figure 9.20. The next problem, ²/₃ – ³/₈, uses common fractions related to earlier unit fractions.

FIGURE 9.20

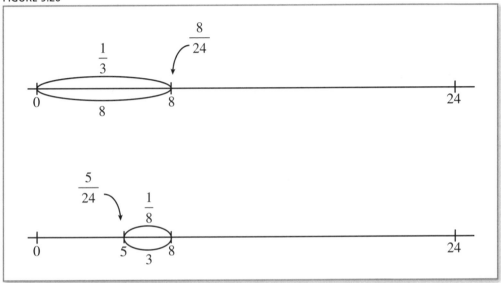

The string continues with another pair of problems, unit fractions ¹/₄ + ¹/₉, and then common fractions ³/₄ + ²/₉, and then ends with a single problem, ²/₅ – ¹/₁₅. As students work with the unit fractions, choosing denominators, and then scaling up to work with common fractions, they are working on proportional reasoning and on the operator meaning of fractions, all while adding and subtracting fractions.

Fraction Addition and Subtraction with Ratio Tables

As students do multiple choose your denominator strings and discuss their different choices for denominators, they begin to work on finding the lowest common denominator by comparing the denominators of the equivalent fractions. You can refer back to their work with prime factorization in doubling/halving strings in multiplication to help them understand how the least common denominator relates to the two denominators.

Ratio tables can help with this process as well. Let's go back to Rick's class. Rick asks students to explain how they would solve ³/₄ + ⁵/₆. As they do, he models their thinking in a ratio table. Notice that each fraction gets its own table, and remember that only equivalent fractions can be in the same ratio table.

Ricks starts with two ratio tables, one for ³/₄ and one for ⁵/₆ (Figure 9.21).

FIGURE 9.21

3		5	
4		6	

Students suggest a denominator of 12 because it is the lowest common denominator. Rick fills in the denominators for each equivalent fraction (Figure 9.22).

FIGURE 9.22

3		5	
4	12	6	12

His students have worked with ratio tables often for multiplication and division, so it is natural that they can see that since 4×3 is 12, they must also multiply the 3×3 to get an equivalent ratio (Figure 9.23).

FIGURE 9.23

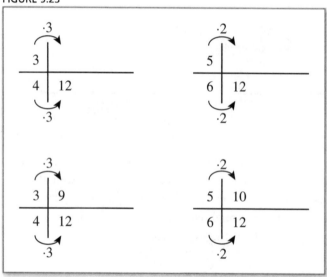

Rick wants to connect the ratio table to their work on the double number line. "When we were using a double number line to represent a race course, how did you find ¾ of 12? How does it relate to the ratio table?" asks Rick.

Students reply:

"Both times we chose 12 because it's a multiple of 4 and 6."

"Since 4 times 3 is 12, ¼ of 12 is 3."

"Since you multiply 4 times 3, you have to multiply 3 times 3 too."

"Whatever you do to the numerator, you have to do the same to the denominator to keep the fractions equivalent."

"The double number line shows you the distances on the course and the fractional amounts of the course. The ratio table just shows the fractional amounts."

After they discuss the similarities and differences, Rick asks students to work on another addition problem, the rational expression addition problem in Figure 9.24.

FIGURE 9.24

$$\frac{2}{3(x-2)}+\frac{x}{(x-2)(x+1)}$$

As students work, they realize they need to find equivalent expressions. Rick models the strategy on the board, beginning by setting up the two ratio tables as in Figure 9.25.

FIGURE 9.25

2	
$3(x-2)$	

x	
$(x-2)(x+1)$	

Students identify that they need to include the factors of each denominator in the equivalent expression, and Rick writes the denominator in each table as in Figure 9.26.

FIGURE 9.26

2	
$3(x-2)$	$3(x-2)(x+1)$

x	
$(x-2)(x+1)$	$3(x-2)(x+1)$

Students then continue using their experience with ratio tables to find the numerators by multiplying, as modeled in Figure 9.27.

FIGURE 9.27

$\cdot(x+1)$

2	$2(x+1)$
$3(x-2)$	$3(x-2)(x+1)$

$\cdot(x+1)$

$\cdot 3$

x	$3x$
$(x-2)(x+1)$	$3(x-2)(x+1)$

$\cdot 3$

"So, we used ratio tables to make equivalent expressions and now we can add them together. That's kind of cool how you all are able to bring all of this together to add these rational expressions. Great job!" says Rick, as he summarizes the result as in Figure 9.28.

FIGURE 9.28

$$\frac{2(x+1)}{3(x-2)(x+1)}+\frac{3x}{3(x-2)(x+1)}$$

Comparing Strategies: Fractions

Here are some more fraction addition and subtraction problems. Which strategy would you use for each one?

  a. $4\frac{1}{2} + 7\frac{1}{3}$

  b. $\frac{1}{5} + \frac{3}{10} + \frac{7}{100}$

  c. $4\frac{1}{6} - 1\frac{1}{4}$

  d. $1\frac{1}{4} - \frac{5}{6}$

For $4\frac{1}{2} + 7\frac{1}{3}$, Troy said, "First, 4 and 7 is 11. Then $\frac{1}{2}$ is like 30 minutes and $\frac{1}{3}$ is like 20 minutes so that's $\frac{50}{60}$ or $\frac{5}{6}$. So $11\frac{5}{6}$." Danny said, "I added the 4 and 7; that's 11. Then I used a denominator of 12. One half is $\frac{6}{12}$ and $\frac{1}{3}$ is $\frac{4}{12}$, so 11 and $\frac{10}{12}$."

For $\frac{1}{5} + \frac{3}{10} + \frac{7}{100}$, Craig said, "That's easy to do with decimals. It's just 0.2 + 0.3 + 0.07. So 0.57 or $\frac{57}{100}$."

For $4\frac{1}{6} - 1\frac{1}{4}$, Samantha said, "It's like 4 hours and 10 minutes minus 1 hour and 15 minutes. So 4 hours and 10 minutes minus 1 hour is 3 hours and 10 minutes. Then subtract 15 minutes and end on 2 hours and 55 minutes, so $2\frac{55}{60}$ or $2\frac{11}{12}$." Trent said, "I used twelfths. So $4\frac{2}{12}$ minus 1 is $3\frac{2}{12}$. Now subtract $\frac{1}{4}$, which is $\frac{3}{12}$, so that's $2\frac{11}{12}$."

For $1\frac{1}{4} - \frac{5}{6}$, Jeremy said, "The difference between $1\frac{1}{4}$ hours and $\frac{5}{6}$ of an hour is $\frac{1}{6} + \frac{1}{4}$. That's just 10 minutes and 15 minutes, so $\frac{25}{60} = \frac{5}{12}$."

Clarifying Understanding

As Close as It Gets

The "As Close as It Gets" exercises like those in Figure 9.29 help students make sense of fraction problems and promote understanding of place value and magnitude as students discuss their strategies. For example, for a problem like $\frac{9}{8} + \frac{4}{5}$, students can reason that a little more than 1 plus a little less than 1 is about 2. For a problem like $\frac{4}{9} + \frac{8}{15}$, a student can reason that about half plus about half is about 1 whole. The last problem supports students' thinking in both fractions and decimals. A student could reason that 2.4 minus about 1.2 is about 1.2, which is close to 1.25.

FIGURE 9.29

As Close as It Gets		
3.1 + 0.8 a) 3 b) 4 c) 5.1 d) 11	187.4 − 1.81 a) 187 b) 186 c) 170 d) 0	4.287 + 3,658.2 a) 3,600 b) 3,670 c) 3,700 d) 4,000
6.438 + 0.465 a) 6 b) 7 c) 10 d) 11	$\frac{9}{8} + \frac{4}{5}$ a) 0 b) 0.5 c) 1 d) 2	$5\frac{1}{5} - 1\frac{8}{9}$ a) 0 b) 2 c) 3 d) 4
$\frac{4}{9} + \frac{8}{15}$ a) 0 b) 0.10 c) 0.25 d) 1	$7 - 3\frac{4}{9}$ a) 3 b) 3.5 c) 4 d) 4.5	$2\frac{4}{10} - 1.24$ a) 0.5 b) 0.75 c) 1 d) 1.25

Relational Thinking

The problems in Figure 9.30 can help encourage students to think relationally. For a problem like 7.3 − 4.9, a student can shift the distance up by 0.1 to get 7.3 − 4.9 = 7.4 − 5. But for an almost identical problem, 7.3 + 4.9, a student can give and take to get 7.3 + 4.9 = 7.2 + 5. The true-or-false questions can help students differentiate between give and take, which works for addition, and take and take, which works for subtraction. They can also help encourage students to use these strategies to make problems easier. For example, when students investigate to see if 87⅕ − 10½ = 87⁷⁄₁₀ − 11 is correct, the ensuing discussion about the ease of 87⁷⁄₁₀ − 11 can intrigue the students enough to try this kind of reasoning when they see a similar problem.

FIGURE 9.30

Relational Thinking

Fill in the blank:

1. $7.3 - 4.9 = \underline{\hspace{1.5cm}} - 5$

2. $7.3 + 4.9 = \underline{\hspace{1.5cm}} + 5$

3. $2.53 + \underline{\hspace{1.5cm}} = 2.55 + 1.98$

4. $4.5 - 3.1 = 4.4 - \underline{\hspace{1.5cm}}$

5. $\frac{5}{6} + \frac{2}{3} = \underline{\hspace{1.5cm}} + 1$

6. $13 - 3\frac{5}{6} = \underline{\hspace{1.5cm}} - 4$

True or false? Why?

1. $35.97 + 14.23 = 36 + 14.26$

2. $7.63 + 0.87 = 7.5 + 1$

3. $7.1 - 1.7 = 6.8 + 2$

4. $2.82 - 2.39 = 2.83 - 2.4$

5. $15\frac{1}{4} + 1\frac{7}{8} = 15\frac{3}{8} + 2$

6. $7\frac{1}{2} + 3\frac{9}{10} = 7\frac{4}{10} + 4$

7. $8\frac{2}{5} - 2\frac{3}{10} = 8\frac{7}{10} - 2$

8. $87\frac{1}{5} - 10\frac{1}{2} = 87\frac{7}{10} - 11$

With students more confident in their ability to reason through addition and subtraction of decimals and fractions, they are ready to tackle decimal and fraction multiplication and division.

ten **10**

Decimals and Fractions: Multiplication and Division

The students really do think more about what they are doing when using these strategies. It is so nice to see them think on their own.

NUMERACY WORKSHOP PARTICIPANT

In this chapter, you'll find strings and activities to help your students build their understanding of decimal and fraction multiplication and division. You'll also see how these strings can, in their turn, help reinforce whole number computation.

Decimal Multiplication

With multiplication of whole numbers, we stressed the power of multiplying by 10 and multiples of 10. In multiplication of decimals, it is very important that students internalize what happens when you multiply by $\frac{1}{10}$ and multiples of $\frac{1}{10}$. The strings in Figure 10.1 can help.

FIGURE 10.1

The Power of a Tenth	
8 · 0.1	12 · 3
8 · 0.3	1.2 · 3
8 · 0.05	12 · 0.3
8 · 0.15	0.12 · 3
8 · 0.35	3.2 · 2
3 · 0.1	32 · 0.2
3 · 0.2	32 · 0.02
3 · 0.05	0.32 · 2
3 · 0.01	6.1 · 2
3 · 0.06	61 · 0.2
3 · 0.26	

The first string sets the stage for multiplying decimals as students find chunks that make sense. The first problem, 8 · 0.1, can be solved by thinking about dimes or percents: "How much money is 8 dimes?" or "What is 10% of 8?" Now that you have 8 · 0.1 = 0.8, you can triple to get the next problem, 8 · 0.3 = 2.4. Some students might find 8 × $0.30, thinking about 8 × 3, then 8 × 30¢ and then writing that in decimals. As you compare the two strategies during class discussion, students can make connections between the two. The third problem, 8 · 0.05, can be solved by thinking about nickels, or by halving the first problem, 8 · 0.1 = 0.8, to get 8 · 0.05 = 0.4. The fourth problem, 8 · 0.15, is the sum of the first and third problems; the fifth problem, 8 · 0.35, is the sum of the second and third problems. The string continues similarly, working toward using earlier problems as "chunks" to solve the last problem, 3 · 0.26.

The second string is designed to prompt students to examine the place-value shifts that occur when multiplying by decimals. You can encourage students to work with money to see the pattern in the first four problems: $12 · 3 = $36, $1.20 · 3 = $3.60, 12 · $0.30 = $3.60, and $0.12 · 3 = $0.36. If students tell you to "just move the decimal point," encourage them to explain why. Use language such as, "If the factor is one-tenth the original factor, the product must be one-tenth of the original product," as shown in Figure 10.2. The string continues with two more sets of related problems. These strings could segue easily into secondary conversations about powers of ten and scientific notation.

FIGURE 10.2

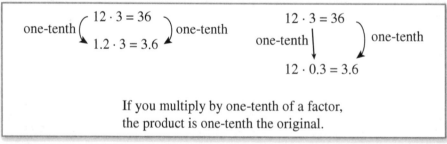

If you multiply by one-tenth of a factor,
the product is one-tenth the original.

The Distributive Property: Chunking

We can use the distributive property of multiplication to chunk decimal numbers in multiplication problems, just as we did for whole numbers. We previously found products like 12 × 16 with chunks like (10 + 2) × 16 = (10 × 16) + (2 × 16). The same type of reasoning gets us 1.2 × 1.6 = (1 + 0.2) × 16 = (1 × 16) + (0.2 × 16). Once students have a feel for multiplying by tenths, hundredths, and so on, then you can use chunking strings like those shown in Figure 10.3 to encourage them to seek manageable chunks when multiplying decimals.

FIGURE 10.3

Decimal Multiplication: Chunking		
1.8 · 2	3 · 0.1	16 · 0.5
1.8 · 0.2	3 · 2.1	16 · 0.25
1.8 · 4	3 · 6	16 · 0.75
1.8 · 4.2	3 · 0.06	16 · 1.25
2.3 · 2	3 · 2.06	12 · 0.5
2.3 · 0.2	2 · 5	12 · 0.25
2.3 · 1.2	0.2 · 5	12 · 0.75
1.2 · 1.6	3.2 · 5	12 · 0.125
	3.2 · 5.1	12 · 0.375

These strings nudge students toward finding handy multiples and then scaling up or down. For example, the first problem of the first string, 1.8 · 2 = 3.6, sets up the next problem, 1.8 · 0.2 = 0.36. The next problem can be found by doubling the first, 1.8 · 4 = 7.2. The next problem, 1.8 · 4.2, is the sum of the second and third problems. These problems are modeled on open arrays in Figure 10.4.

FIGURE 10.4

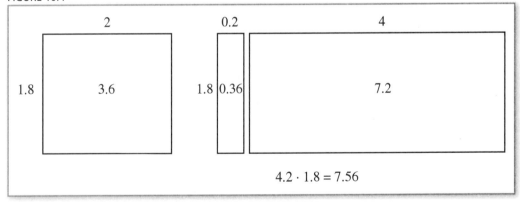

The string continues with related problems 2.3 · 2, 2.3 · 0.2, and 2.3 · 1.2. Notice that in both of these sets, students end with a two-digit decimal times a two-digit decimal that they can find using only two chunks. Make sure students notice this efficiency. Strategic chunking pays off!

The middle string is similar but makes use of the 5 is half of 10 strategy students learned for whole numbers: 3.2 · 5 = ½(3.2 · 10) = 16. The string finishes with 3.2 · 5.1, which is just $0.1 \cdot 3.2 = 0.32$ more than the previous problem, so $3.2 \cdot 5.1 = 16 + 0.32 = 16.32$.

The last chunking string uses the friendly chunks of halves and quarters, and also draws on students' knowledge of money. Students can reason up and down with quarters to find products such as $16 \cdot 0.75$ and $12 \cdot 0.375$, as shown in the ratio tables in Figure 10.5. If a factor is close to 0.25, 0.50, or 0.75, or even 0.125, 0.375, or 0.875, students can think in terms of halves, quarters, and eighths. When the numbers get particularly ugly, in a problem like $159.46 \cdot 0.38$, students can use these landmark fractions (in this case, ⅜, or 0.375) to find estimates. The problems in the string follow a similar pattern, moving from ½, to ¼, to ¾, to ⅛, and finally ⅜.

FIGURE 10.5

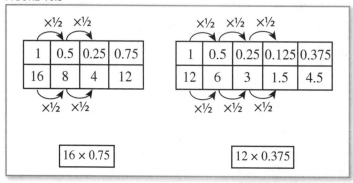

The Distributive Property: Over and Under

The over and under strings in Figure 10.6 encourage students to build on their understanding of multiplying by 0.1 and its multiples, and to use those multiples as friendly numbers.

FIGURE 10.6

Decimal Multiplication: Over and Under	
$3.4 \cdot 1.1$	$4.6 \cdot 0.5$
$3.4 \cdot 0.9$	$4.6 \cdot 0.25$
$0.51 \cdot 4.2$	$4.6 \cdot 0.76$
$0.49 \cdot 4.2$	$30.8 \cdot 0.26$
$10.1 \cdot 7.4$	$30.8 \cdot 0.24$
$9.9 \cdot 7.4$	$30.8 \cdot 0.74$
$99.9 \cdot 12.4$	$202 \cdot 0.76$

In the first string, students can start by adding or subtracting $0.1 \cdot 3.4 = 0.34$ from 3.4. For $0.51 \cdot 4.2$ and $0.49 \cdot 4.2$, students can just add or subtract $0.01 \cdot 4.2 = 0.042$ from half of 4.2. The string ends with another pair of related problems and then $99.9 \cdot 12.4$, which can be found by finding $(100 - 0.1) \cdot 12.4 = 1{,}240 - 1.24 = 1{,}238.76$. That's a three-digit-by-three-digit decimal multiplication problem solved in two chunks!

The next string continues the theme of over and under by using the friendly chunks of halves and quarters. The first two problems, $4.6 \cdot 0.5$ and $4.6 \cdot 0.25$, lead to the third, $4.6 \cdot 0.76$; since $0.5 + 0.25 = 0.75$, three-quarters of $4.6 = 2.3 + 1.15 = 3.45$. Then, $4.6 \cdot 0.76$ is just $0.01 \cdot 4.6 = 0.046$ more, or 3.496. The next three problems are similarly related. For the last problem, $202 \cdot 0.76$, students will have to find their own helper problems.

The Associative Property: Doubling/Halving

The string in Figure 10.7 is a doubling/halving string for decimal multiplication. The first problem, $0.51 \cdot 4.2$, was also in an over and under string, so students may use that strategy at first. However, it is followed by a doubled/halved equivalent, $1.02 \cdot 2.1$. This should get the conversation started about doubling and halving with decimal multiplication. The next two problems are also doubled/halved equivalents. The rest of the string consists of problems that lend themselves to doubling and halving because at least one of the factors halves easily and one of the factors doubles to a nice number. In several of the problems, you can double and halve more than once to get even easier problems to solve. For example, $8.4 \cdot 3.5 = 4.2 \cdot 7 = 2.1 \cdot 14$, which is simply $2.1 \cdot 14 = (2 \cdot 14) + (0.1 \cdot 14) = 28 + 1.4 = 29.4$.

FIGURE 10.7

Doubling/Halving
$0.51 \cdot 4.2$
$1.02 \cdot 2.1$
$1.5 \cdot 1.8$
$3 \cdot 0.9$
$1.6 \cdot 3.5$
$2.5 \cdot 3.2$
$8.4 \cdot 3.5$

Decimal Division

Before you embark on decimal division, make sure your students have enough experience with whole number multiplication and division and decimal multiplication. The multiplicative thinking they develop through work with those operations is crucial for their understanding of decimal division.

Using the Distributive Property in Chunking Strings

The first strings for decimal division (Figure 10.8) give students experience with using the distributive property of multiplication to solve decimal division problems in manageable chunks. Model these strings on arrays so that students can see and manipulate the chunks. As they sketch each array, the relationship of one problem to the next is more obvious: the divisors are the same, so one of the dimensions is the same. The dividend is bigger, so the area is bigger. When they have two related chunks next to each other, they can ask, "How can I put these together to make an array so that it helps me solve this next problem?" In all three strings, the problems look difficult, with lots of digits and decimals, but they chunk relatively easily. Students can make connections between decimal division and the strategies they've used for whole number division.

FIGURE 10.8

Decimal Division: Chunking		
2.5 ÷ 2.5	1.2 ÷ 1.2	2 ÷ 0.02
5 ÷ 2.5	0.6 ÷ 1.2	0.2 ÷ 0.02
7.5 ÷ 2.5	1.8 ÷ 1.2	0.08 ÷ 0.02
0.75 ÷ 0.75	4.8 ÷ 2.4	2.28 ÷ 0.02
3 ÷ 0.75	1.2 ÷ 2.4	2.4 ÷ 2.4
3.75 ÷ 0.75	6 ÷ 2.4	4.8 ÷ 2.4
4.5 ÷ 0.75	2.1 ÷ 1.4	7.2 ÷ 2.4

In the first string, the first problem (2.5 ÷ 2.5) is easy, but is a useful chunk for the later problems. The second problem (5 ÷ 2.5) gives students several options. They may ask, "How many 2 and a halves are there in 5?" or they may work from the first problem, reasoning that since the dividend is twice the dividend in the first problem, the quotient must also be doubled. The arrays in Figure 10.9 model this relationship. Students could also write $\frac{5}{2.5} = \frac{50}{25}$ by finding an equivalent ratio, but for now, emphasize the arrays so that students can see the chunks of area. Students can combine the first and second problems to find 7.5 ÷ 2.5 = (5 + 2.5) ÷ 2.5 = 3.

The next four problems are similarly related. The first two, 0.75 ÷ 0.75 and 3 ÷ 0.75, lead to the third and fourth, 3.75 ÷ 0.75 and 4.5 ÷ 0.75. Arrays for these problems are also shown in Figure 10.9. This is a good first decimal division chunking string because the chunks combine relatively obviously to help with the related harder problems.

FIGURE 10.9

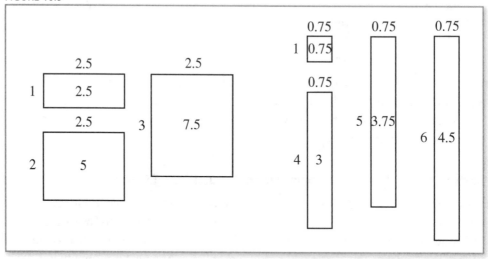

The second chunking string in Figure 10.8 uses halves to make helper problems. It starts with the easy 1.2 ÷ 1.2 = 1, followed by 0.6 ÷ 1.2. This is another good string to model with arrays, because they will show that the area is half the area from the first problem. Therefore the missing dimension (quotient) must also be half, so 0.6 ÷ 1.2 = 0.5. Then they can use those two chunks to get 1.8 ÷ 1.2. The next set of problems is related similarly. The more experience your students have with halves, the more they will begin to use them in both multiplication and division.

The last chunking string continues the theme of sets of related problems that lead to a more difficult problem. The four related problems use smaller numbers than the other strings, giving students experience reasoning with a divisor as small as 0.02. As students solve the first three problems, 2 ÷ 0.02, 0.2 ÷ 0.02, and 0.08 ÷ 0.02, they build the answer to the fourth problem, 2.28 ÷ 0.02 (see Figure 10.10). Most students who have not previously memorized a digit approach prefer to work from left to right, large to small, and putting the problems in order from greatest to smallest dividend helps students develop the inclination to do so on other similar problems.

FIGURE 10.10

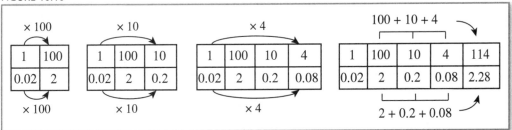

The Distributive Property: Over and Under with Partial Quotients

In Chapter 7, the models for the over and under strings were ratio tables. To see these strings with both models, we'll use arrays here. The first two strings in Figure 10.11 might not look very much like decimal division strings, but the answers to the later problems in each string are decimals. Progressing from whole number division with whole number answers to whole number division with decimal answers helps students make sense of decimal division no matter what the numbers are.

FIGURE 10.11

Decimal Division: Over and Under	
160 ÷ 4	32 ÷ 8
164 ÷ 4	40 ÷ 8
162 ÷ 4	36 ÷ 8
161 ÷ 4	38 ÷ 8
160.5 ÷ 4	37 ÷ 8
163 ÷ 4	39 ÷ 8
166 ÷ 4	

The first string begins with 160 ÷ 4 and 164 ÷ 4. Students can use a 40 × 4 array and a 1 × 4 array to find answers of 40 and 41, respectively. The next problem, 162 ÷ 4, increases the area from 160 to 162, so the question becomes "What array will give an area of 2 if one dimension is 4?" Some students might suggest adding a 1 × 2 array; if they do, discuss with them whether this would maintain the array as a rectangle. As they look for a way to maintain the known dimension of 4 units, they should eventually see that adding a ½ × 4 array adds an area of 2. Thus the missing dimension is 140.5 (see Figure 10.12). This is not trivial. For students to reason about the area of rectangles when one dimension is less than 1 can be a cognitive struggle. How can the area be less than the side length? Some students may benefit from using grid paper models at this point, so they can count the number of half squares.

FIGURE 10.12

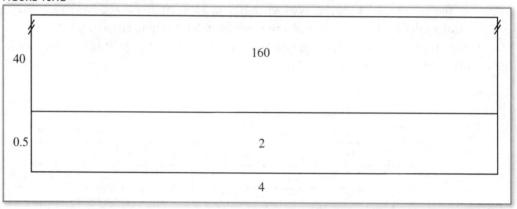

For the next problem, 161 ÷ 4, the question becomes "What array will give an area of 1 if one dimension is 4?" Some students might interpret this to mean "What times 4 is 1?" You can help make the connection by looking at the series of arrays they have used: 1 × 4 = 4, ½ × 4 = 2, and now ¼ × 4 = 1 (see Figure 10.13). Each time you cut the area (dividend) in half, keeping the side length (divisor) constant, the other side length (quotient) must also be cut in half. So 161 ÷ 4 = 40.25. The array helps because it gives students a model to act on. The string continues by cutting the added array in half again, 160.5 ÷ 4. Since we already know 160 ÷ 4, we just need to find an array with area of ½ and one dimension of 4. This yields a dimension that is half of the quotient to the previous problem, and ½ of ¼ is ⅛. Half of 0.25 is 0.125, so 160.5 ÷ 4 = 40.125. The string ends with two more related problems, 163 ÷ 4 and 166 ÷ 4, where students are using the same pieces but are now building up from the 162 ÷ 4 chunk.

FIGURE 10.13

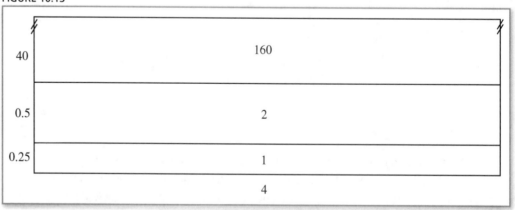

The second string in Figure 10.11 has a similar progression. Many students will need to work with these kinds of strings over a few days to solidify their tentative learning about quotients less than 1. The first string used the divisor of 4 and this string uses the divisor of 8 because the multiples of both of those are fairly easy to partition. Once students reason that 32 ÷ 8 = 4 and 40 ÷ 8 = 5, then the next problem's dividend, 36, is right in the middle, so 36 ÷ 8 = 4.5, which is right in the middle of 4 and 5. If the divisor had been 7, it would not be so easy to find a halfway point. A strategy for finding 37 ÷ 8 is shown in the array in Figure 10.14. As you give each problem in the string, model the chunks on the array and elicit from students the ways they are finding the quotients. Are they thinking in terms of rectangles and area? Are they using the previous problems to add on to? Are they using the previous problems to find the new added part? If there is a remainder, where do they see it in the array?

FIGURE 10.14

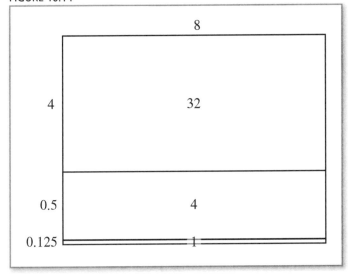

Constant Ratio

As students think through the problems in the strings in Figure 10.15, they may begin to see that the answers to two problems are the same if the ratio between the dividend (numerator) and divisor (denominator) remains constant. In other words, if you multiply the dividend and divisor by the same number, the quotient remains the same. Students can then begin to employ the constant ratio strategy by scaling the ratio up or down until they get to a friendlier problem, such as 5.4 ÷ 0.9 = 54 ÷ 9 = 6.

FIGURE 10.15

Constant Ratio		
56/7	164/8	220/22
5.6/0.7	164/0.8	198/22
56/0.7	1.64/0.8	19.8/2.2
5.6/7	616/56	1.98/0.22
0.56/7	6.16/56	0.198/2.2
0.56/0.7	61.6/0.56	0.22)‾19.8
56/0.07	0.616/5.6	126/12
138/12	616/5.6	

Let's join Amy in her middle school class. In the first string, students begin with the easy $56 \div 7 = 8$. With the next problem, $5.6 \div 0.7$, many students use money, and reason, "Since 8×7 is 56, 8×70¢ is 560¢ or $\$5.60$. So $5.6 \div 0.7 = 8$."

Some students notice that the answers to the first two problems are the same. Amy writes $\frac{56}{7} = \frac{5.6}{0.7} = 8$ and asks, "What's going on?"

"They are equivalent because if you divide the first fraction by 10, you get the other one," begins Raul. "I mean, divide both the numerator and the denominator by 10."

After discussing the relationship, they continue with $56 \div 0.7$. Some students continue to reason with money, deciding how many groups of 7¢ are in 5.6 dollars, scaling up from the previous problem to get 80. Some students find an equivalent fraction. "I multiplied by one 10 to both the numerator and denominator and I got $560 \div 7$. That's like $56 \div 7$ then $\times 10$, so I got 80 too."

Amy writes $\frac{56}{0.7} = \frac{560}{7} = \frac{56 \cdot 10}{7} = 80$. For the rest of the problems, Amy models mostly the constant ratio strategy. For $5.6 \div 7$, Amy asks students to estimate the answer because she wants them to think about the problem and not just immediately start finding equivalent ratios. Students discuss that the quotient must be less than 1. Many of them find the solution by first multiplying by 10 and then factoring out a 7: $\frac{5.6}{7} = \frac{56}{70} = \frac{7 \cdot 8}{7 \cdot 10} = \frac{8}{10} = 0.8$. Similarly, they find $0.56 \div 7 = 56 \div 700 = 8 \div 100 = 0.08$ and $0.56 \div 0.7 = 56 \div 70 = 0.8$. Each time, Amy asks them to estimate and then compare the numerator and denominator and explain the relationships. Students discuss that the relationship of the numerator to the denominator determines whether the quotient is greater or less than 1. Many students also find it easier to solve the equivalent problems that use only whole numbers (such as finding $56 \div 700$ rather than $0.56 \div 7$).

One student asks, "Is that why you move the decimals in long division?" Amy takes a few minutes to connect the "move the decimal" rule with the equivalent ratios that they have been finding by multiplying the numerator and denominators by powers of 10. She writes the $0.56 \div 7$ problem both in fraction and in long division notation. Then she asks students to make an equivalent fraction so that the divisor is a whole number. They find the equivalent fraction $\frac{56}{700}$. After she writes that in long division notation, $700 \overline{)56}$, she asks students to compare and discuss (see Figure 10.16). Students note that when you move the decimal, it's because you're creating equivalent fractions, and that moving the decimal twice is like scaling up by 100.

FIGURE 10.16

Write the original problem	Make an equivalent fraction	Write the equivalent problem
$7 \overline{)0.56} = \dfrac{0.56}{7}$	$\dfrac{0.56 \cdot 100}{7 \cdot 100} =$	$\dfrac{56}{700} = 700 \overline{)56}$

The string finishes with one more related problem, $56 \div 0.07$, and then a new problem to see what students will do with different numbers. For $138 \div 12$, the numerator and denominator are not decimals, but the quotient is. This will challenge students to see if they understand what's happening and it will give Amy good information about where to go in tomorrow's string.

The second string in Figure 10.15 gives students more experience with the constant ratio strategy, but this time the quotients are not whole numbers. The last string is similar but also introduces the long division notation if it hasn't already come up.

Comparing Strategies: Decimals

As with the other operations, it is crucial for you to discuss and compare strategies with your students so that they have a good sense for which strategies work best with which numbers. What strategy would you use to solve each of these problems?

a. $0.26 \cdot 24$

b. $0.48 \cdot 8.2$

c. $142.1 \div 1.4$

d. $1 \div 7$

e. $0.16 \cdot 76$

f. $4.9 \cdot 34.8$

For $0.26 \cdot 24$, Jose said, "I decided to first find $0.25 \cdot 24$. So $\frac{1}{4}$ of 24 is 6. Now I just need $0.01 \cdot 24$. That's 0.24. So 6.24."

For $0.48 \cdot 8.2$, Reba said, "First I'll find $\frac{1}{2}$ of 8.2, 4.1. So $0.5 \cdot 8.2 = 4.1$. Now I need $0.02 \cdot 8.2 = 2 \cdot 8.2 \cdot 0.01 = 16.4 \cdot 0.01 = 0.164$. So $0.48 \cdot 8.2 = (0.5 - 0.02) \cdot 8.2 = 4.1 - 0.164 = 4 - 0.064 = 3.936$.

For $142.1 \div 1.4$, David said, "I used the constant ratio strategy to get $1,421 \div 14$. Then I noticed that both are divisible by 7, so $^{142.1}/_{1.4} = {}^{1,421}/_{14} = {}^{203}/_2 = 101.5$.

For $1 \div 7$ (finding the decimal equivalent for $\frac{1}{7}$), Michelle used a ratio table to show her strategy (see Figure 10.17). She said, "I started with the 7 and multiplied by decimals so that I could get as close to 1 as possible, because another way of saying the problems is $7 \cdot \_\_\_\_ = 1$." She continued adding smaller and smaller chunks until she got to 0.9996, when she decided she was close enough. While problems like this can be tedious, a few well-placed examples help build students' sense of place value, division, and the decimal equivalent for fractions.

FIGURE 10.17

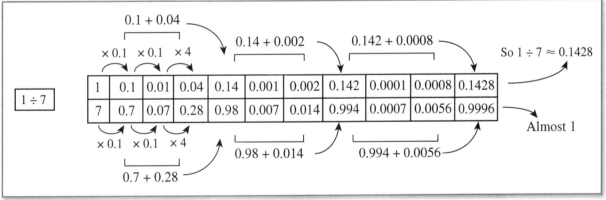

For 0.16 · 76, John said, "I thought ¾! I know that I can find 76 · 0.16 by (75 + 1) · 0.16. To find 75 · 0.16, I found ¾ of 0.16, which is 0.12, and scaled back up for 12. I just needed one more 0.16, so 12 + 0.16 = 12.16."

For 4.9 · 34.8, Craig said, "I'll do half first, that's like times 0.5. So half of 34.8 is 17.4, but then I need to scale it up by 10, so 174. Then I found 0.1 times 34.8, 3.48. So subtract 3.48 from 174 and that's 170.52."

Fraction Multiplication

Teachers have told me that their students do well on fraction multiplication quizzes, but have trouble when this operation is combined with others because they mix up the rules and the steps in those rules. The students can easily "multiply straight across," but may lack an understanding of what fraction multiplication really means.

Area Models for Unit Fractions

The short string in Figure 10.18 can help students establish the product of two unit fractions using the array model.

FIGURE 10.18

Product of Unit Fractions
$\frac{1}{3} \cdot \frac{1}{2}$
$\frac{1}{2} \cdot \frac{1}{4}$
$\frac{1}{3} \cdot \frac{1}{4}$

We can model the portions of a rectangular array using fractional amounts of the array. For example, in the context of a brownie pan, we could say that after the faculty meeting, ⅓ of that pan was left over. I'll just take ½ of what's left. How much of the original amount do I get? What is ⅓ of ½? See Figure 10.19 for one model of this problem. Students could also use a 2 × 3 array to model the problem: How much of the array do I get?

FIGURE 10.19

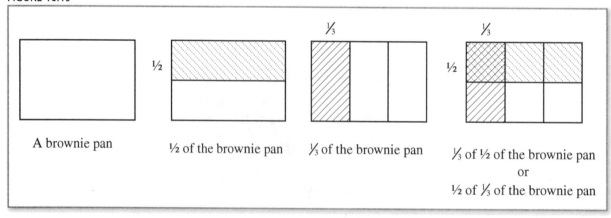

A brownie pan   ½ of the brownie pan   ⅓ of the brownie pan   ⅓ of ½ of the brownie pan
or
½ of ⅓ of the brownie pan

The other two problems in the string continue the theme. By the end, students should see that the product of two unit fractions is another unit fraction whose denominator is the product of the unit fractions' denominators—the sizes of the pieces of the brownie pan. It's a unit fraction because you only get one piece. Through this students should begin to construct what fraction multiplication means: a portion of a portion.

Scaling Up

When your students are firmly grounded in unit fraction multiplication, you can use the following strings to help them see that they can scale up to find products involving common fractions.

The first string in Figure 10.20 strengthens the operator meaning of fractions as students find $\frac{1}{5}$ of a number and then scale up to find $\frac{2}{5}$ and $\frac{3}{5}$. They reason that if $\frac{1}{5}$ of 20 is 4, then $\frac{2}{5}$ of 20 will be twice as much, so $\frac{2}{5} \cdot 20$ is 8. The next problem uses similar reasoning. The fourth problem, $\frac{6}{5} \cdot 20$, uses an improper fraction and students see that $\frac{6}{5}$ of 20 is $\frac{1}{5}$ more than 20. The string continues with two more sets of paired problems.

FIGURE 10.20

Scaling Up		
$\frac{1}{5} \cdot 20$	$\frac{1}{3} \cdot \frac{1}{5}$	$\frac{1}{4} \cdot \frac{1}{2}$
$\frac{2}{5} \cdot 20$		
$\frac{3}{5} \cdot 20$	$\frac{2}{3} \cdot \frac{1}{5}$	$\frac{5}{4} \cdot \frac{1}{2}$
$\frac{6}{5} \cdot 20$		
$\frac{1}{4} \cdot 60$	$\frac{2}{3} \cdot \frac{4}{5}$	$\frac{5}{4} \cdot \frac{3}{2}$
$\frac{3}{4} \cdot 60$		
$\frac{1}{3} \cdot 12$		
$\frac{2}{3} \cdot 12$		

The next two strings work on scaling up to find the product of two common fractions. Let's join Rick in algebra 2 just after his students have solved the first problem in the second string. Notice that he interchanges *of* with *times* throughout the conversation so that students connect the word and the operation with the meaning they are constructing.

"So, you've all got $\frac{1}{15}$ for $\frac{1}{3}$ of $\frac{1}{5}$. So, then what's *two*-thirds of $\frac{1}{5}$?" Rick emphasizes the *two* slightly. "Show me how those two problems relate on the array." Students draw arrays similar to those in Figure 10.21. Some students have just started over, drawing the new array, but Justin sees a connection.

FIGURE 10.21

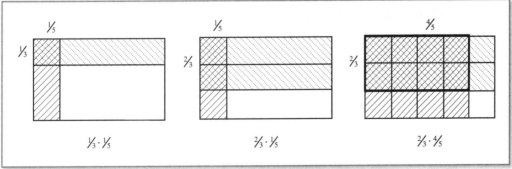

"The area just doubles," says Justin. "First you have ⅓ of ⅕, which is 1/15. Then you asked us for double that, so 2/15."

After students briefly discuss the doubling, Rick asks, "The next problem is ⅔ × ⅘. What does that look like and what is the answer?"

Again, many students draw a new array, shade ⅔ horizontally and then ⅘ vertically, and look at the pieces that are double shaded. Rick wants students to consider scaling up from the last problem to this one. "How are the arrays from ⅔ of ⅕ and ⅔ of ⅘ related?"

"It's 4 times bigger. It's like, if I read the problem backward then you have *four*-fifths of ⅔. That's 4 times bigger than *one*-fifth of ⅔," suggests Melik.

As students continue to work with strings like this, they construct the idea that when multiplying fractions, the product of the denominators is the denominator of the answer, the size of the pieces of the brownie pan. Then you can scale up by each numerator to get the numerator of the answer, the number of pieces you take.

Another outcome is that students learn that the denominators in a fraction multiplication problem determine the dimensions of the outside array and that the numerators determine the dimensions of the double-shaded inside array. For ⅔ · ⅘, we cut the brownie pan into a 3 × 5 array, and there is a 2 × 4 array double shaded.

Once students have established an understanding of fraction multiplication, you can move on to engaging them with trading places and doubling/halving strings.

The Commutative Property: Trading Places

The first string in Figure 10.22 consists of two sets of paired problems. When students find that the answers to ⅗ × 4/7 and ⅘ × 3/7 are the same, they can be intrigued to figure out what is happening. Does the product always stay the same when the numerators trade places?

FIGURE 10.22

Trading Places		
$\dfrac{3}{5} \cdot \dfrac{4}{7}$	$\dfrac{9}{16} \cdot \dfrac{4}{3}$	$\dfrac{8}{3} \cdot \dfrac{9}{16}$
$\dfrac{4}{5} \cdot \dfrac{3}{7}$	$\dfrac{16}{5} \cdot \dfrac{15}{8}$	$\dfrac{6}{5} \cdot \dfrac{25}{18}$
$\dfrac{3}{4} \cdot \dfrac{2}{5}$	$\dfrac{3}{5} \cdot \dfrac{1}{2}$	$\dfrac{33}{4} \cdot \dfrac{4}{11}$
$\dfrac{3}{7} \cdot \dfrac{2}{4}$		

Have students compare the arrays for the first two problems in the first string (as in Figure 10.23), focusing especially on the interior array. The two inside arrays have the same area; one is a rotation of the other. Since the areas are the same, the products are also the same. The second set of paired problems confirms the result.

FIGURE 10.23

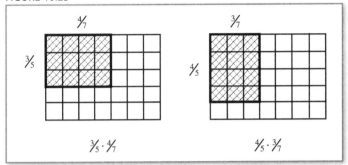

At the end of the string, ask students which of the last two problems they would rather solve. By trading places, which is really using the commutative property, ¾ · ⅖ becomes ²⁄₄ · ⅗ = ½ · ⅗, an easier problem to reason through—just find ½ of ⅗.

The next two strings give students experience looking for opportunities to use the trading places strategy to make problems easier. The problem ⁹⁄₁₆ · ⁴⁄₃ is equivalent to ⁴⁄₁₆ · ⁹⁄₃ = ¼ · 3. How about ³³⁄₄ · ⁴⁄₁₁? It is equivalent to ³³⁄₁₁ · ⁴⁄₄ = 3 · 1 = 3. Notice that by writing the problem this way, using the commutative property to trade places, students end up simplifying the fractions but without the confusing language of "canceling." Students trade places and then simplify each of the resulting fractions by using equivalence, a strategy they can also use with rational expressions.

At the end of such a string in an algebra class, Abby asks students to consider how this strategy might relate to a problem like simplifying $\frac{2x}{(x+1)} \cdot \frac{(x+1)}{4}$. Students reply that they could swap the numerators to get $\frac{(x+1)}{(x+1)} \cdot \frac{2x}{4}$. Now the problem is just $1 \cdot \frac{2x}{4} = \frac{1}{2}x$.

Doubling/Halving

If your students have worked with doubling and halving whole numbers, the strategy transfers readily to some fraction problems. Figure 10.24 shows a string to promote this strategy. The first two problems are paired whole number problems, 6 · 8 and 12 · 4, to get students thinking about doubling and halving. The next three problems are related by halving/doubling and doubling/halving. They can lead to a discussion on which number is asier to double and which is easier to halve. The last two problems lend themselves to doubling and halving by turning into 10 · 3 and 3 · 3 (doubling/halving twice), respectively. A good check is to ask students to write some problems for which doubling/halving is a good strategy and some for which it is not, and discuss why.

FIGURE 10.24

Doubling/Halving
$6 \cdot 8$
$12 \cdot 4$
$24 \cdot 1\frac{1}{2}$
$\frac{3}{4} \cdot 48$
$12 \cdot 3$
$20 \cdot 1\frac{1}{2}$
$\frac{3}{4} \cdot 12$

Fraction Division

Fraction division is complex. This is perhaps the reason for the adage "Ours is not to reason why, just invert and multiply." However, using the following strings, students can construct solid understanding of fraction division and powerful strategies for different problems. Just as with whole numbers, division can have both quotative and partitive meanings. Students will benefit from experience reasoning through problems before getting to general strategies, which will help them look to the numbers first before deciding on a strategy.

Using Quotative Division: Whole Numbers Divided by Fractions

Students can use the quotative meaning of division when working the problems in the whole number divided by fractions string in Figure 10.25. The string begins with unit fraction divisors and works up to common fraction divisors, with the quotients scaling up and down so students can reason proportionally about what is happening as the different elements change. If there are 3 one-thirds in one array, how many one-thirds are in 2 arrays? If there are 10 one-fifths in two arrays, then how many two-fifths are there in those same two arrays?

To find $2 \div \frac{1}{3}$, you can ask "How many one-thirds in 2?" You can use a rectangular array with thirds shaded to help students visualize the quantities (see Figure 10.24). As you sketch the array, ask students how many one-thirds are in the array and then partition the array to match. Ask students how that one array with thirds can help you figure the problem that asks about two arrays. Draw the second array if needed. The next problem, $4 \div \frac{1}{3}$, doubles the arrays. Continue to use the quotative language of "How many one-thirds are there in 4?" The next two problems are similar and deal with fourths. The next two problems go from $6 \div \frac{1}{3}$ to $6 \div \frac{2}{3}$. Since two-thirds take up twice as much of the array as one-thirds, there must be half as many two-thirds as one-thirds. The last two problems give students a chance to try that reasoning.

FIGURE 10.25

Whole Number Divided by Fractions

$2 \div \frac{1}{3}$

$4 \div \frac{1}{3}$

$3 \div \frac{1}{4}$

$6 \div \frac{1}{4}$

$6 \div \frac{1}{3}$

$6 \div \frac{2}{3}$

$2 \div \frac{1}{5}$

$2 \div \frac{2}{5}$

$2 \div \frac{1}{3}$ How many ⅓s in 2? $4 \div \frac{1}{3}$ How many ⅓s in 4?

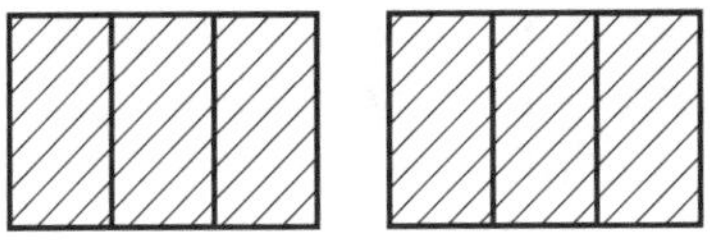

$3 \div \frac{1}{4}$ How many ¼s in 3? $6 \div \frac{1}{4}$ How many ¼s in 6?

$2 \div \frac{1}{5}$ How many ⅕s in 2? $2 \div \frac{2}{5}$ How many ⅖s in 2?

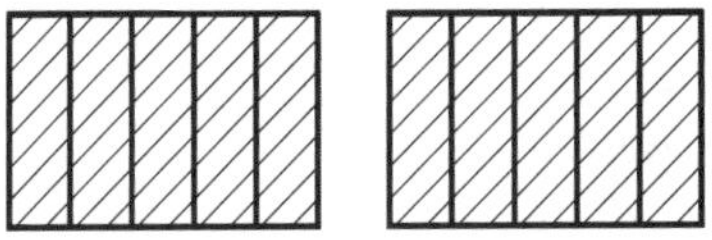

Using Quotative Division: Fractions Divided by Fractions

Students can also use the quotative meaning of division to divide fractions by fractions. The first two strings in Figure 10.26 concentrate on making sense of dividing a fraction by a fraction by using many problems where the fractions have the same denominator.

FIGURE 10.26

Fractions Divided by Fractions		
$6 \div 3 = 2$	$3 \div 1\frac{1}{2}$	$3 \div 2$
$\frac{5}{6} \div \frac{1}{6}$	$3\frac{1}{2} \div \frac{1}{4}$	$\frac{3}{5} \div \frac{2}{5}$
$\frac{5}{8} \div \frac{1}{8}$	$2\frac{1}{2} \div 1\frac{1}{4}$	$1 \div 2$
$\frac{2}{3} \div \frac{1}{3}$	$4 \div 1\frac{1}{3}$	$\frac{1}{3} \div \frac{2}{3}$
$\frac{3}{2} \div \frac{1}{2}$	$2\frac{2}{3} \div \frac{1}{6}$	$\frac{5}{3} \div \frac{4}{3}$
$\frac{3}{2} \div \frac{1}{4}$	$1\frac{1}{2} \div \frac{3}{4}$	$\frac{9}{3} \div \frac{5}{3}$
$3\frac{1}{2} \div \frac{1}{4}$	$\frac{3}{4} \div \frac{3}{8}$	$\frac{5}{2} \div \frac{3}{2}$
$\frac{2}{3} \div \frac{1}{3}$	$\frac{1}{3} \div \frac{2}{3}$	$\frac{3}{5} \div \frac{9}{10}$
		$\frac{1}{7} \div \frac{1}{5}$

The first string starts with the problem 6 ÷ 3 = 2. You could start by asking students to quickly recall the two meanings of division using the problem. This serves to remind students of both meanings so that they might try both.

The rest of the problems are similar to $\frac{5}{6} \div \frac{1}{6}$, which can be interpreted as asking "How many one-sixths are in five-sixths?" (see Figure 10.27). Because the denominators are the same, students can reason that there are 5 one-sixths in five-sixths, and begin to generalize that this is true for any denominator—there are 5 $\frac{1}{a}$s in $\frac{5}{a}$. The sixth and seventh problems have different denominators, but they draw on the understanding that students have of the relationship between halves and fourths. They nudge students toward the idea that, since there are 4 fourths in 1, there are 6 fourths in 1.5, or $\frac{3}{2}$.

FIGURE 10.27

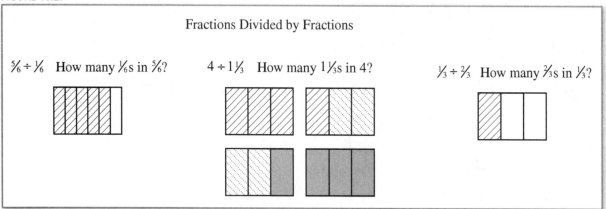

Fractions Divided by Fractions

$\frac{5}{6} \div \frac{1}{6}$ How many $\frac{1}{6}$s in $\frac{5}{6}$?   4 ÷ 1$\frac{1}{3}$ How many 1$\frac{1}{3}$s in 4? $\frac{1}{3} \div \frac{2}{3}$ How many $\frac{2}{3}$s in $\frac{1}{3}$?

The second string continues the theme but throws in some mixed numbers so that students can reason with bigger chunks. For a problem like 4 ÷ 1$\frac{1}{3}$, students can draw 4 arrays and look for the number of one and one-thirds in the 4 arrays (see Figure 10.27). By the end of the string, many students are finding equivalent fractions so that they have a common denominator and then dividing the numerators. As you work through strings like this, ask students to articulate what they are doing. For example, if they say that the answer to $\frac{3}{4} \div \frac{3}{8}$ is 2, because there are 2 three-eighths in $\frac{6}{8}$, ask students how that answer relates to the numerators. The quotient of the numerators is the same as the quotient of the problem—but only if both fractions have the same denominator. The last problem foreshadows the next string by asking $\frac{1}{3} \div \frac{2}{3}$. You can use an array to help student visualize the relationship that there is $\frac{1}{2}$ of $\frac{2}{3}$ in $\frac{1}{3}$. If students find this difficult, you may need to do more problems similar to those in the first and second strings.

The last string begins with the problem 3 ÷ 2 to get students thinking about what they do to solve a division problem where the divisor does not divide evenly into the dividend, or in other words, when the quotient is not a whole number. Students can use this first problem to help them solve $\frac{3}{5} \div \frac{2}{5}$. Asking how many two-fifths divide into three-fifths is equivalent to asking how many twos divide into 3, so $\frac{3}{5} \div \frac{2}{5} = 3 \div 2 = \frac{3}{2}$. The string continues by pairing 1 ÷ 2 with $\frac{1}{3} \div \frac{2}{3}$. The next three problems, $\frac{5}{3} \div \frac{4}{3}$, $\frac{9}{3} \div \frac{5}{3}$, and $\frac{5}{2} \div \frac{3}{2}$, have common denominators so that students can just divide numerators. Keep asking questions to help students clarify that the answer to the fraction division is equivalent to the quotient of the numerators. If students are struggling, you could insert more problems with common denominators, like $\frac{5}{4} \div \frac{3}{4}$ and $\frac{9}{3} \div \frac{6}{3}$. The string ends with two problems, $\frac{3}{5} \div \frac{9}{10}$ and $\frac{1}{7} \div \frac{1}{5}$, for which students have to find the common denominator and then divide the numerators. Model student strategies that find equivalent fractions and then ask students why that is helpful. This strategy may feel strange to those of us who learned invert and multiply, but it is a transparent and meaningful strategy for students who have constructed a strong understanding of fraction equivalence.

Using Partitive Division: Rates and the Constant Ratio Strategy

We can use rates to help students construct a different way of looking at fraction division with a partitive meaning. A context, such as the ratio of cups of cheese to pizzas, helps students visualize situations: how much of a pizza can we make if we have certain amounts of grated cheese?

FIGURE 10.28

Constant Ratio Strings		
$2 \div \frac{1}{2}$	$\frac{1}{5} \div \frac{1}{3}$	$4 \div \frac{3}{5}$
$2 \div \frac{1}{3}$	$\frac{2}{5} \div \frac{2}{3}$	$\frac{3}{4} \div \frac{1}{5}$
$1 \div \frac{1}{5}$	$\frac{1}{4} \div \frac{1}{5}$	$\frac{2}{3} \div \frac{1}{4}$
$2 \div \frac{2}{5}$	$\frac{3}{4} \div \frac{3}{5}$	$\frac{4}{3} \div \frac{1}{4}$
$2 \div \frac{1}{5}$	$\frac{1}{5} \div \frac{1}{3}$	$\frac{2}{3} \div \frac{3}{4}$
$4 \div \frac{2}{3}$	$\frac{4}{5} \div \frac{4}{3}$	$\frac{4}{x^2} \div \frac{2}{x}$
$4 \div \frac{1}{3}$	$\frac{3}{5} \div \frac{3}{4}$	

Abby starts the first string in Figure 10.28 in her algebra class by introducing a pizza context. "So, let's say that it takes 2 cups of cheese to make ½ a medium pizza. How much cheese do we need to make a whole pizza?" She models their answer of 4 cups in a ratio table (Figure 10.29).

FIGURE 10.29

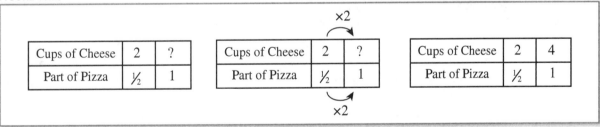

"What math problem does this represent? How would you write an equation to represent this scenario?" asks Abby.

"Well, we could write the ratio of cheese to pizza like 2 cups: ½ pizza," suggests Tania.

"What are some of the other ways to write ratios?" asks Abby. As the class makes suggestions she writes them on the board: *2:½, 2/½, 2 ÷ ½*. "So, just like in division problems, when we could look at constant ratios to find the answers, we can also look at ratios as division problems." She continues with the string. "What if I am making a large pizza and I know that it takes 2 cups to make ⅓ of a pizza. How much cheese do I need to make a whole large pizza?"

"If 2 cups make ⅓ of a pizza, then you'll need 3 times that for a whole pizza, so 6 cups," says Melik. Abby models that on a new ratio table because the ratio has changed (Figure 10.30).

FIGURE 10.30

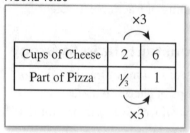

"What if it took 1 cup of cheese to make ⅕ of a pizza? Now how much cheese do we need to make a whole pizza?" asks Abby.

"That one's easy—just 5 cups. You need 5 one-fifths to make a whole," answers Isabelle. Abby adds this ratio table to the board (Figure 10.31).

FIGURE 10.31

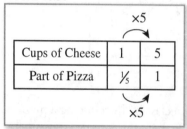

Abby continues, "What if it takes 2 cups of cheese to make ⅖ of a pizza? How much for a whole pizza?"

"That's just double," explains Ryan, "You had 1 cup making ⅕. Now you have 2 cups making ⅖. So that's the same ratio."

"It's double and it's the same?" asks Abby.

The class discusses that when you multiply both the numerator and the denominator by the same factor, the ratios are equivalent. Abby continues by writing the next problem, $2 \div \frac{1}{5}$, on the board and asking students to tell her what question it represents in terms of pizza and cheese.

"That's a cheesy pizza! You're saying that it takes 2 cups of cheese to make only ⅕ of a pizza," answers Maria.

Abby continues the string with the problems $4 \div \frac{2}{3}$ and $4 \div \frac{1}{3}$, keeping the problems in context, asking students to justify their thinking, and discussing the scaling up and down. At the end, she asks students to study the ratio tables from the string and discuss any patterns they find. One of the things students note is that to find the amount of cheese needed for 1 pizza, they ended up multiplying by the denominator of the divisor.

In the second string, students continue to use ratio tables to scale up or down to get to 1 pizza. As they work, they realize that as they divide unit fractions, their goal is to find equivalent ratios such that the divisor equals 1. To do this, they multiply both the dividend and the divisor by the denominator of the divisor. For example, to find $\frac{1}{5} \div \frac{1}{3}$, if you multiply both $\frac{1}{5}$ and $\frac{1}{3}$ by 3, you end up with $\frac{1}{5}(3) \div \frac{1}{3}(3) = \frac{3}{5} \div 1 = \frac{3}{5}$. The next problem, $\frac{2}{5} \div \frac{2}{3}$, is equivalent to the first; if it takes $\frac{2}{3}$ of a cup of cheese to make $\frac{2}{5}$ of a pizza, it takes $\frac{1}{3}$ of a cup of cheese to make $\frac{1}{5}$ of a pizza. As you work through these problems together, students may begin to generalize that they find an equivalent problem using unit fractions by dividing both numerators by the numerator of the divisor. Then they scale the divisor up to 1 by multiplying by the denominator of the divisor. This is modeled in Figure 10.32 for the problem $\frac{2}{5} \div \frac{2}{3}$. The rest of the string continues to develop this idea.

FIGURE 10.32

$\div 2$ $\times 3$

Cups of Cheese	$\frac{2}{5}$	$\frac{1}{5}$	$\frac{3}{5}$
Part of Pizza	$\frac{2}{3}$	$\frac{1}{3}$	1

$\div 2$ $\times 3$

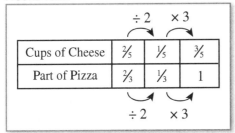

The third string gives students practice answering the question, "How can I scale the problem so that the divisor is 1?" They realize that they can multiply both the dividend and the divisor by the reciprocal of the divisor and they end up with an equivalent ratio in which the divisor is 1 (as in Figure 10.33). This is the standard algorithm—to invert and multiply. Students with a background with ratio tables, multiplicative and proportional reasoning, and equivalent ratios are well equipped not just to use the algorithm, but understand why it works!

FIGURE 10.33

$\times \frac{3}{2}$

Cups of Cheese	$\frac{2}{5}$	$\frac{3}{5}$
Part of Pizza	$\frac{2}{3}$	1

$\times \frac{3}{2}$

$$\frac{2}{5} \div \frac{2}{3} = \frac{2}{5}\left(\frac{3}{2}\right) \div \frac{2}{3}\left(\frac{3}{2}\right) = \frac{3}{5} \div 1$$

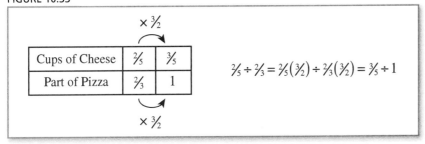

Comparing Strategies: Fractions

Think about the following examples. Which strategy would you use for each? Which strategies make sense for which kinds of numbers?

a. $\frac{4}{9} \cdot \frac{3}{2}$
b. $15 \cdot \frac{2}{3}$
c. $\frac{3}{7} \div \frac{2}{3}$
d. $9 \div \frac{3}{2}$
e. $\frac{2}{5} \div 4$

For $\frac{4}{9} \cdot \frac{3}{2}$, Emma said, "I know that $\frac{1}{9} \cdot \frac{1}{2}$ is $\frac{1}{18}$. Then I scale up by 4 and 3 to get $\frac{12}{18}$, which is equivalent to $\frac{2}{3}$." Kai said, "I traded places so $\frac{3}{9} \cdot \frac{4}{2} = \frac{1}{3} \cdot 2 = \frac{2}{3}$."

For 15 · ⅔, Grace said, "So, ⅓ of 15 is 5. Double that to get 10."

For ³⁄₇ ÷ ⅔, Raphe said, "I want to make the divisor 1, so I'll multiply both by ³⁄₂, so ³⁄₇ ÷ ⅔ = (³⁄₇ · ³⁄₂) ÷ (⅔ · ³⁄₂) = ⁹⁄₁₄ · 1 = ⁹⁄₁₄." Gabi said, "I know that the problem is equivalent to ⁹⁄₂₁ ÷ ¹⁴⁄₂₁ = ⁹⁄₁₄."

For 9 ÷ ³⁄₂, Taylor said, "That's like ¹⁸⁄₂ ÷ ³⁄₂, so 18 ÷ 3 = 6." Hannah said, "I'll keep the ratio constant by multiplying both by ⅔ to get (9 · ⅔) ÷ (³⁄₂ · ⅔) = 6 ÷ 1 = 6."

For ⅖ ÷ 4, Corey said, "2 ÷ 4 is ½, so it's ½⁄₅ so that's ¹⁄₁₀."

Angel said, "I'll make them both fifths, so ⅖ ÷ 4 = ⅖ ÷ ²⁰⁄₅ = ²⁄₂₀ = ¹⁄₁₀."

April said, "I know that ⅖ is 0.4 so 40¢ divided by 4 is 10¢, so $0.10."

Clarifying Understanding

As Close as It Gets

To help your students estimate and consider the magnitudes in problems, use the problems in Figure 10.34. Have students share their strategies and compare. Encourage students to use decimals and fractions interchangeably when possible.

FIGURE 10.34

As Close as It Gets		
24.2 · 0.11 a) 0.242 b) 2.42 c) 24 d) 240	0.51 · 3,102 a) 15 b) 150 c) 1,500 d) 15,000	512 ÷ 9.9 a) 5 b) 50 c) 500 d) 5,000
3.68 ÷ 101 a) 0.0368 b) 0.368 c) 3.68 d) 36.8	$\frac{3}{4} \cdot \frac{15}{16}$ a) 0 b) 0.75 c) 1 d) 2	$\frac{9}{10} \cdot \frac{11}{5}$ a) 0 b) 0.5 c) 1 d) 2
$\frac{26}{5} \div 5$ a) 0.1 b) 1 c) 10 d) 100	$\frac{9}{10} \div \frac{1}{8}$ a) 0 b) 1 c) 8 d) 9	$1\frac{1}{2} \cdot 4.1$ a) 0.5 b) 2 c) 6 d) 12

When discussing strategies for the "As Close as It Gets" problems, you may find the following helpful.

▶ For 0.51 · 3,102, we want students to see 0.51 as about ½, reasoning that about ½ of 3,000 is about 1,500.

▶ For 512 ÷ 9.9, a student might reason that about 500 divided by about 10 is about 50. Division by 10 is very important and needs attention until students master it.

▶ For ¾ · ¹⁵⁄₁₆, students can estimate that ¾ of about 1 is about ¾.

▶ For ⁹⁄₁₀ · ¹¹⁄₅, students can think of about 1 times about 2 is about 2.

► For $^{26}\!/_5 \div 5$, a student could reason that about 5 divided by 5 is about 1.

► For $^9\!/_{10} \div \frac{1}{8}$, a student might think about how many one-eighths are in about 1: about 8.

► For $1.5 \cdot 4.1$, a student might reason, "I thought about 1.5 times 2 and then doubled. So that's 3 doubled is 6." Another might think about $1\frac{1}{2}$ fours, which equals $4 + 2$, or 6.

Relational Thinking

You can use the relational thinking problems in Figure 10.35 to help students clarify strategies, why they work, and when to use them. Several of the problems are designed to help students think about maintaining correct place value. For example, in the first fill-in-the-blank problem, students need to decide how to keep the expressions equivalent. Other problems help students focus on keeping ratios equivalent by scaling up or down by powers of 10, as in $^{237.8}\!/_{3.7} = {}^{2378}\!/_{?}$. Other problems have students fill in the parts to make the distributive property work, such as $2.7 \cdot \underline{\hphantom{xxx}} = (2 \cdot 5) + (0.7 \cdot 5) = \underline{\hphantom{xxxx}}$. All of these problems are subtle hints about possible solution strategies. They can be helpful to you to assess how students are thinking and reasoning.

The true-or-false questions give you opportunities to help students sort out which strategies can be used with which operations. The equivalent ratio problems in questions 3 and 4 ask students to make sense of the place values—did they multiply the numerator and denominator by the same number? Considering $^2\!/_{15} \div ^5\!/_2 = ^2\!/_2 \div ^5\!/_{15}$ leads students to think about whether "trading places" works in division as well as multiplication.

FIGURE 10.35

Relational Thinking

Fill in the blank:

1. $36 \cdot 76 = 36(0.76 \cdot \underline{\hspace{1cm}}) = (36 \cdot 0.76) \cdot \underline{\hspace{1cm}}$

2. $2.7 \cdot \underline{\hspace{1cm}} = (2 \cdot 5) + (0.7 \cdot 5) = \underline{\hspace{1cm}}$

3. $\dfrac{237.8}{3.7} = \dfrac{2{,}378}{}$

4. $60.4 \div 0.6 = 60 \div 0.6 + 0.4 \div \underline{\hspace{1cm}}$

5. $\dfrac{4}{15} \cdot \dfrac{3}{4} = \dfrac{}{15} \cdot \dfrac{4}{4}$

6. $5\dfrac{1}{3} \cdot 12 = 16 \cdot \underline{\hspace{1cm}}$

7. $\dfrac{4}{3} \div \dfrac{1}{2} = \dfrac{8}{6} \div \dfrac{3}{6} = \underline{\hspace{1cm}} \div \underline{\hspace{1cm}}$

8. $\dfrac{4}{3} \div \dfrac{1}{2} = \left(\dfrac{4}{3} \cdot \dfrac{2}{1}\right) \div \left(\dfrac{1}{2} \cdot \underline{\hspace{1cm}}\right)$

True or false? Why?

1. $7.5 \cdot 81 = (10 \cdot 0.75) \cdot 81 = 10 \cdot 60.75$

2. $0.26 \cdot 0.29 = 0.25 \cdot 0.30$

3. $\dfrac{73.29}{8.32} = \dfrac{7{,}329}{832}$

4. $\dfrac{0.146}{617} = \dfrac{146}{0.617}$

5. $\dfrac{7}{16} \cdot \dfrac{4}{7} = \dfrac{7}{7} \cdot \dfrac{4}{16}$

6. $18 \cdot 2\dfrac{1}{3} = 6 \cdot 7$

7. $\dfrac{2}{15} \div \dfrac{5}{2} = \dfrac{2}{2} \div \dfrac{5}{15}$

8. $2 \div \dfrac{3}{5} = \left(2 \cdot \dfrac{5}{3}\right) \div \left(\dfrac{3}{5} \cdot \dfrac{5}{3}\right)$

Conclusion: Bringing It All Together

Critics of recent reform efforts to improve numeracy in elementary schools claim that student strategies are too cumbersome and inefficient. However, when students have a repertoire of strategies that include whole number, fraction, and decimal operations, they can flexibly solve all kinds of problems efficiently and accurately.

Using the strings and activities in this book can empower your students to think and reason through problems. They can look to the numbers first and then decide on a strategy. They can be intrigued by patterns and equivalent answers and seek to find clever solutions. They can gain confidence and staying power. They will know when to apply sophisticated strategies and when to pick up a calculator.

Some of the strategies in this book might seem a bit much. After all, many of us have been successful without them. However, if you approach them from the perspective that the steps are transparent and that the strategies are constructed within the learner, then they don't seem as daunting or foreign. I have seen this work with students and teachers time after time. Students are engaged, willing to think, and more confident in their justifications. They will be able to transfer their understandings born from reasoning through complex concepts to higher math.

references

Booth, Julie L., and Robert S. Siegler. 2006. "Developmental and Individual Differences in Pure Numerical Estimation." *Developmental Psychology* 41: 189–201.

Burrill, Gail. 1997. "Computation, Calculators, and the 'Basics.' NCTM News Bulletin President's Message: November 3.

Carpenter, Thomas P., Megan Loef Franke, and Linda Levi. 2003. *Thinking Mathematically: Integrating Arithmetic and Algebra in Elementary School.* Portsmouth, NH: Heinemann.

Common Core State Standards Initiative. 2011. National Governors Association Center for Best Practices (NGA Center) and the Council of Chief State School Officers (CCSSO). "Common Core State Standards Initiative: The Standards." Available at: www.corestandards.org/the-standards. Accessed February 4, 2011.

Dehaene, Stanislas. 1999. *The Number Sense: How the Mind Creates Mathematics.* New York: Oxford University Press.

Dowker, Ann. 1992. "Computational Estimation Strategies of Professional Mathematicians." *Journal for Research in Mathematics Education* 23 (1): 44–55.

Fosnot, Catherine Twomey, et al. 2008. "Contexts for Learning Mathematics." Portsmouth, NH: *first*hand. Available at: www.contextsforlearning.com. Accessed January 26, 2011.

Fosnot, Catherine Twomey, and Maarten Dolk. 2001. *Young Mathematicians at Work, 1: Constructing Number Sense, Addition, and Subtraction.* Portsmouth: Heinemann.

Fosnot, Catherine Twomey, and Maarten Dolk. 2001. *Young Mathematicians at Work: Constructing Multiplication and Division.* Portsmouth, NH: Heinemann.

Fosnot, Catherine Twomey, and Willem Uittenbogaard. 2007. *Minilessons for Extending Addition and Subtraction: A Yearlong Resource.* Portsmouth, NH: *first*hand/Heinemann.

Gravemeijer, K. P. E. 1999. "How Emergent Models May Foster the Constitution of Formal Mathematics." *Mathematical Thinking and Learning* 1 (2): 155–77.

Lamon, Susan J. 2005. *Teaching Fractions and Ratios for Understanding: Essential Content Knowledge and Instructional Strategies for Teachers.* Mahwah, NJ: Lawrence Erlbaum Associates.

Lesh, R., T. Post, and M. Behr. 1988. "Proportional Reasoning." In *Number Concepts and Operations in the Middle Grades,* 93–118. Reston, VA: Lawrence Erlbaum & National Council of Teachers of Mathematics.

Liu, Nina, Maarten Dolk, and Catherine Twomey Fosnot. 2007. *Organizing and Collecting: The Number System.* Portsmouth: *first*hand Heinemann.

Miller, Jane Lincoln, and James T. Fey. 2000. "Proportional Reasoning." *Mathematics Teaching in the Middle School* 5 (5): 310.

Siegler, Robert S., and Julie Booth. 2004. "Numerical Estimation in Young Children." *Child Development* 75 (2): 428–44.

Siegler, Robert S., and Elida V. Laski. 2007. "Is 27 a Big Number? Correlational and Causal Connections Among Numerical Categorization, Number Line Estimation, and Numerical Magnitude Comparison." *Child Development* 78 (6): 1723–43.

Stein, Rob. 2008. "How One's 'Number Sense' Helps With Mathematics." *Washington Post.* September 8. Available at: www.washingtonpost.com/wp-dyn/content/article/2008/09/07/AR2008090701899.html?nav=emailpage. Accessed February 4, 2011.

Texas Education Agency. 2003. *TAKS (Texas Assessment of Knowledge and Skills) Grade 5, Mathematics, Reading, Science.* Available at www.tea.state.tx.us/student.assessment/take/released-tests/. Accessed on April 13, 2011.